ECONOMICS
FOR MANAGERS

ECONOMICS
FOR MANAGERS

P. C. F. Crowson & B. A. Richards

Edward Arnold

© P. C. F. Crowson and B. A. Richards 1978
First published 1975 by
Edward Arnold [Publishers] Ltd
41 Bedford Square, London WC1B 3DP

Reprinted 1977
Second Edition 1978

British Library Cataloguing in Publication Data
Crowson, Phillip C F
   Economics for Managers. – 2nd ed
   1. Managerial economics
   I. Title   II. Richards, Basil Anthony
   330'.02'4658   HD30.22

ISBN 0-7131-3397-X

Printed in Great Britain at
The Camelot Press Ltd, Southampton

PREFACE

Since the first publication of *Economics for Managers* in 1975, there have
been various changes and developments in the economic environment
necessitating a revision, particularly in the macro-economic chapters of
the book. This being so, and with the encouraging reception given to the
original edition in mind, it has been decided to publish a second edition.
The general structure of the book remains unchanged, but the opportunity
has been taken to bring the whole text up to date and to revise many of the
charts in line with recent reports and statistics.

The book has been written for both the practising manager and the
management student. Indeed, since the Diploma in Management Studies
became a reality in Britain in 1961 it has become increasingly the case that
the practising manager is also a management student. Accordingly, the
contents of *Economics for Managers* are designed to meet the needs of the
manager in the daily process of decision making, and those of the
management student taking Part I of the Diploma in Management Studies,
for those reading for a degree or professional qualification with a
management-economics content, or as an introductory text for students
taking the new Business Studies courses at Higher level.

Today's economic environment is subject to increasingly rapid change
and the manager's task of adapting his company to such change becomes
progressively more difficult. He is no longer only concerned with the
traditional business decisions of finance, production and marketing. His
decisions, if they are to be effective, must be based on an understanding
of the economic concepts which underlie all business activity, and a
knowledge of the economic environment in which the firm operates. He
must also be capable of applying such understanding and knowledge
through modern management techniques. The object of this book is to
provide the basic groundwork for a wider understanding of the economic
aspects of management. Other books in the same series provide the
corresponding information on the quantitative, financial and behavioural
aspects.

As there is no economics syllabus common to all colleges for the

Diploma in Management Studies, we have had the great advantage of being guided in our task by management needs rather than by set academic guidelines. However, with teaching experience at the Polytechnic of Central London in mind, we have tried to ensure that the subject matter is sufficiently comprehensive to meet the needs of most students. Our aim throughout has been to present sufficient of the theory to satisfy academic requirements, and sufficient of the practice to make it meaningful in the management situation.

P. C. F. C. and B. A. R.

CONTENTS

I

BUSINESS OBJECTIVES

The changing environment

Had this book been published fifteen, or even ten, years ago it would have been relatively simple to describe accepted views and practices concerning company objectives and corporate planning. Today the political, economic, sociological, and technological framework within which companies must operate is changing so rapidly that it is perhaps appropriate to identify at the outset some of the more critical factors which may affect the setting of company objectives and the planning required for their realisation. The manager's first step should be to identify the characteristics of the real world in which he must operate.

One of the most profound changes, particularly in the United States, has been in public attitudes to business generally, and to large-scale industry in particular. Leading industrialists were highly regarded, even up to a decade ago, and their companies were looked on with favour. Today, however, industry is often held in low esteem, and the brightest graduates no longer wish to enter it. The pursuit of profit is widely regarded with suspicion, irrespective of political affiliation. Improvements in material standards of living, and economic growth, once thought the greatest of virtues, have been toppled from their lofty pedestals. A less materialistic youth is rediscovering the beauties of nature, the shade of Malthus is again abroad, and conservation is the keynote of the age. Science and technology have been the mainsprings of modern industrial development, but science is now widely considered to be a false god. It is not the purpose of this book to explore in any depth these socio-logical and moral changes, which may easily represent a fashion rather than a dramatic change in trend, but all managers must be aware of them.

Rapid technical change, particularly since 1945, has profoundly influenced every aspect of industry. Complete new industries such as petrochemicals and electronics have developed, the techniques of production in all industries have been transformed, and new transport and communication techniques have made possible a revolution in industrial organisation and management. A general feature has been the great increase in the most economic scale of plant in all industries, which has involved an increase in capital intensity. Rapid air travel and telecommunications advances have enabled far-off managements to exert close control over subsidiaries at opposite sides of the earth. The world has truly become a 'global village', with a vast increase in the interdependence of all economies. This growing interdependence has especially affected the advanced industrial nations of Europe, North America and Japan. The development of faster data-processing equipment and computer systems has enabled individual firms to grow more rapidly even than the most efficient scale of plants. Whereas management was formerly believed to be a bottleneck inhibiting the growth of firms, technical change has greatly eased this constraint and raised it much higher up the size range in many, but not all, industries.

Ownership and control

Public policy and economic theory have not always kept pace with the technical and economic changes that have occurred in recent years. Company law especially has lagged markedly behind economic reality. Even though a new UK company law was passed in 1976, this merely tinkered with the systems and still failed to adapt organisational forms to present-day realities.

Economic theory has tended to lag even more. The dominant model of the firm in many elementary textbooks is based on the small, owner-managed business which emerged in modern industry in the early and mid-nineteenth century. The entrepreneur, combining the functions of management, risk taking, and provision of capital, remains the ideal. Yet even in the nineteenth century rapid growth of demand often led to a need for much more capital for expansion than the owner and his immediate associates could supply.

The joint stock company, whose prototype was the chartered companies of Elizabethan days and earlier, was adapted to the needs of nineteenth-century industry and commerce. The device of limited liability enabled outside investors to sink their savings in industry, secure in the knowledge that the rewards might be unlimited whilst their losses would be restricted to their initial subscription. Originally the privilege of limited liability required a special Act of Parliament for each case, a restriction which became increasingly cumbersome and was eventually repealed.

As industry developed, the stock exchange traded in shares of limited-liability companies, and ownership and control became increasingly divorced from management. The owners of the shares might have no connection with the firm apart from their annual dividend. Even up to 1945, however, ownership of most firms was concentrated in relatively few hands, and the scale of firms was such that the dominant owners could still effectively manage their investments. Dramatic growth in the next decades, however, with tremendous needs for capital, has severed close links between original shareholders and management in all but a handful of companies. Increasing organisational complexity, and the need to keep abreast of rapid technological changes and market developments, increased the demand for specialist managers with particular skills. Professionally trained managers were widely recruited to supplement firms' existing pools of entrepreneurial talent. As companies have become larger and more complex these hired managers have increasingly displaced those with shareholdings in the firm. At the same time, growing capital needs have increased the number of shares issued by large firms, and ownership has become very widely spread both in private hands and also in large institutions, such as pension funds, insurance companies, and banks. The issue of loans and debentures has further increased corporate capital. Today even the largest shareholders in leading companies may control a negligible proportion of the voting powers.

The situation has thus developed whereby the functions of ownership and effective control have become separated. The balance of power has shifted markedly in favour of the professional manager, or board of directors, and the shareholder has become emasculated. His only effective weapon is moral pressure, which can admittedly be important. If he dislikes a company's policies he can always sell his shares on the stock exchange. Company law has not kept pace with this organisational change and scarcely recognises the place of the professional manager. Companies must be run in the interests of their members, i.e. shareholders, yet the possibility of conflicts between the interests of shareholders and managers is almost completely ignored.

Even though the directors of the largest US public corporations tend to have large shareholdings, this is not generally true of the United Kingdom. The average shareholdings of directors and senior managers in the main British public companies tend to be very low. The merger wave of the last decade has often diluted family interests and widened the gap between ownership and control. Also stock option schemes for senior executives are not regarded by the tax authorities as favourably as in the United States, and their introduction has frequently been delayed by prices and incomes restraint. Such schemes do, of course, give senior managers a direct interest in their companies, but it is highly debatable whether even senior managers should be unduly encouraged to invest their savings as well as their livelihoods in their employing company.

Quite apart from the possibility of their own interests conflicting with those of the shareholders which the law enjoins them to pursue, directors of large companies face increasing pressures from other interests. Whereas shareholders can transfer their investments relatively easily, most employees cannot readily change their jobs. Strong social and economic ties bind them to a particular locality in which the opportunities for transfer between employers may be strictly limited. Often firms owe as much to the professional skills or contributions of their employees as to the providers of capital. This reaches an extreme in the professions and service industries, such as advertising, where the expertise of the staff is all-important and capital needs are minimal. Although employees have a strong interest in working for a prosperous and efficient employer, decisions which may conflict with their interests are frequently made by directors. Such conflicts of interests are most likely to be acute when large capital projects, mergers, or redundancies are being considered. Yet, according to the law, all employees are merely servants of a company and directors must not have regard to employee interests if they conflict with those of the shareholders. In practice, of course, directors of public companies pay considerable attention to employee interests.

Companies must maintain harmonious relationships with their customers if they are to remain profitably in business over the long term. They must ensure that they give their customers a 'fair deal' and this might occasionally conflict, at least in a narrow legal sense, with the interests of the shareholders. Another interest directors must consider is the wider public interest. This is expressed through such vague phrases as the need to be 'good corporate citizens', or have a 'sense of social responsibility'. In recent years companies have fallen over themselves, particularly in the United States, to show that their activities are beneficial to mankind and are having a positive effect on the environment. At the local level, firms may finance social facilities, or set up scholarships in the cause of public relations, or they may subscribe to charities. Yet these activities are peripheral to their central activities and might be overruled in the courts. The main point is that companies often see a need to do more to meet the vaguely defined public interest than is strictly required by the law.

The modern manager has to balance the interests of all his constituents—himself, his employees, his customers, his shareholders, and the general public whether at local or national level—with little help from an outdated company law. The legal view is that the law sets the ground rules and constraints within which industry must operate, but the manager is then on his own. Such ground rules might include regulations governing working hours and conditions of work, safety, permissible effluent levels, or air-purity standards, or required product quality controls, apart from the more general framework of the tax and company-law system. Increasingly this legal view is being regarded as insufficient, and managers will face new pressures in the 1980s. One of the strongest will be a growing demand by employees for a more secure role and for a much greater degree of participation in management's decisions, on the general direction of the business as well as on more narrowly defined employment questions. This demand affects all organisations and is not confined to companies in the private sector.

In this respect British company law has not only lagged behind industrial developments, but also behind movements on the European mainland. In Germany and the Netherlands, for example, company law requires directors to have regard to the interests of employees and the general public in addition to those of shareholders. A company is regarded as rather more than a collection of property rights. There is a developing tendency throughout Europe for employees to be officially represented in the company's organs of government, as well as in works or company councils. In Germany, as is well known, employee representatives sit on the Supervisory Board, the company's policy-making body concerned with long-term strategy. Employees also have an important role in the Netherlands and the Scandinavian countries. Whilst due account must be taken of the different pattern of development of employer-employee relations in the UK and mainland Europe—a strong voluntary tradition versus legal restraints, for example, and strong and widespread unionism versus relatively weak and narrowly based unions—European trends do have some lessons for the UK. Membership of the EEC has already stirred controversy on the appropriateness of company law to modern circumstances, and it will in due course force some profound changes in company organisation. This does not mean that the UK will or should slavishly adopt existing European patterns, but that these patterns will be modified to fit UK traditions and circumstances.

In 1977 a government committee chaired by Lord Bullock recommended that boards of directors should have equal numbers of shareholders' and employees' representatives plus one independent member agreed by the two interest groups. This $2x + y$ formula and the accompanying proposals were widely criticised; the committee was not asked whether workers' representation was a good idea but to advise on the best means of achieving it. The majority accepted the official TUC line that worker directors could only be elected by unionists, irrespective of the extent of a company's union membership. The principle of worker directors is not fully accepted by all unions, and many union leaders as well as employers were bitterly opposed to the Bullock Committee's recommendations. The employers' views were set out in a minority report which argued that worker directors were an irrelevance without fundamental changes in industrial relations lower down. The government's precarious minority position in Parliament and the Liberal Party's opposition to the Bullock proposals prevented quick legislation in the 1976–78 sessions of Parliament.

In some European countries pressure is also developing for direct representation of the public interest on company boards through state or local government appointment of a proportion of directors. The great danger is that boards of directors will end up as collections of representatives of widely disparate interests. Either their decisions will be reduced to the lowest common denominator, or their functions will be usurped by the company's executive organs. An alternative, and more likely, development is the extension of *social audits*, which are being developed in the United States. The idea is that the company should not only subject its books to annual scrutiny by external auditors, but that it should also analyse its impact, for good or ill, on the environment, considered in its widest sense. Although social audits are not backed at present by any legal sanctions they are undoubtedly a possible development. Another common trend is the appointment in large companies of advisers on environmental affairs to acquaint management with the external impact of their actions and to seek means of minimising any adverse effects. A UK government Green Paper of July 1977 on the Future of Company Reports recommended that companies should publish more information about their activities 'to reflect the wider accountability of directors and cover the interests of people other than shareholders'.

Company objectives

The above and similar developments cloud the simple position of company law that a board of directors' sole and overriding duty is to further the interests of shareholders. Management's need to balance a wide range of apparently diverse interests raises in an increasingly acute form the question of company objectives. It may, of course, be strongly argued that commercial managements are not competent to balance all the interests. Such a balancing role can only be performed by the state, and managements should be left to concentrate on their primary role. Management's view of the public interest, for example, may not be the same as that held by the mass of the electorate. This means that the State should require industry to operate within defined guidelines and constraints. This is merely a continuation of the present legal view already set out above. The main objection is that society's priorities and objectives are continually changing, and that the law is too inflexible in response to such changes. It is, in another guise, the argument for Britain's unwritten constitution rather than the precise written document of the United States. There is, however, a general presumption that industry should concentrate its energies on fairly narrowly defined objectives. Unless a company has clearly defined goals and targets, or at the very least some generally accepted criteria of success, management will have no yardstick against which to judge its effectiveness.

The overriding objective of companies in traditional economic theory, as set out in subsequent chapters, was maximisation of profits. The sole aim of economic man in business was to expand his output until profits were maximised. Obviously this had to be considered over a sufficiently long period, as short-term profit maximisation might spell long-term ruin. Short-term maximisation might, for example, mean pushing workers so hard for such low wages that they eventually strike, or selling shoddily made goods at such exorbitant prices in periods of shortage that new entrants come in with better-quality products sold at lower prices. The need for long-run, as opposed to short-run, profit maximisation is often used to justify the legal view that company directors should have regard solely to the shareholders' interests. If long-run profit maximisation meets the shareholders' interests it will only be achieved by ensuring that other interests are appeased, if not completely satisfied. Up to a point this may be true, but the public interest may often lose out, because it may often have no direct impact on profits. The annual accounts do not, for example, reflect costs of damage to the environment, nor the beneficial multiplier effects on regional employment of siting a factory in a development area. Consideration of the public interest, however, requires some acknowledgment of such external effects. Yet companies in the private sector are unable to take full account of any external effects of their actions lest they lose out to competitors who might be less socially conscious. Although it is by no means clear that simple profit maximisation is the only or most important goal of modern industry, it is not certain that it should be jettisoned as a guide to corporate behaviour. Even if it were decided that managers should no longer solely consider the shareholders' interests, the pursuit of profit might still remain the most appropriate objective. This is examined below.

The profit-maximisation goal of traditional economic theory was a device for determining the scale of output once a firm had decided on its product scope in market conditions where price was given. The firm would expand output until the marginal cost of producing and selling an additional unit equalled the marginal revenue obtained from selling that unit. At this output, and this output alone, profits would be at a maximum, because any increase in output would add more to costs than to revenue, and any reduction in output would mean that profits were less than they could be. The assumptions made of perfect competition in the supply of labour and capital meant that the optimum output would also give the highest return on capital.

Profits are the difference between a firm's total receipts and its total expenses. Not only do they reward the equity, risk-bearing capital put into the business, but they also encourage entrepreneurship. In the conditions of perfect competition that characterised economic theory, all moderately efficient firms would earn some 'normal' rate of profit, which might vary between industries according to the degree of risk or uncertainty involved. The difference between the rate of interest on government funds and the average rate of profit would be the reward for risk and entrepreneurial skill. Where there were imperfections in the market, profits might additionally include a scarcity element, which competitive pressures would usually prevent emerging. Even in imperfectly competitive industries, firms would still fix their output or prices at levels ensuring maximum profits.

The development of modern capitalism with its divorce of ownership and control, and the growth of a managerial class within industry, has severely damaged the view that pursuit of maximum profits, even in the longer term, is a firm's main objective. Classical theory had always recognised other motives such as the pursuit of power, both economic and political, and of social status, but these were always considered as subsidiary goals that could best be achieved by profit maximisation itself. Most large companies appear to pursue a hierarchy of objectives in which profit maximisation, suitably defined, is but one element. These objectives may not always be mutually consistent.

In the classical firm making few products and selling in a restricted market, and where the owner and manager were the same person, profit maximisation was a relatively straightforward goal. Maximum profits for the shareholders may, however, conflict with the needs of management in modern firms, and in any case need translating into operationally useful objectives for transmission throughout the various levels of the organisation.

The personal goals of managers are more likely to be directed towards personal security, and status, both within the firm and in the wider community, than to maximum profits for their firm. These goals are likely to be achieved if the manager's company earns a profit consistently above a level likely to be regarded by shareholders as an acceptable minimum, but below a level which might involve excessive risks of failure or is likely to attract new entrants into the industry. Above all, the goal of security will ensure that the firm earns sufficient profits to pay an acceptable dividend, that it at least maintains its place in the market, and that it remains secure from a take-over which would adversely affect the incumbent managers. The goal of an 'acceptable level of profits' implied by security is less easy to define than profit maximisation. Possible criteria, which can be used operationally within the company, are a rate of return on capital employed at least as good as the average of all firms in the industry, and a rate of return no worse than the firm has earned in the past. The firm needs to earn sufficient to pay an acceptable dividend, both to satisfy shareholders and, if necessary, to attract new capital, whilst earning sufficient to finance expansion schemes from internal sources. Such a pursuit of 'satisfactory' profits is known as *satisficing*. The reasons advanced for limiting profits are management's goal of security, its strong desire to maintain the goodwill of customers by earning only a 'fair return', a wish to limit trade-union demands for a greater share of high profits, a need to discourage competitors from encroaching on the firm's geographical or product territory, and a desire not to attract the attention of civil servants responsible for anti-monopoly regulations.

Whilst this view does not dethrone profits as an extremely important goal of modern companies, it moderates their influence. The other aims of security and status can best be achieved by ensuring long-run profitability and can best be expressed through some measure of profits. Nonetheless these are still goals of the organisation, and will apply if management is considered as an entity, but they may not embody the aspirations of individual managers. It is strongly argued, notably by Professor J. K. Galbraith, that, in practice, professional managers will not subordinate their own personal and pecuniary interests to those of ineffectual shareholders. Self-interest will ensure a safe goal of prevention of losses rather than maximisation of profits. Whilst salaried managers do not receive any of the super profits associated with successful high-risk projects unless they earn a commission based on profits, their status and position would be seriously affected adversely if their actions caused a loss.

It is often a mistake to regard large companies as unified organisations working steadfastly towards common goals. They are living and changing entities in which individual managers and departments may be striving for status and power. As in all organisations there will normally be interdepartmental jealousies and rivalry. Perhaps the only method to subordinate these individual rivalries to the goals of the enterprise as a whole is to stress size and growth as corporate objectives. Many writers have pointed out that profitable growth serves the interests of both managers and shareholders in profits, security and status. Growth will create new opportunities for promotion and higher salaries within the organisation, and will nullify personal jealousies between managers.

Obviously the goal of growth must be subject to some constraint of minimum profits and dividends; otherwise it will offend against the objectives of security and company survival. The cheapest method of growth is through internally generated expansion, which requires healthy profits. The goal of growth is not therefore necessarily inconsistent with the pursuit of 'satisfactory' profits, suitably defined. Security also is interlinked with the other objectives through their impact on stock-market expectations and the company's share price. Provided the latter is maintained, and the company is not regarded as, in some sense, 'cheap', the company will be relatively safe from unwelcome takeovers.

Growth and profits need defining more narrowly to be of any value to management. The vague goals must be turned into precise, and prefer-ably numerical, targets whose form will vary with each company. Given a growing industry and economy, the growth objective might be defined as a rate of growth of sales volume, the maintenance or increase of the firm's share of a product or geographical market, a defined annual extension of plant capacity, an expansion of the labour force, an annual percentage or absolute increase in profit, or a target increase in earnings per share. The last target is linked with the profit goal, which might variously be defined as a given rate of return on total capital employed or on shareholders' funds, or a given rate of profit retention. There may, therefore, be a whole range of interlocking targets and objectives which the company uses to plan its pursuit of its twin primary goals. To a marked extent, the initial size of the company and management's attitude to risk will qualify the various targets. A sleepy and highly security-conscious management will place greater emphasis on present-day profits; a more adventurous team will push growth. Quite apart from deliberate targets, companies may set constraints for security reasons. These might include some minimum dividend distribution rate to satisfy shareholders' current income expectations, and perhaps some maximum gearing ratio. This is the ratio between loans and other debts bearing a fixed return and total capital employed. The higher the gearing ratio, the greater the volatility of rewards to shareholders because of the greater burden of fixed interest, and the more the risk. But a high gearing ratio allows a faster growth rate than a lower one.

The interrelationship of the various targets can be demonstrated through simplified schematic balance sheets and trading accounts as shown in Table 1.1. This table also brings out the relationship between the various definitions of capital and profits.

Table 1.1 The interrelationship between major company targets

Balance-sheet liabilities		Trading account	
Share capital	A	Sales	F
+ Reserves	B	− Costs	G
= Shareholder's funds:		= Trading profits	H
Equity capital	C	− Depreciation	I
+ Debt capital	D	= Profit before tax and interest	J
= Total capital employed	E	− Interest	K
		− Taxation	L
		= Earnings for ordinary shares	M
		− Dividends	N
Constraints		= Retained profits	O
Gearing ratio = D/E			
Payout ratio = N/M			
Dividend rate = N/A			
Objectives			
Earnings per share = M/A (if £1 share)			
Return on capital employed = J/E			
Return on shareholders' funds = M/C			
Rate of growth = O/C			

Corporate strategy and the environment

In one sense the discussion of targets and objectives in the previous section has put the cart before the horse. Even before defining their pecuniary and non-pecuniary goals and targets, companies must determine their overall strategy in relation to their environment. They must decide on the products they wish to make, the markets they intend to serve, and the geographical areas they wish to sell in. The type of process and raw materials they will use and the location of their plants are also important strategic questions. We have already touched on the dramatic sociological changes in attitudes to business that have taken place in recent years. It is now worth emphasising the equally profound organisational and political changes.

Nowhere has change in business been more manifest than in the post-war growth of the international company. Increasing economies of scale, managerial and financial as well as technical, have greatly widened industry's horizons. National frontiers have in many cases become a nuisance, if not an irrelevance, to large manufacturing corporations. Many companies have developed operations in more than one country, and these firms have been given the collective title of 'multinationals', even though there are probably more differences between any two than between two companies in any one country. This is an area shrouded in confusion and drenched in prejudice, where national emotions are easily aroused, and facts are often scarce. This is not, however, the place to go into the role or nature of multinational companies. They are merely used as a potent symbol of changes in the business environment. The export marketing of twenty years ago, for example, which aimed to satisfy consumer needs by sending goods from their point of production beyond national frontiers, is rapidly giving way to international marketing strategies which seek to meet the same objectives by moving any combination of goods, financial resources, capital equipment, and people across national frontiers. The switch has been rapid and fundamental. Where multinational businesses have developed furthest, in the American manufacturing firms with large foreign operations, goods and resources are no longer exported. They are moved, sometimes with startling rapidity and frequency, to that location anywhere in the accessible world which will best serve corporate objectives. These companies have a world market, and growth (often regardless of product) is their objective. Only thus can they adapt to, and meet, the rapidly escalating technological and other requirements of today's business environment.

Most companies, of course, are not yet multinational in this sense, and there is no strong reason why they should become so. They are still concerned with achieving their declared objectives within a modified national context. They do not necessarily engage in international marketing development, and may not wish to. Nonetheless, all managers, whatever their industry, need to take the new patterns of world business into account. To do otherwise is to ignore the changing dynamics of the market and the changing structure of its financial, commercial, human, and technological institutions. The achievement of company and other objectives, through the optimum utilisation of corporate resources in satis-fying consumer needs, is today an increasingly trans-national process.

In essence, management needs to formulate its objectives and strategies with a clear view of the changing nature of the external environment faced by the company, and its own position within it. It needs to draw up appropriate strategies and tactics to meet its own goals and targets, and to be sufficiently flexible to adapt all these to changing circumstances. This is the purpose of sound and effective corporate planning—to make management rise to the challenge of the external environment, and to overcome internal limitations.

Once the general corporate goals have been defined, and then established as precise targets, it is necessary to plan an appropriate strategy. The necessary strategic decisions focus attention on the external climate facing the firm and are primarily marketing decisions about geographic markets and product mix. A key component of such a strategy is a clear-sighted examination of external economic constraints and opportunities at the present time and in the future. The firm's broad strategies must next be related to its own internal constraints, and its strengths and weaknesses *vis-à-vis* its existing and potential competitors. The firm needs to carry out a careful audit of its resources of all types and to match these against its proposed strategies and available opportunities. Such a resources audit, if conducted carefully and honestly, may itself suggest avenues for profitable development and parts of the business which require close attention.

Quite often companies have vague aspirations about future development, but no clear ideas either on how to achieve them, or on the resources needed. Yet they may go ahead regardless, and wonder why their targets are never achieved. This is especially the case with mergers and take-overs, where vague desires for growth and size often overcome all reason. Yet effective mergers require exhaustive analysis of underlying motivations and a clear and unprejudiced knowledge of the relative strengths and weaknesses of the companies involved.

A careful resources audit may easily highlight areas where the company is exceptionally weak and should withdraw from the business in question to use its scarce resources more effectively. Disinvestment of this nature seems to be one of the most difficult decisions management is called upon to make. It means, at least temporarily, a reduction in the scale of operations, and also implies that past decisions may have been wrong, an admission that few people will make voluntarily.

This brief sketch of some of the main steps in the planning process clearly demonstrates that effective planning is inseparable from the other functions of management, and especially of senior management. Too often corporate planning is hived off into a separate department with no direct communication with the board of directors and no clear commitment on the part of the board. The annual corporate plan becomes a complex rigmarole totally separate from management's normal functions. In practice that is not planning, but lip service to planning.

Once the company has defined its objectives, has properly identified its opportunities, strengths and weaknesses, and has drawn up its strategies, the next step is to translate these into plans for action. Corporate planning establishes the framework within which management makes its short-term decisions and controls the daily operations. Obviously such planning must be sufficiently flexible to cope with sudden changes in the environment. If planning has been done properly, however, external changes should not create profound shocks to the company and it should be able to adapt relatively smoothly. Plans should be living entities rather than fossils.

The broad company targets and strategies will be translated into more detailed targets for each profit centre and department. Thus an overall requirement for a given return on capital might, at a lower level, be translated into a target of £100000 profit with a new capital allocation of, say, £50000. A broad strategy of penetration of the European market might be redefined as sales of £250000 of a particular product via the Brussels office in six months' time, with the establishment of a processing plant in eighteen months. In this manner, company targets can be transformed into means of management control, through all levels of the management hierarchy. The precise planning routes taken by individual companies, however, depend so much on individual circumstances that further generalisations are not possible. A common theme, not only of planning, but of management's tasks broadly defined, is the central role of economic analysis. This is obvious when applied to external developments and changes in the broad legal framework within which firms must operate. Analysis of cost and price trends, raw material availability, interest-rate movements, and market developments obviously requires people with at least a nodding acquaintance with economics. A sound knowledge of managerial economics is also central to the internal aspects of planning and development. The economist's tool kit, described in the next chapter and developed in subsequent chapters, is the most useful collection of weapons for clear and concise analysis of the central issues facing the business. The method of thinking imposed by a study of economics is also a considerable asset.

II

FUNDAMENTAL ECONOMIC CONCEPTS

Economics defined

There are almost as many definitions of economics as there are economists. One of the most useful, given by Professor Samuelson in his world-famous textbook, is 'Economics is the study of how men and society choose, with or without the use of money, to employ scarce productive resources, which could have alternative uses, to produce various commodities over time and to distribute them for consumption, now and in the future, among various people and groups in society.'[1] If all resources were abundant there would be no difficulty in making a choice either between alternative uses or between the present and future. Moreover, the distribution of the fruits of these resources would be relatively simple. In practice man's basic needs are few, but his wants are unlimited and tend to rise over time. Resources, however, are, in the last analysis, finite, and of varying quality and accessibility. The main economic resources are land, labour, and capital, which is essentially stored-up labour. Other resources, such as water and air, have been regarded as so abundant that they have been termed 'free goods', but growing concern about pollution, and increasing demands on natural resources, are rapidly changing attitudes.

Unlike physical scientists, economists are rarely able to perform controlled experiments to test how their theories operate in practice. They are mainly concerned with the activities of human beings and man-made organisations that are never entirely predictable. The world is so richly complex that economists must necessarily abstract what they regard as the key variables, and build simplified theories and models. Moreover, both to keep themselves sane and also to provide a firm basis for analysis, they must assume that man, in his economic activities at least, is a rational being working to maximise his self-interest, however this might be expressed. This need to build operationally useful theories from an analysis of the real world explains why economists, like weather forecasters, often fail to predict accurately; both the economic

[1] *Economics. An Introductory Analysis*, by P. A. Samuelson, 5th edition 1961, McGraw-Hill.

environment and the atmosphere are highly complex systems. It also explains the oft repeated gibes about two-handed economists, and their frequent failure to agree amongst themselves; each can emphasise different aspects of the real world.

A common fallacy, frequently encountered, is that the type of behaviour that is right for the individual also works for the economic system as a whole. For example, the virtue of increasing private savings might be a public vice in a recession. The whole is not always equal to the sum of the parts, nor are micro- and macro-economic aims necessarily congruent.

The remainder of this chapter describes some of the most useful tools for managers available from the economist's tool box. In the last analysis they may seem to be merely commonsense, but it is a very rigorous commonsense. Many of the tools are derived from simple abstractions such as perfect competition in which buyers and sellers have equal bargaining power and equal knowledge, and both are concerned with maximising profits to the exclusion of other targets such as those sketched in the previous chapter. One of the failures of much economics teaching is that too much stress is laid on this over-simple model of the real world and that the necessary adaptations to present-day reality are only acknowledged hurriedly at the end. Nonetheless, the model does allow a clear description of the basic economic tools. This chapter only outlines those aspects of the theory that are directly useful in management; detailed exposition with all the necessary qualifications is available in the standard text-books on economic theory.

Opportunity cost

The appropriate costs to consider in choosing between two alternatives are frequently not the prices dictated by the market place, but the *opportunity costs*. Here examples are easier than description. The opportunity cost of using a machine is the most profitable alternative sacrificed by employing the machine in its present use. The opportunity cost of buying a colour television is the interest or profit that could be earned by investing the purchase money. The opportunity cost of working for oneself in a shop is the salary that one could earn in other occupations, suitably adjusted for all the non-pecuniary satisfactions of being one's own boss. These examples involve clearcut choices between two tangible alternatives, but opportunity costs are not always as obvious.

If a machine has been standing idle the opportunity cost of bringing it into production is nil. There is no need to make a charge for it nor to apportion overheads and other fixed costs to its output. In making pricing decisions relating to under-utilised production capacity, it is not necessary to include all the costs allocated to the machine in the past, as they have already been incurred, but merely the cost of employing it in that use rather than in any other. If it has no other use it has no opportunity cost. An annual depreciation charge calculated on original cost for accounting purposes has little relevance to the opportunity cost of employing assets. Only the additional sacrifices forgone in making the decision need be considered.

Not all opportunity costs involve actual monetary payments. A man on a desert island might have the choice between picking coconuts or fishing. The opportunity cost of coconuts is the weight of fish that might be obtained with similar time and effort—irrespective of how much the man likes shinning up trees.

Opportunity costs are important when considering make-or-buy decisions, and also when deciding whether or not to sell. For example, the alternative to using business premises which one owns as offices is to rent or sell them. The opportunity cost is the rental forgone, or the difference between the expected market value at the beginning and end of the year, whichever is the higher. Decisions on whether to make or buy a component or material are very common in industry. Account must be taken of the opportunity costs of each alternative, such as the effect of using equipment that might profitably be used now or later for producing another product, the difficulties of ensuring adequate quality, or possible disruption to delivery because of transport trouble or strikes in the supplying firms.

Whilst consideration of opportunity costs is essential for the correct choice of alternatives, most accounting systems are not organised to provide accurate direct estimates. This means that they must be separately assessed for each decision. Cost-accounting systems that allocate fixed costs and depreciation on the basis of some formula such as direct-labour and raw-material costs, or sales turnover, obviously fail to reflect the opportunity costs of idle capacity in different departments.

One form of opportunity cost which is widely used is in the analysis of capital projects. The discount rate used to work out net present values when evaluating capital projects is theoretically an opportunity cost of capital. The alternative to carrying out the project is to invest the money in a safe alternative and the evaluation is designed to ascertain whether the project yields a higher return. This aspect of opportunity cost is discussed in more detail later in this chapter.

Marginal and incremental costs

The concept of the *margin* is perhaps the most fundamental of all economic theories. In decision making, the most important costs and revenues are not those operating over the whole range of output or sales but those at the margin. *Marginal costs* are the costs involved in producing one extra unit of output in the cheapest way possible. This involves making a distinction between *fixed costs* which are independent of changes in output, and *variable costs* which change with output. The *average cost* per unit of output is the total cost divided by the number of units produced, and the *marginal cost* is the difference between the total costs of producing (x) units and $(x + 1)$ units. Economic theory assumes that output can change by infinitely small amounts, and the marginal cost can be obtained by differential calculus.

Once a firm has installed its equipment, its prospective output is limited in the short run by its capacity. Overheads such as rent, insurance, rates and office staff, and depreciation are fixed. These fixed costs per unit will decline as output increases to the limit of capacity. The variable costs per unit such as raw material, power and process labour will initially tend to decline with output because of increasing returns to the variable factors, but as the plant nears capacity variable costs per unit will rise faster than output because of management difficulties, the extra costs of overtime and so on. Traditionally, therefore, a firm's *short-run* costs can be graphically depicted as shown in Chart 2.1.

Because the fixed costs continue whether or not anything is produced, marginal costs in the short run depend only on variable costs. As long as the marginal cost per unit remains below the price received it will pay the firm to produce. In Chart 2.1, *P* is the critical point. The firm will cover its variable costs and make some contribution towards overheads at outputs greater than OP' and prices above OA. From *P* the firm will move along its marginal cost curve, as price rises, to *Q* and beyond. *Q* is the point at which the firm is covering its total costs, and any subsequent price rise will enable it to earn profits. The more rigorous theoretical analysis includes a 'normal' profit in fixed costs. In a perfectly competitive climate *Q* is the point of long-run equilibrium both for the firm and for the industry with a price of *OB*. Chapter III discusses the cost side in more detail, and Chapter V sets out the equilibrium price.

The above cost structures of course only operate in the short run, which economists define as that period of time in which the capital equipment and overheads of the firm are fixed. Even in the short run, however, the firm has a certain flexibility in varying the inputs of factors of production such as process labour and raw materials. As time passes the firm obtains greater and greater flexibility; its equipment becomes worn out, obsolete, or is replaced, and overhead expenses can be altered. Thus in the long run all costs are variable; short-run marginal costs are less flexible than long-run costs and are below them. The difference between the long and short run varies considerably between products and

Chart 2.1

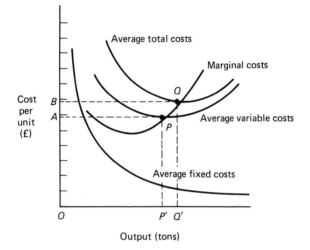

Output (tons)

industries. In an industry such as fashion with virtually no capital commitment, the short run is very short indeed, whereas in something like mining it is measured almost in decades.

The cost model of Chart 2.1 is derived from the perfect-competition theories of the nineteenth century. In practice, empirical studies suggest that marginal costs do not vary greatly with output, but are constant over much wider ranges. One reason is that managements increasingly regard labour as a fixed cost, particularly in large capital intensive plants, and power consumption may also vary little with output. The main variable costs then become raw materials, the price of which is only likely to vary with the firm's output if the firm is a very large buyer relative to the available supply. In many manufacturing firms the cost curves look more like those in Chart 2.2 than in Chart 2.1.

Average variable costs remain approximately constant until capacity output is reached, when they start to rise sharply. Constant marginal costs mean that marginal costs and average variable costs are the same. This cost structure inevitably eases the problems of decision taking.

Whilst economists may indulge in elegant theories, a manager does not have the time or scope for precise calculation of cost curves even if his accounting system is sufficiently refined, which is doubtful. Nonetheless, the marginal analysis of the economist can be suitably coarsened for use by management. The relevant concept is *incremental costs*. Whilst marginal costs refer to a unit of output, incremental cost is defined as the

Chart 2.2

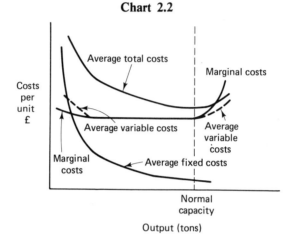

change in total cost resulting from a decision, and incremental revenue as the change in total revenue. Marginal analysis suggests it is profitable for firms to expand output until marginal costs equate with the price. Similarly, for the businessman a decision is profitable as long as the incremental costs of that decision are less than the incremental revenues. Again this means distinguishing between those costs that are fixed for the duration of the decision, and those that can vary. Only the latter are relevant in any incremental analysis.

The decision involved in considering incremental costs may have nothing to do with changes in output. The problem may be whether or not to close down a factory, rationalise the product range, or change the manufacturing process. Nonetheless, one of the most important decisions is whether or not to take low-priced orders which fail to cover full costs. Incremental analysis shows that if there is idle capacity it may well pay to take such business. Orders at prices below full costs are worthwhile as long as the *additional* revenue associated with them exceeds the *additional* costs involved. Depreciation or overheads that would be incurred irrespective of the decision are not relevant.

Obviously the comparison of incremental costs and revenues is not the only relevant factor involved in such decisions, even though important. Long-term policies may require a decision contrary to incremental analysis. For example, acceptance of one order below full cost may lead to pressures for similar treatment by other customers which the firm might be in too weak a position to resist. In practice, of course, this possibility would be covered by an opportunity-cost analysis. Another factor might be the impact of a decision to price below full cost on demand in the long term, or on the possibility of government price control, or anti-monopoly action.

Examples of the incremental-cost approach are common in public-utility pricing decisions. Off-peak charges for electricity and railway travel, the post office's telephone tariff, and the practice of coal merchants, central-heating installers and double-glazing firms of reducing prices in the summer all illustrate incremental analysis in action. Off-peak charges cover the incremental costs of supply and contribute to overheads, and it is therefore often useful to reduce prices in order to utilise spare capacity and encourage demand. If an additional effect is to reduce demand at the peaks that is all to the good, as it will lower the total capacity needed and allow a more efficient allocation of resources on a national basis.

It is often useful to reformulate the incremental principle in terms of *contribution*. In the short run, an activity may be justified as long as it makes a contribution to overheads and profits. The total cost of producing, say, deep-freezers, may be £100 when all fixed costs and overheads are allocated, but the price obtainable may be only £90. There is an apparent loss of £10 per deep-freezer, and there seems to be a case for stopping production. The incremental cost may only be £50, so that the contribution to overheads and fixed costs is £40. If production were to stop, some other method would be required of covering these fixed costs. Decisions are rarely so simple in practice, and usually different product lines are being compared. The appropriate comparison is of contributions, rather than estimates of profits or losses based on some arbitrary allocation of all non-attributable fixed expenses.

Frequently management must decide how to divide limited resources between competing product groups. For example, an injection-moulding machine in a plastics fabricating factory may be adaptable to turn out three different products—buttons, toys, and name tabs. Buttons may give a contribution of 30 pence each, toys 60 pence each and name tabs only 20 pence each. Initially the choice would seem to be to maximise the production of toys, followed by buttons, with name tabs a poor third. But this takes no account of the machine cycle time involved in each product, which may be 5 minutes for buttons, 10 minutes for the far more complicated toys, and only 2 minutes for name tabs. If there is a limited number of machines, the firm may wish to maximise contribution per machine minute, and the appropriate figures are buttons 6 pence, toys 6 pence and name tabs 10 pence. This suggests a completely different decision from that implied by the crude figures. More usually, real decisions are far more complex with several different restraints in operation. The correct choice becomes a conventional linear programming exercise.

The contribution concept underlies break-even analysis, which is discussed in Chapter III. In this connection a basic assumption is that marginal costs (incremental average costs per unit) are similar in form to those of Chart 2.2, rather than those of Chart 2.1. In other words, an increase in output will not cause any increase in marginal costs; costs (and prices) are presumed to be linear over relevant outputs. Where the cost functions are non-linear the contribution concept can be adapted, although it is inevitably more complex.

Marginal utility

Marginal utility is an abstract concept formulated by nineteenth-century economists in attempts to explain the typical shape of demand curves. Customers buy products because they fulfil needs, and give some satisfaction or 'utility'. A first unit purchased will give a certain amount of utility. Purchase of subsequent units will raise total utility, but the marginal utility of each additional unit purchased will tend to fall. Total utility will grow at a slower and slower pace as purchases rise because man's psychological ability to appreciate more and more of the product normally declines. The first pint of beer consumed may taste marvellous, but after, say, the sixth (depending on individual capacity), each additional pint does little to raise total satisfaction. The law of diminishing marginal utility states that as the amount of a product purchased increases its marginal utility to an individual tends to decrease.

Economists have engaged in prolonged discussions on whether or not it is possible to add or compare the utilities of different people, or indeed whether the concept is operationally useful. Suffice it to say that the concept is used for demand theory and also underlies cost–benefit analysis. In this connection it is useful to remember that cost and utility are the joint determinants of *value*. Unless a product gives someone utility it will have no value or price, irrespective of the cost of production. Conversely, something such as air may give utility, but normally have no economic value because it costs nothing to produce.

The generalised marginal principle

The cornerstone of the economist's marginal analysis is that purchases, activities, or productive factors should be allocated so as to ensure that the marginal utilities, benefits, or value-added accruing from each are identical in all uses. It should not be possible to increase the total benefit, or reduce the total cost by moving one unit from one application to another. If this equimarginal condition is not met, the system is operating below its optimum, and it is always possible to gain some improvement by reallocation of inputs or purchases. The key assumption underlying this result is the 'law of diminishing returns' or variable proportions, which has already been touched on in the previous section in dealing with utility. For the *equimarginal principle* to operate, diminishing returns are held to apply. In the case of production the 'law' implies that the marginal product will decline as more and more of one resource is combined with fixed amounts of another. This proposition in fact holds over a wide range of economic activity. For example, successive applications of fertiliser tend to raise cereal yields per acre, but increasing quantities of fertiliser are successively required to give equal output increases.

A simplified example might clarify the principle. A firm has two departments A and B, and a fixed labour force which it can allocate in the most efficient manner possible. With the present labour distribution the marginal product per worker (incremental revenue less incremental costs) in A is £100, and in B it is £60. Obviously it would pay the firm to move workers from department B into department A because each worker moved would raise the firm's total product by £40. Clearly the effect would be to raise the marginal product of workers in department B and reduce it in A, until the marginal product is the same in the two departments at, say, £80. To the objection that workers are not sufficiently divisible as to ensure complete equality of marginal products, it may be argued that the hours they work are; on this basis, fractions of men are perfectly feasible.

The equimarginal principle is one of the most common theorems of economics, and it is applied in varying situations in the remainder of this book. One use, for example, is in the analysis of pollution control where the cost of installing, say, smoke-stack precipitators, should be compared with the benefit. The proper aim should never be the elimination of all pollution as that might be unnecessarily expensive. Rather the costs of control should be traded off against some acceptable level of pollution, which will vary according to geographic and other circumstances. The equimarginal principle is also the basis of capital allocation, where the aim is to utilise available funds in such manner as to ensure that the discounted returns are equalised in all uses. This entails expanding those activities that yield a high return, and withdrawing from those with a low return, until the marginal returns are equal. This is simple in theory but very difficult to achieve in practice.

Whilst the equimarginal principle has a very wide range of uses, its practicable application can be far more complex than this section suggests. One important complication is that over wide ranges of output diminishing marginal returns may not operate. Returns may be constant or even increase. A firm may be able to allocate all its labour in one department without meeting diminishing returns until the department reaches full capacity. In this situation it may not be possible to equate marginal products in all departments, but the principle can be applied nevertheless. As far as possible resources should be applied to those activities which yield the highest returns before starting less productive activities. In many factories, of course, it is technically necessary to produce products with high and low marginal products simultaneously. It is worth re-emphasising that the marginal products have been defined as incremental revenues less incremental costs. Account should always be taken of any possible change in revenues, such as a price drop, involved in altering the allocation of resources.

Time and the discounting principle

We have already seen that the nature of costs varies with the passage of time. In the short term most costs are fixed, whereas the longer the period under consideration, the more costs become variable, until in the long run all costs can be varied. No decision is likely to be correct which fails to take time into account—or the changing nature of costs and revenues over time. The main role of company managements is to foster the interests of shareholders. These interests must, however, be considered in a long-run context with the firm as a continuing entity, and short-term profit maximisation may run counter to this aim. Managers must pay adequate attention to the conflicting demands of employees, customers, and the public interest, and these interests must temper short-term profit maximisation. If, for example, prices are set too high in a period of temporary shortage so that the firm enjoys monopoly profits, customer goodwill may be sacrificed and alternative suppliers encouraged. Similarly the management may keep variable costs as low as possible by neglecting employee welfare to such an extent as to promote high labour turnover and serious unrest. Yet again, too little attention may be paid to the environmental aspects of the firm's activities, and no provision initially made for effluent control. Public authorities may then impose rigid requirements involving heavy capital expenditure. The message is that management's time perspective must not be too short. The consequences of an action can vary over time, and it is important to take any long-run effects into account when making a decision.

A basic human characteristic is the preference for consumption today over consumption tomorrow. Jam today is always better than jam tomorrow, unless sufficient incentive is offered to forgo the immediate enjoyment of today's jam. This is not because of uncertainty about the likely receipt of tomorrow's jam, but merely a property of the passage of time. Given a choice between a sum of £250 now or the same sum next year, only a lunatic would accept the money next year, even if all prices were completely stable. Investing the money, even in the National Savings Bank at say 8% per annum, would make it worth more than £250 in a year's time. £250 today is worth £270 in a year's time. Conversely, next year's £250 is worth £231.48 today at the same 8% per annum interest rate. Obviously the interest rate a person is prepared to accept to forgo present consumption can vary considerably according to his economic circumstances. That required by an ascetic monk may be very low indeed, whilst a starving father of ten would demand a very high interest rate. The opportunity cost of present consumption is infinitely higher for the father than for the monk.

The possibility of earning interest with the passage of time means that even in a world without price inflation all future costs and revenues must be discounted back at an appropriate interest rate before they can be properly compared with expenses incurred or revenues received today. The proper evaluation of alternatives requires the use of an appropriate discount rate.

The general formula for converting future money to present-day values is a derivation of the formula for compound interest. Its generalised expression is:

$$P = \sum_{t=1}^{T} \frac{S_t}{(1+r)^t}$$

where
    P = present value
    S = future sum
    r = rate of interest
    t = number of years elapsing before S is received

The rate of interest in this equation is an opportunity cost. An example makes the discounting principle clearer. A firm is due to receive royalties of £500 per annum for the next five years, and the appropriate rate of interest is 10%. The present value of these royalties is:

$$P = \frac{500}{(1+0.10)} + \frac{500}{(1+0.10)^2} + \frac{500}{(1+0.10)^3} + \frac{500}{(1+0.10)^4} + \frac{500}{(1+0.10)^5}$$

$$P = \frac{500}{1.10} + \frac{500}{1.21} + \frac{500}{1.331} + \frac{500}{1.4641} + \frac{500}{1.61051}$$

$$P = £454.55 + £413.22 + £375.66 + £341.51 + £310.46$$

$$\underline{P = £1895.4}$$

The present value of £1 895.4 may be compared with alternative receipts, similarly discounted, so that the firm may discover the most appropriate method of deploying its funds. Use of published discounting tables simplifies the necessary computations; appropriate computer programs are also available.

Whilst the discounting principle is appropriate for all decisions involving money in the future, its main use is in the evaluation of investment decisions and the choice of appropriate capital projects. Typically, an investment decision involves the commitment of resources today in order to achieve an annual stream of outputs in the future. Once the resources are committed, they are tied up during the life of the assets; the management's time perspective in regard to these resources has been altered from the long to the short run.

The analysis of capital projects is a complex process which cannot be adequately covered in this description of basic economic concepts. The only point emphasised here is that correct analysis must take into account the life of the assets, their residual value, and the size and timing of cash expenditures and receipts over this life. This inevitably requires some form of discounting method to convert money earned at different times into present values. Failure to discount could easily involve faulty investment decisions, particularly when two projects are being compared. For example, two projects each with the same £1 000 initial outlay may give completely different cash inflows. Project A may be for a new product which takes a long while to build up a market, so that inflows remain low in the early years. Project B, however, may be for a product which has a large assured outlet in the first few years, but which will then be made obsolete in most uses. The undiscounted value of cash inflows may, as in the example below, be identical for both projects, so that the undiscounted average return on initial capital would be the same. Management might, therefore, invest in the project with the long-term future, yet project B would probably be that preferred on a discounted basis. Receipts in the near future are preferable to inflows in the more distant future, even if both are equally certain (which is not so here). It would pay the firm to invest in project B with the higher net present value.

| | Project A | | | Project B | | |
Year	Net cash flow £	Discount factor (10%)	Present value £	Net cash flow £	Discount factor (10%)	Present value £
1	50	0.909	45.5	500	0.909	454.5
2	100	0.826	82.6	500	0.826	413.0
3	150	0.751	112.7	500	0.751	375.5
4	250	0.683	170.6	400	0.683	273.2
5	350	0.621	217.4	300	0.621	186.3
6	500	0.565	282.5	200	0.565	113.0
7	600	0.513	307.8	100	0.513	51.3

		Project A	Project B
Undiscounted net cash flow	£	2 000	2 000
Present value of net cash flow	£	1 219.1	1 866.8
less Cost	£	−1 000	−1 000
Net Present Value	£	219.1	866.8

An alternative way of analysing projects is to find the rate of return required to bring the net present value to zero. This method, known as DCF analysis, treats the net cash flows arising from a project as a mixture of interest on capital plus the recovery of the capital. It involves calculating the net return (after tax) earned on the capital remaining in a project and is done by interpolating in annuity tables. In the example project A gives a DCF rate of return of just over 14.4% and project B a rate of almost 39.4%.

The discussion has assumed that the firm is aiming to maximise profits from its investment, and that no other objective is more important. On the other hand, when the discounted rates of return of projects A and B are correctly calculated, the firm may still prefer A on the ground that it would be gaining entry into a strategically important market. Nonetheless, the use of discounted expenditures and receipts would at least ensure that its decision was soundly based and management was fully aware of the consequences. The use of appropriate discounted-cash-flow (DCF) techniques is particularly important where governments use the tax system, or direct incentives such as grants, to stimulate investment.

Risk and uncertainty

Nearly all management decisions are made in an atmosphere of *uncertainty*, because it is never possible to predict the future with complete confidence. Although they are closely intertwined, a distinction is made between *risk*, which can be assessed on the basis of past experience, and insured against, and *uncertainty* which is not insurable. A life assurance company, working on the basis of past experience, can assess the risk of people in certain age groups dying, whereas there is no means of insuring against the uncertainty attaching to most business decisions. One theory of profit is that it is the reward necessary to induce firms to take risks and accept uncertainty. The greater the degree of uncertainty attaching to a business (e.g. mineral exploration versus operating a mine) the greater the required profit.

One of the main decision areas in which risk and uncertainty are particularly important is investment project evaluation. Estimates of a project's future cash flow (and often its cost) are inevitably *uncertain*. Any single measure (e.g. a DCF rate of return) is an unreliable guide to its worth as it gives no guide to the degree of uncertainty attached to it. Also there is always a *risk* that the actual return will differ markedly from the expected return. It is necessary to estimate both the risk of a project not achieving the required rate of return, and also the risk of not recovering the money invested.

The estimated return is built up from assumed capital costs and cash flows. The probability of this return being achieved will generally take the form of the normal distribution shown in Chart 2.3. The normal distribution is the mathematical 'law' for dealing with quantities whose magnitude is continuously variable. The area under the curve represents the probability that the return will lie between two given values. The most likely return is E, but there is a strong probability that the actual return will diverge from it, in either direction, if the assumptions have been made completely objectively.

In general more uncertainty surrounds completely new plants, than the

Chart 2.3

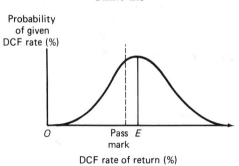

DCF rate of return (%)

replacement of existing assets with plants that have already been proved in use, because the cost data of the latter can be forecast with some confidence. It tends to be higher in new markets (either product or geographical) than in markets in which a company already has extensive knowledge. The degree of uncertainty cannot be specified in advance for different types of project, but varies with the individual circumstances of each proposal. In Chart 2.4 both projects A and B have the same expected DCF rate of return, but project B is relatively certain (a high percentage of the area under the curve lies within a narrow range of E), whilst project A is much less certain to achieve E. In statistical terms their mean DCF rates of return are identical, but B has a much lower

Chart 2.4

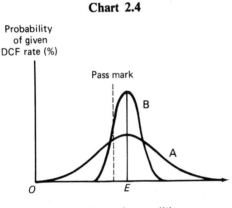

standard deviation than A. Some measure of this standard deviation is needed to allow for uncertainty.

Use of a required rate of return without any measure of probability carries a risk that the returns calculated for a project may be biased. This risk is negligible for projects of the B type, but can be significant in the A type. A manager may have a pet project and it would be natural for him to adopt those assumptions which show the project in the best light, even if this is subconscious rather than conscious optimism. Thus in Chart 2.5 the most likely estimate of the expected return is E, but R could easily be predicted with minor variations in the assumptions. This might make all the difference between a project's authorisation or rejection. A single measure of profitability hides such optimistic bias, which means that projects are more likely to fall short of the predicted rate R than to reach it.

The risk involved in a project is connected with the degree of

Chart 2.5

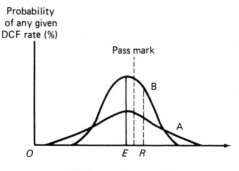

DCF rate of return (%)

uncertainty attached to estimates of the return. Two companies may, however, adopt different attitudes to the degree of uncertainty involved in identical projects. The faster the company's rate of growth, the greater its need to accept riskier projects. The available projects offering acceptable and virtually certain returns are limited, so that the company must branch out into new markets or novel processes. Unless it expands through acquisition its knowledge of these new areas will be more sketchy than for its existing business. A higher degree of risk here does not necessarily mean that expected returns will be higher than for low-risk projects. Indeed the reverse could hold. The greater the size of a project in relation to the size of the company and its available resources, the greater the risk. If a project is small the risk of failure will have little effect on the company, which will be willing to sacrifice some safety for the probability of higher returns. If, however, the project is very large relative to the company's assets or cash flow, the company will seek to minimise the possibility of loss. Of course, the simultaneous failure of a large number of small projects could also have a disastrous effect, but the chances of this occurring are smaller than the chance of failure of a single project. Possible methods for coping with the uncertainty and risk underlying investment decisions are:

(a) *A higher required rate of return*

Different pass marks might be set for projects carrying different degrees of uncertainty. This approach, however, provides no criteria for deciding what types of project should be counted as relatively certain and what as relatively uncertain.

The assumption seems to be that there is a much greater probability that the actual return will fall below the predicted level than that it will be exceeded. A further assumption is that any predicted return is the most likely outcome E, and not some biased estimate such as R. If bias does exist, a higher pass mark will not necessarily ensure that undesirable projects are excluded; it might just entail greater subjectivity on the part of those making the cash-flow forecasts.

A far more serious objection is that this approach assumes that the probability of an estimated cash flow materialising will diminish each year (the future is more uncertain than the present) and furthermore will diminish by a fixed percentage of the probability in the preceding year.

In practice not all uncertainty is of this type. If, for example, the plant is to manufacture a new product for which the company has an assured source of raw materials and a long-term contract at a fixed price, the major uncertainty will be associated with the capital cost and timing of the investment. To require a higher discounting rate for future revenues, which are fairly certain, is inappropriate for such situations where the proposed capital expenditures are uncertain.

(b) *Calculation of 'super-profits'*

This involves discounting the cash flows of the project at a standard discount rate to determine the net present value of 'super-profits' available as a protection against failure. It involves the implicit assumption that the basic cash-flow estimates are relatively certain, even though the project may be risky to the company (because, say, of its size and the amount of capital committed). The project is assumed to be of the B rather than A type, although the A type is more likely in practice. No amount of apparent 'super-profits' will protect against failure if the chance of such failure is relatively high.

(c) *Risk analysis*

Each variable in the cash-flow forecast is assigned a range of values with an associated probability. Using a computer, different random values of the variables are successively generated to produce a probability curve of the expected DCF rate of return. The computer simulates sufficient combinations of the expected variables to measure not only the most likely rate of return (E), but also the shape of the curve (i.e. both the mean and standard deviation). The number of computer runs required normally lies between 100 and 500. The main advantages claimed are:

1. More accurate assessment of the expected result than is given by a single-figure estimate.

2. Knowledge of the range of possible outcomes, and hence an indication of the risks attached to the proposal.

3. Knowledge of the probability of each outcome, and hence of the likelihood of the decision being a bad one.

(d) *Sensitivity analysis*

Full risk analysis, though the most satisfactory approach, is both expensive and time consuming, requiring a considerable amount of management involvement, preparation, and computer time. The main variables in an investment decision are usually the capital cost, the costs of production and the level of sales and prices. Sensitivity checks show the effect on the expected return of varying any one of these factors independently. Whilst providing no overall measure of the degree of uncertainty, sensitivity analysis is useful in showing the most critical areas of an investment project.

(e) *Weighted returns*

Quick indications of a project's worth may often be needed. One possibility is to make three estimates of the expected cash flows:

> The most likely outcome.
> A fairly optimistic estimate.
> A moderately pessimistic view.

This shows the expected range of the rate of return (or if discounted at the standard pass mark, of the net present values of the project). The three estimates are then weighted, using standard weights, to give some indication of the uncertainty involved. The weights normally proposed are 50% for the most probable and 25% for the optimistic and pessimistic predictions. The weight could, however, be varied according to circumstances, perhaps assigning a greater weight to the pessimistic estimate if there were a need to ensure that all projects adopted stood a good chance of success. This approach has the merit of simplicity and relative ease of calculation when compared with sensitivity analysis, but it still runs the risk of bias. Only certain parameters are assigned to a probability distribution (the most-likely, pessimistic and optimistic values) without the distribution being fully defined.

Summary

Since the concepts described in this chapter will be encountered throughout the book a summary may be useful.

Economics is concerned with the choice of alternatives in a world of scarce resources.

The appropriate cost to consider in choosing between alternatives is the opportunity cost—the cost of the most profitable alternative sacrificed in making the decision.

The most important costs and revenues in decision making are those operating at the margin. In practical terms, a decision is correct if the incremental revenue (change in total revenue created) in taking it exceeds the incremental costs (change in total costs involved).

This requires distinguishing between those costs that are effectively fixed for the period of the decision and those that are variable, but care must be taken to choose the appropriate time perspective.

Decisions based on full costs may be incorrect, particularly in short-run periods of excess capacity.

Decisions may have different consequences in the long run than in the short run, and allowance must be made for this.

An activity may be justified in the short term as long as it makes a contribution to fixed expenses and overheads. Contribution is the difference between revenue and incremental costs.

Resources should so be allocated as to ensure that their net marginal products (incremental revenues less incremental costs) in each activity are equal. This equimarginal principle applies wherever there is an allocation problem.

As the amount of a product purchased by an individual increases, the amount of extra satisfaction, or marginal utility derived from each extra unit, tends to decrease.

Money today is worth more than money tomorrow. All future costs and revenues involved in a decision must be discounted back to present values to give appropriate yardsticks for comparison.

The need to discount is particularly acute in investment decisions.

Because it is impossible to predict the future with confidence, all business decisions are uncertain. Sufficient allowance must be made for this uncertainty, and single-figure forecasts regarded with suspicion.

Uncertainty is uninsurable, whereas risk can be assessed on the basis of past experience and can be insured against. Different firms have different attitudes to risk.

III

COST ANALYSIS

General issues

The previous chapter has introduced some basic concepts such as marginal and incremental costs, and fixed and variable costs, which will now be discussed in more detail. First, a word of warning is necessary; comparisons are drawn between the economist's and accountant's methods of looking at costs. These comparisons are not intended to attach any praise to the former or blame the latter. Both economists and accountants have different, and, at times, overlapping roles; like Britain and America, however, they share a common language which is often a cause of mutual confusion and incomprehension.

At any time a firm's cost structure reflects decisions made in the past about the size of plant, the technical process adopted, the factory's location, the product range, the social organisation of management and the labour force, and so on. These are all influences on long-run costs to be considered later in this chapter. Once these decisions have been made, however, costs reflect the firm's short-run production function. That is, they mirror the precise combination of factors of production, such as land, labour and capital, that the firm has decided it needs to make its product range. In essence they result from a technical decision about the production process; so many men are required using so much raw materials to work a given range of machines to produce a particular output. Even in the short run, however, management can in many instances vary the precise combination of factors of production within limits. Most firms do not have sufficient market power greatly to influence the price they pay for labour, raw materials and other inputs. They must, therefore, vary resource inputs so as to minimise their unit costs. Firms which do have sufficient market power to dominate one or more factors of production are known as *monopsonists*. Frequently they tend to be publicly owned. Major examples are the Post Office in its purchase of telecommunications equipment and the Central Electricity Generating Board in heavy electrical equipment. The National Coal Board is a monopsony in the employment of coal miners, and the Post Office in the employment of postmen.

Classification of costs

The need for management to be able to respond to changes in the market price of inputs highlights the importance of very careful analysis of short-run costs. A distinction has already been drawn between fixed and variable costs, but it is now necessary to explore this more deeply.

The terms 'fixed' and 'variable' are in relation to output and not to the passage of time. The former do not change regardless of the number of units produced whereas the latter move proportionately with output. It is always important to be clear whether one is discussing total costs or average costs per unit of output. Most economic and accounting theory is expounded in terms of average unit costs. There is no absolute yardstick of what costs are fixed and what are variable, even in the short run, when the physical equipment of an enterprise is unchanged. Indeed, there is no absolute yardstick for measuring costs at all; it depends entirely on the purpose of the analysis. Accounting is as much a matter of judgment as economics, and is not just an exercise in adding up numbers fitting into predetermined rigid categories. Thus, for some purposes, process labour may appropriately be treated as fixed when it is underemployed and a decision is required on whether or not to take on extra work which requires no overtime working. This highlights the fact that the short and long run merge into each other, and that what is fixed for one decision may well be variable for a similar decision at a different level of output. Thus, in the above example, if output were to rise still further, process labour would become a variable cost if it were necessary to pay overtime. Moreover, process labour would also be a variable cost at much lower levels of output; if output fell back the firm would first eliminate overtime, then introduce short-time working, and then lay off some of the workers.

Few costs can be easily separated into those that are completely fixed and those that are perfectly variable with respect to output changes. There are many intermediate categories that are neither fish nor fowl, but are partly fixed and partly variable. For example, domestic gas and electricity consumers are usually charged on a two-part tariff; the charge is fixed up to a certain level of consumption, regardless of the units consumed, but subsequently a variable element comes in which varies directly with additional consumption. Many rental charges, as for photocopying equipment, are of this type, as are earnings of workers paid both salary and commission. Another example of a semi-fixed cost is depreciation, even though it is usually treated as completely fixed. The greater the output from a machine, particularly when it is operating near capacity, the greater may be wear and tear. Moving parts may deteriorate more quickly, and the machine may fall to pieces faster. Thus above a certain output depreciation may in part be a variable cost. In some cases costs may be fixed over wide ranges of output, but then jump in a step-wise fashion when output increases by an extra unit. This is because of what are known as *indivisibilities* in a particular input. An oft-quoted example is the salaries of first-line supervision; they may remain constant up to a certain level of output and then jump as a new supervisor is added. The cost of transport might follow the same pattern; lorries can only be added as complete units and a new one will be needed when the others are fully utilised. This example suggests that management can usually overcome indivisibilities, and smooth out step-like costs so that they are rarely encountered in practice. Thus a firm would probably contract out its additional transport needs until an extra lorry became economic, rather than run an under-utilised new vehicle. Some variable costs, particularly of raw materials, may move in a complex manner with output. For example, a firm may be able to take advantage of larger quantity discounts as its demand grows for a particular material; its unit costs for the input will tend to decline in a series of shallow steps as output increases.

In Chapter II the economist's marginal costs were shown in the form of a U-shaped curve, and it was suggested that in many companies marginal or incremental costs are constant over a wide range of output up to capacity working. We have now seen that costs of individual inputs can take more complicated shapes. The charts opposite show in pictorial form the examples cited above.

It has already been stressed that the distinction between fixed and variable costs or expenses changes depending on whether the decision is short or long run. Even when the size of plant is given, there are no hard and fast distinctions. The nature of costs varies with the requirements of the decision. Some costs, such as lighting and heating the factory, or supervisory staff, may be virtually fixed whilst the plant is operating, but can be forgone if the plant is shut down. Even when the plant is closed, however, some fixed costs are incurred to keep the factory on a standby basis, but are escapable if the company is liquidated. It may, for example, be necessary to incur certain ongoing maintenance expenses to keep the plant in a state of production readiness.

Some costs, though invariate with regard to output, can easily be altered at the discretion of management, and are thus not in the same category of fixed costs as, for example, depreciation. Selling expenses, research and development, and advertising are typical examples. Indeed it might be argued that the size of output varies according to the level of such costs. Certainly advertising has an impact on sales revenue.

Discretionary fixed costs of this type are usually programmed in advance. This introduces another complication. The nature of costs depends on the unit under consideration, whether it is an individual machine, a production department, a plant within a factory, a complete factory, or the company as a whole. Costs that might be fixed as far as a machine is concerned may be variable for the whole factory. Thus, in a textile factory fuel consumption might vary directly with output, but for each individual machine or department it will be fixed irrespective of output, as soon as one unit is produced.

Chart 3.1   Some simple forms of cost function

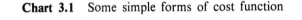

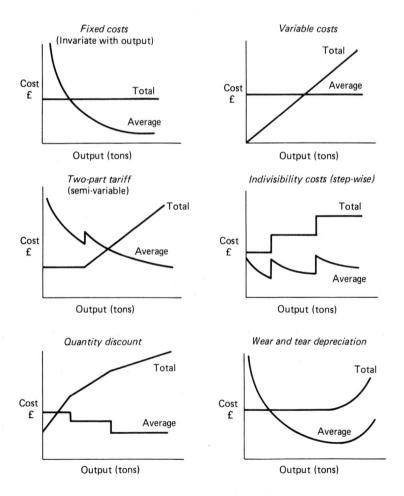

Although various types of cost function have been distinguished, the remainder of this chapter adopts the usual simplifying assumption that variable costs move linearly with output, at least up to a plant's capacity. Again capacity is not an unambiguous concept, but is highly elastic. It should properly be regarded as a series of constraints and bottlenecks of increasing severity which gradually inhibit further output increases. Frequently organisational changes, such as the adoption of three shift working in a factory that previously worked only one shift, or productivity agreements abolishing craftsmen's mates and allowing process workers to perform simple maintenance, can allow plants to run

Chart 3.2   Transportation cost for 16″ diameter pipeline

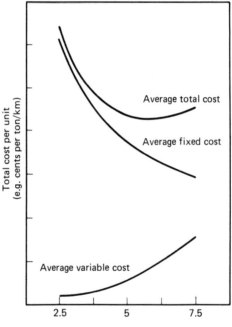

Throughput (million tons per year)

SOURCE: *Shell Information Handbook*, 1971–72; OECD, *Oil: The Present Situation and Future Prospects*, 1973.

far above their rated or design capacity. In many process industries it is possible to alter raw-material inputs or the plant's operating charac- teristics to give considerable output variations, particularly where the plant produces more than one product. Simply cutting out the need for maintenance shut down, or deferring it, may raise capacity by about 4%.

The constancy of marginal costs over wide ranges of output is supported by many empirical studies. Some writers go too far in asserting that sharply increasing costs with size are rare. Apart from the fertiliser type of example mentioned in Chapter II, Chart 3.2, redrawn from an OECD report on the oil industry, gives a clear case of costs increasing with size. As the flow through a pipeline of a given diameter is increased, variable costs per unit rise sharply.

Some US studies of manufacturing plants also support the view that costs may rise above a certain output although the rate of rise may be very gentle. Even if cost curves are slightly curved, however, a straight line may give a reasonable approximation for business decisions over the range of outputs likely to be encountered in practice. It is easier to see this if total costs rather than average costs per unit of output are plotted as in Chart 3.3.

Moreover, the typical U-shaped cost curve and constant costs can be reconciled if it is assumed that no factor of production is entirely fixed. The U-shaped curve is the counterpart of the law of variable proportions, whereby successive units of variable factors combined with one fixed factor tend to give successively smaller marginal products. In many manufacturing plants it is possible to vary all factors over wide output ranges. No single input is one-dimensional; each has several dimensions. Although the input may be fixed in one dimension it may be variable in others. Thus the number of men employed may be constant but the hours they work can vary; the number of machines may be constant but some may be closed down or the time they are operating may be changed. This ability to vary all productive factors within broad limits is widespread throughout large-scale manufacturing industry but less common in small-

Chart 3.3

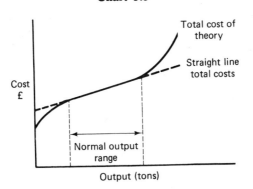

scale manufacturing and in other industries. It provides an adequate theoretical justification for assuming constant costs, provided allowance is always made for the possibility of diminishing returns to scale.

So far we have illustrated the need to subdivide and allocate costs according to the decision under review. Most costs can readily be allocated, but in some cases regression analysis or similar techniques might be required to determine the exact relationship between costs and output. One of the main functions of accounts departments is to record, and keep a close check on, costs—in a word, cost control. This means comparing actual costs with some predetermined standards for convenient cost centres within the company, such as departments. It is obviously impracticable always to present costs in all the available detail, even if it is recorded. Accountants, therefore, aggregate costs by centres in as little detail as is practicable. Yet, in order to take sensible management decisions, cost information is frequently required in different forms and for different groupings from those normally produced by cost accountants. Only where decisions have become routine can the accounting system regularly provide the necessary information in a standard form. Major decisions are rarely of this routine nature, so that special cost analyses are needed involving either a reallocation of the original data or estimation from what is available. Accountants are consequently often blamed for not making cost analyses for any conceivable eventuality, yet this would hardly be a productive use of their time.

The distinction between fixed and variable costs, though the most useful, is not the only one encountered in industry. Sometimes the terms *indirect* and *direct* costs are used in place of fixed and variable; direct costs vary with output, whilst indirect costs do not. The concepts of marginal and incremental cost and opportunity cost have already been discussed in Chapter II. Often a distinction is drawn between incremental and *sunk* costs; the former are those that result from a particular decision whilst the latter would be incurred regardless. Thus the obsolescence component of depreciation is a sunk cost which should be irrelevant for decisions once the equipment is installed, but any extra wear and tear incurred would be very relevant. Closely allied to the incremental or sunk costs dichotomy is that between *escapable* and *inescapable* costs. Escapable costs are those that would be reduced (or increased) if a particular decision was made, whilst inescapable costs would remain unchanged. In the discussion of opportunity costs it was pointed out that not all relevant costs were necessarily incurred; some might be *implicit*. In small businesses these might be the salary the owner might earn as an employee, or the interest and dividends on the capital he has tied up. These costs are implicit in that they probably do not enter into pricing decisions. Another breakdown is between *period* costs which are a function of time rather than activity, and *activity* costs which change with activity. Depreciation or rent would be period costs and raw materials an activity cost. From management's point of view it is useful to distinguish between those costs they can control—*controllable* costs—and those they cannot—*uncontrollable* costs. The higher up the management hierarchy, the greater the proportion of controllable costs facing a manager.

Few firms merely produce one product, but most have a wide range of different products which may even be produced on the same machinery. In process industries such as chemicals or oil refining the production of several products simultaneously is frequently inescapable, regardless of whether a market is always available for the by-products. This raises the question of dealing with *common* or *joint* costs. At one extreme such as the chemical works, all costs, both fixed and variable, might be common, whilst in engineering plants the only common costs may be certain fixed expenses. The correct allocation of common costs is one of the most difficult problems in cost accountancy and there is no easy solution. Economists might argue that incremental analysis of the effects of varying the output of one product on the various costs would resolve much of the problem, and that tracing the paternity of a cost is an irrelevant philosophical exercise. In many cases this may well be true, but this attitude does not help to price true joint products, or determine the most profitable product mix in process plants.

Normally accountants are forced to fall back on arbitrary rules of thumb when allocating joint costs. The usual methods are to apportion such costs either according to the sales value of each product or on some quantitative basis such as the weight of the output. Neither is entirely satisfactory. For example, allocation by turnover means that a change in the market price of one product would affect not only its own cost but also that of its co-products, which is hardly a rational way of looking at things. A price rise would increase the turnover of product X relative to Y and Z which would mean that its share of common costs ought to rise, thereby lowering the costs of Y and Z. If the reason for the allocation is to determine initial prices this method is nonsense. It is necessary to check the reason for allocating costs, and the appropriate method of allocation may vary with the reason. It may be necessary for pricing, inventory control, tax purposes, or merely for organisation reasons. Some allocation of costs may be necessary, for example, between cost centres, or for determining interdepartmental transfer prices. The main point is that the method of allocation chosen should not be shrouded in too much precision; otherwise a crude rule of thumb might take on the appearance of some divine law.

Historic and economic costs

We have already said that one of the main functions of accounts departments is to record and control costs. This requires the logging of all costs at the time they are incurred. Correct recording of historic costs is vital for the stewardship function of accounts departments. These costs form the backbone of the annual balance sheets and profit-and-loss statements required legally for presenting to shareholders. Yet these historic costs incurred are often irrelevant for decision making, because they fail adequately to reflect the opportunity costs of decisions. Enough has already been said about opportunity costing and incremental analysis to demonstrate this, but it is worth emphasising in the area of fixed assets. Most companies show plant, machinery, buildings and land in their books at the cost of acquisition. A depreciation charge is deducted from the year's trading profit by spreading this cost of acquisition over the asset's expected life. Tax arrangements and investment incentives are complicating factors but the usual procedures are either to spread the cost evenly over the expected life (*straight-line depreciation*) or to weight the earlier years more heavily (*reducing-balance depreciation*). The depreciation charge calculated in this manner is often used for costing exercises, even though opportunity costing shows that this historic charge is irrelevant. What matters is the opportunity cost of the assets at the time a decision is made. This requires considerable analysis and means that the appropriate charge (which may often be zero) cannot be calculated according to predetermined formulae. Perhaps more important, depreciation based on historic cost may completely fail to show the cost of replacing the underlying assets in a period of rapid price and cost inflation. Moreover, expressing fixed assets in the books at their acquisition costs may seriously undervalue a company's underlying asset base, particularly where it owns lands and buildings. Spotting such asset situations was an important feature of takeover bids in the UK in the late 1960s and early 1970s. Acquiring companies could revalue the assets of bought companies to show a large paper profit on their bid, which could be realised either as security for loans to finance further bids or by selling off the underlying assets. Such 'asset stripping' has now fallen out of favour. Most large companies tend to revalue their assets at periodic intervals both to avert such takeover situations and to ensure the fullest use of their resources.

As long as the going rate of inflation is moderate, say under 4% per annum, depreciation based on historic cost may not seriously underestimate replacement costs. For one thing technical improvements often tend to lower the capital cost per unit of output in a new plant, and few firms rarely replace obsolete or worn-out machines with identical equipment. The pace of inflation accelerated markedly in the UK from 1967–68, however, and historic-cost depreciation is no longer a good measure of replacement cost. This means that part of the profit shown in annual accounts should more accurately be treated as depreciation; conventional accounts will not correctly state either the capital or the profit. If all companies were forced to depreciate on replacement rather than historic costs, and to value fixed assets at replacement costs, relative stock-market valuations of different industries would change radically. Apparent profits shown by many manufacturing firms might be greatly reduced, but the earnings of property companies would fall even more because of the exclusion of any inflationary gain in land prices.

The rapid inflation of the early 1970s prompted the government to establish a Committee to study the best means of adapting accounts to the problems it posed. The Sandilands Report of 1975 recommended a comprehensive system of current cost accounting to provide a much better indication of the underlying state of a business than traditional accounts. The UK accounting profession in turn set up a Committee to study the best means of implementing the Sandilands proposals, and this reported in the autumn of 1976. Progress was interrupted in mid 1977 when a majority of the accounting profession voted against the proposed programme. This was, though, a Pyrrhic victory; UK company accounts will eventually be presented in such a way as to distinguish between real and inflationary developments.

Break-even and profit volume analysis

A common method of presenting cost information to management is in the form of break-even charts. Graphical presentation enables the salient features of a situation to be grasped quickly and a decision to be made on the basis of the main variables. It helps management to see the wood without too close a look at all the component trees. In practice, most managers suffer from a desire to see all the 'pertinent facts', and call for all the detailed costs behind break-even charts until they become over-borne by detail. Such a habit should be firmly resisted; only the *relevant* facts are necessary for a decision, and it is rarely necessary to know all cost details.

Most break-even charts are drawn on the assumption that costs move linearly with output, which we have already seen is a reasonable simplifying assumption. They plot total costs and revenues against the volume of output to show the impact on profits of decisions concerning output, prices or costs. The two most common types of chart are shown below as Charts 3.4 and 3.5. Obviously far more complex charts can be drawn to illustrate situations with more complex cost structures.

Chart 3.4 shows what happens to total revenues and total costs as output changes. If the product of the plant is homogeneous, output can be shown in physical terms, but usually the various products will be reduced to a common measuring rod of money. Just as constant unit costs are assumed, the chart also assumes a linear total-revenue function. It is assumed that variations in output have no impact on the price, something that may hold for small firms producing standardised goods in

Chart 3.4   Conventional break-even chart

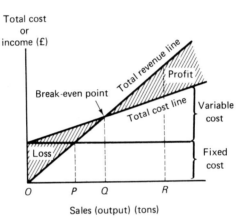

competition with many other sellers (i.e. in conditions of perfect competition) but is rarely true for modern manufacturing industry. The simple revenue curve used in break-even charts greatly limits their practical applications; although costs may approximate to a straight line, revenues do only rarely. The factors acting on demand and the shape of the revenue curve are discussed in Chapter IV. One possibility is to show total revenue as a convex curve, but this would unduly complicate presentation and arithmetic. Another is to plot a family of revenue curves, with each curve showing what happens to total revenue with a different product price. Such an approach is useful but ignores the considerable difficulties involved in measuring how the relationship between volume and price varies.

In Chart 3.4, *OQ* is the output required to break even, with higher outputs resulting in a profit. If output falls to or below *OP* the firm will fail even to cover its fixed costs. Frequently break-even charts are designed for monitoring the annual budget or profit plan. Thus the planned output may be *OR*, and *QR* shows the amount by which output can safely fall below *OR* before a loss is incurred. Break-even charts of this nature are obviously only useful for monitoring short periods; if there were serious danger of output falling consistently below *OP*, or even below the planned *OR* level, management would take steps to alter the underlying costs and revenues.

Chapter II has shown the usefulness of the contribution concept and Chart 3.5 is a break-even chart reformulated to illustrate this concept. In this chart variable costs are plotted below fixed costs, which are shown as

Chart 3.5 Contribution break-even chart

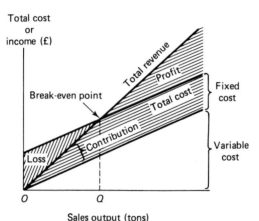

Sales output (tons)

a constant addition to variable costs. The contribution is the difference between total revenue and variable costs, and at the break-even point, *OQ*, it exactly equals the difference. For monitoring plans over the course of the year the lines of Chart 3.5 are often redrawn to show planned total revenue less variable cost (i.e. contribution), actual contribution and profit/loss as in Chart 3.6.

Charts such as 3.6 are normally most useful for individual products or small departments of a firm rather than for a company as a whole. This is because they make no allowance for the impact of changing product mix on either revenues or costs. Such changes are often frequently encountered in practice. Break-even analysis can, however, be adapted to compare the break-even points and profit contributions of different products as an aid to decisions about product mix, as in Chart 3.7.

This chart compares two products A and B. At output *OA*, product A covers its variable costs and also the fixed costs directly attributable to it.

Chart 3.6   Profit contribution chart for controlling plans

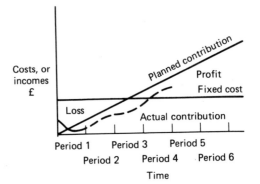

At higher outputs it contributes to general overhead expenses and the company's profit. Product B, with different cost structures, has a higher break-even point OB, and makes a smaller contribution to company overheads as the slope of the contribution curve is shallower. This type of analysis is often known in cost-accountancy textbooks as cost–volume–profit analysis.

The uses of break-even analysis are not confined to study of the relationships between output and costs. Similar charts can be used for comparing the impacts of different capital expenditure decisions, or for showing the effects of variations in raw material prices or wage rates. One of the defects of this analysis is that it is completely static and assumes fixed relationships between the variables. Not only is no

Chart 3.7   Profit contribution comparisons for two products

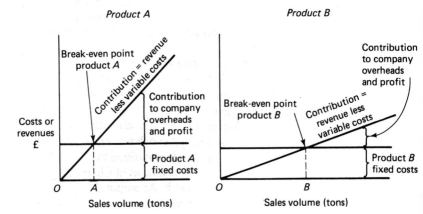

allowance made for changes in the prices underlying the cost curves, but the technical nature of the business is also assumed to be fixed; profits are assumed to be a function of output alone. As stated earlier, break-even charts can normally only be used for short periods, and normally to monitor plans rather than guide major decisions. They suffer the weaknesses of the dichotomy between recorded and economic costs, and oversimplify cost functions. No allowance is made for costs which influence sales volume, such as advertising, nor for costs incurred in one period which affect output in other periods. Development spending or plant maintenance are examples of such lumpy costs which do not vary necessarily with output. Work in progress and stocks of finished goods are also complications. This formidable list of potential drawbacks means that break-even analysis can only be used with discretion and that its validity will vary between industries. Industries with stable cost functions and techniques will find it useful, whereas firms facing frequent product, unit-cost, or technical changes will seldom use it on a widespread scale. Nonetheless, as the introductory remarks to this section indicated, a technique which enables managers to see the wood rather than the trees is useful.

Short-term and long-term costs

The definition of the long run advanced in Chapter II is the period in which all a firm's costs are variable and no irrevocable decisions have been made about location, plant size, product range and so on. For practical purposes management is more concerned with the short run, as established firms rarely embark on greenfield expansion projects. Nonetheless knowledge of long-run cost factors is of value.

A discussion of long-run cost curves can be on two planes. They might be defined as the spectrum of costs incurred in plants of varying sizes, technical configurations and efficiency at a given time, or as the likely trend of costs over time. In the first instance the state of technique is given and the firm can choose that best suited to its needs, whilst in the second techniques are changing rapidly. A new process may be discovered tomorrow which renders all existing processes obsolete, but no firm can be expected to know this (though it may assess the risk) when it chooses between techniques. 'Long run', in the economic sense, refers to all the present choices facing a firm.

A clear distinction is needed between the long-run cost curve for a particular plant or process and that facing the firm as a whole, as the two may differ considerably. One of the most famous economic theorems is that increasing the output of a product allows specialisation. Instead of carrying out all the tasks associated with producing one product, workers can specialise on one component task, and specialised machinery can be installed for each step. In other words, growing output will allow the adoption of more efficient techniques, so that long-run costs will tend to fall as output increases; there are major economies of scale. The assembly line allows much lower production costs for motor vehicles than an individual workshop; so that the mass-produced family car is far cheaper than the custom-built saloon. Whereas in the workshop each mechanic must be skilled at a wide variety of tasks, and large mechanical handling devices may be uneconomic, the assembly line has very sophisticated equipment and mechanics concentrating on single tasks. As output is increased, very large or expensive machines can be fully utilised which would be uneconomic at smaller output levels. The indivisibility of much capital equipment means that it is inaccessible to plants operating at sub optimum levels. Moreover, in process industries such as chemicals, the capital costs of construction do not rise proportionately with the scale of the plant. Larger plants can spread their fixed costs over a much larger output, so that average fixed costs fall. Chart 3.8, showing the costs of operating crude oil tankers over a specific voyage, gives a good example of these technical economies of scale at plant level.

Chart 3.8 Technical economies of scale: comparative transportation costs by various sizes of tanker

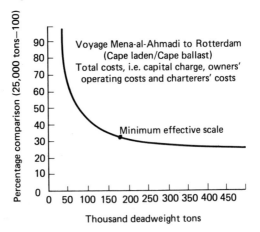

SOURCE: *Shell International,* 1970; OECD, *Oil: The Present Situation and Future Prospects,* 1973.

The chart shows a typical L-shaped pattern. Above a certain output, which may be very large, further increases in size will not allow major cost reductions; this output is the minimum effective scale.

Apart from specifically technical economies, an increasing scale of output, particularly at the lower end, may enable the firm to gain quantity discounts on raw material purchases, bought-in services or freight charges. Where several manufacturing processes are involved and each one has a different technical optimum, increased output will enable the firm to use that combination of plants, or material purchases, that minimises unit costs. Smaller firms will be forced to adopt less economic arrangements. In process industries, increasing scale may allow a change from batch or campaign production to lower-cost continuous processes.

Technical economies of scale are related mainly to production plants or factories rather than firms. As the scale of the firm increases, however, it too is able to exploit economies of scale in the financial, managerial, and marketing spheres. As the firm expands it is able to employ functional specialists, enabling managers to concentrate on running the business. It is able to utilise complex managerial techniques, and to staff research and development departments which were previously too expensive. It is even able to pay higher salaries to attract the best talent. Some managerial or organisational economies are also available at plant or factory level. For example, specialist maintenance departments may become economic at higher output levels.

Traditional economic theory suggested that 'diseconomies' would set in above a certain size level because there would be administrative difficulties in effective coordination and control. In practice, no such size barrier appears to have been reached in efficiently organised companies. Delegation of decision making to profit centres, use of financial controls, advances in communications equipment and the introduction of computers have enabled firms to prevent the emergence of managerial diseconomies. Whereas the traditional theory implied that the long-run cost curve would turn upwards above a certain output, there now appears no mandatory reason for such a cost pattern. The implications of this are discussed later.

As firms expand they are able to employ specialised sales organisations, to finance larger stocks to meet sudden surges of demand without delay, to incur heavier marketing expenses such as advertising, and to install a more effective distribution network. Whereas the smaller firm may rely exclusively on small advertisements in local newspapers, larger firms may be able to afford national papers or television. The large firm can wield more power over both suppliers and customers because it may be a major element in demand for its raw materials or in the supply of its finished goods.

The financial field is one of the most important areas where large firms have advantages over smaller. Investors may have more confidence in a large company than a small one, and trade creditors may be more willing to lend. The large firm can also borrow at lower interest rates from the banks, and has access to sources of funds such as the stock market which most small firms cannot tap. Moreover, most large firms are better able to absorb shocks such as poor trading conditions, or major plant breakdowns, than small or even medium-sized firms. This is likely whether or not the large firm has a more diversified output range than the smaller.

Not everything works in favour of the large plant or the large firm in every industry. If it did, and there were no diseconomies of scale, there would be a general tendency towards monopoly in all industries. Despite frequently expressed fears that a handful of multinational companies will soon control world industry, the empirical evidence, discussed in Chapter IX, is contradictory; it is possible to argue that there is no general tendency to monopoly at least in the UK. Some people have suggested that this implies that the long-run cost curve must be U-shaped in those industries where monopolies do not emerge. Further discussion must await Chapter IX.

The evidence suggests considerable variations in the technical economies of plant size between different industries. Moreover, plants of different size appear to coexist equally in the same industry. One defect of larger plants, particularly in process industries, is that they lack flexibility, and increase risks. The costs of operating a 500 000 t.p.a. ethylene cracker, for example, rise sharply when the plant operates below capacity. In many instances the characteristics of demand may dictate a plant size somewhat below the technical optimum. Such may be the case if demand is subject to pronounced seasonal or cyclical fluctuations. Also the technical optimum must be balanced against other market characteristics; one optimum plant may be more costly than two smaller ones if its advantages are offset by transport costs to the outlying areas. In many manufacturing industries the technical optimum may exist at low output levels, and further output increases are covered by increasing the number of units rather than their scale. The technical optimum plant does not impose a minimum economic scale on the size of the firm in the way that it might in certain heavy chemical operations. Industries subject to frequent changes in fashion or taste, or which require frequent design modifications, tend to have a much larger number of smaller firms than those where demand is inherently stable. Smaller firms are more prolific in market-orientated industries whilst large firms and plants dominate commodity-manufacturing businesses such as cement, bread, or heavy chemicals. Both small firms and batch plants are often far more flexible than their larger rivals.

Recently many assembly-line industries have increasingly realised that pushing technical scale economies and specialisation to their limits may become self-defeating. Such industries are very vulnerable to strikes and other output disruptions whose cost far outweighs the scale economies. Moreover, much of the labour unrest apparently endemic in such industries may well result from their too great attention to technical factors in disregard of their labour forces. Many motor firms are now experimenting fruitfully with production lines which allow workers a far greater variety of tasks and control over their own operations. There are social and psychological drawbacks to the full exploitation of technical optima, and the most economic solution may lie at a sub-optimum technical position.

Chart 3.9 shows how the long-run curve is related to short-run costs in a particular industry, in this case oil pipelines.

Chart 3.9   Long-run and short-run costs: typical pipeline cost curves. Total costs per unit for various unit sizes and throughputs

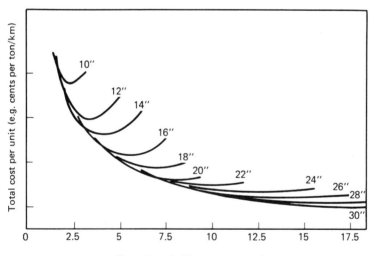

Throughput (million tons per year)

SOURCE: *Shell Information Handbook,* 1971–72; OECD, *Oil: The Present Situation and Future Prospects,* 1973.

Although only a few short-run cost curves are shown on the chart there is in theory an infinite number varying with different pipe diameters. The long-run curve forms an envelope or tangent to the family of short-run curves. In this instance the curve is smooth because there are no indivisibilities, which may often limit the range of alternatives.

Once the firm has installed its pipeline it must operate along that particular short-run curve, but in the long run it can choose whichever curve it likes. The choice of pipe diameter will in this instance depend on expected crude-oil throughput. Some cost curves suggest that certain pipe diameters, such as the 18-inch, will rarely be installed, because at all throughputs unit costs exceed those of larger diameter pipes. The limiting factor in such cases may be total capital cost rather than unit cost, because the supply of funds may be limited or there may be more attractive uses than investing in, say, a 30-inch rather than a 28-inch pipe for a 12.5 million t.p.a. throughput.

Once a decision has been made on plant size, it will pay to continue operating on the appropriate short-run cost curve until the marginal or incremental cost of operation exceeds the average total costs of a new and larger plant. In this cost equation all relevant factors such as product obsolescence and technical product competitiveness must be included. Marketing considerations are also relevant. Given a choice between two plants in an uncertain or fluctuating market situation, a firm may not always install the plant that gives the lowest technical operating costs for the output considered most likely. It may rather prefer a plant which has slightly higher unit costs at that output, but lower average costs over a wide range of possible outputs. Empirical evidence suggests that long-run cost curves are normally of the shape shown in Charts 3.8 and 3.9 rather than U-shaped. The point at which the curve begins to flatten out (around 100 000 tons) in Chart 3.8 is known as the minimum effective scale. Irrespective of the preceding remarks about flexibility, no firm is likely to buy a smaller tanker for the voyage specified. The point at which the minimum effective scale is reached varies widely between industries.

Structure of the firm and costs

Aside from plant size, one of the key questions a firm must consider at the outset is the scope of its activities. As it grows it can greatly alter its cost structures by altering this scope. Moreover, since one of the key objectives of modern firms is profitable growth, *diversification*, as changing the firm's scope is called, may be essential. Such diversification may be geographical, as in the decision to export for the first time, or to set up a new plant overseas; it may be into a new or similar product related in some way to the existing range; or it may be into a completely unrelated activity.

Two common motives for diversification are to spread risks by expanding the number of eggs in different baskets, and to employ surplus funds. By manufacturing different products, using different raw materials and serving totally dissimilar markets, a firm may be able to iron out seasonal or cyclical variations and ensure stable earnings. An ice-cream vendor might, for example, sell hot chestnuts in the winter. Moreover, non-specific overhead expenses can be spread over more products. Many firms though suffer from the belief that management is a completely transferable resource, and that a bassoon manufacturer will be equally able to sell guitars. Whilst this may work for some conglomerates which buy companies solely for financial reasons, and still allow considerable managerial independence to their acquired subsidiaries, few managements have this degree of self-control. British industry is riddled with examples of companies that have diversified into fields about which they know too little. This is true even when the diversification has been through acquisition of existing companies. Many firms are affected by a form of hubris which apparently makes them believe that they are more capable of earning profits, or of earning higher profits, than their shareholders if their excess funds were distributed as dividends rather than used for diversification.

This does not mean that diversification is necessarily incorrect, but that it is frequently misunderstood and that too few firms carefully analyse their motives. Also there are far too few cases of companies admitting that they may have made a mistake and contracting their field of operations.

The most common methods of diversifying are to move further down the production chain towards the final consumer, or backwards towards the raw material. This is known as *vertical integration*. Firms usually integrate backwards in order to ensure an adequate and reliable supply of raw materials of acceptable quality. It may be the only possible way of keeping sufficient control of prices, as in some commodities where market prices can fluctuate wildly, or to preserve quality-control standards, as in pharmaceuticals. Sometimes firms may produce part of their own materials and buy in the rest. This gives them greater flexibility and also enables them to keep a close check on the cost structures of their independent suppliers. Forward integration may be the only way in which firms can sell their full output. For example, existing distributive arrangements may be inadequate or fully tied up. More commonly, products early in the production chain tend to be more homogeneous than those further down. The main competition may be on price, given goods of standard quality. Forward integration may enable the producer to command premia for specialities and more sophisticated products.

Where economies of scale become particularly large at one point in the production chain, perhaps through a technical innovation, there may be a tendency towards *horizontal integration* at that stage. A firm may extend the production of its existing product range. Cotton spinning is an example of an industry where horizontal integration was pronounced. Where a firm produces many different types of product, perhaps linked by common processes or raw materials, or similar markets, the process is known as *lateral integration*. This is particularly common in the chemical industry or some branches of engineering. The firm can obtain economies through use of a common marketing, selling and distribution organisation serving one market, or through buying raw materials in bulk for several products. One of the main motives for diversification is to enable the firm to supply a complete product range for a particular purpose. There may also be surplus plant or selling capacity which can profitably be utilised by widening the product range.

The oil industry provides an interesting example of the various types of integration at work. The major oil companies are basically producers, transporters and marketers of crude oil. They have vertically integrated backwards into exploration and exploitation of crude oil, and forwards into the refining and marketing of petroleum products, and more recently further into chemicals, fertilisers and plastics. They have integrated horizontally into producing crude oil in different areas, or by expanding the scale of their refinery operations, and laterally by going into different forms of energy such as coal, natural gas, and nuclear power. Moreover, they have also diversified out of their basic activities into completely unrelated fields as a means of spreading risks or to use spare cash.

What this section has shown is that the motives for widening the scope of a firm's activities are various. Diversification may lower the firm's costs and greatly increase its market power but this is by no means self-evident. As with all decisions, careful analysis of long-run incremental costs and benefits and of the real motives is essential before any decision to diversify is made.

IV

DEMAND ANALYSIS

No firm is likely to remain in business for very long and make a profit unless it has some knowledge of the demand conditions facing it. Without such knowledge it will not know how much it can expect to sell of each product and thus the likely scale of output, nor whether or not it is likely to make an acceptable profit, given expected cost levels. Contrary to the impressions fostered by concentration on allowable costs in recent government anti-inflationary policies, prices are not solely determined by costs but also by the interaction of supply and demand. This chapter discusses some of the basic economic concepts of demand, the characteristics of demand in differing economic circumstances, and briefly touches on forecasting methods.

The demand curve

In economics, demand means those wants and desires of consumers that are supported by sufficient purchasing power and willingness to buy at the offer price. Most young couples aspire to a house of their own, yet too few have an income large enough to translate this aspiration into the purchase of a house. Their demand is *latent* or unrealised. Similarly, most owners of black-and-white television sets might prefer a colour set, but may be unable to afford one until prices drop substantially.

The demand curve relates price to the quantity demanded. It is usually shown sloping downwards from left to right as in Chart 4.1 because of the existence of latent demand. It is normally drawn as a smooth curve assuming no irregularities in demand conditions over the given price and output range. As price falls from P to P' more people will be able to purchase the product in question, and demand will rise from OQ to OQ'. Some people who have already purchased the product might decide to buy more at the lower price, and others may switch to the product when it becomes cheaper than other products which they previously preferred. The 'law of diminishing marginal utility' discussed in Chapter II is another explanation for demand curves sloping downwards to the right.

More complex or perverse demand functions are discussed later but the downward-sloping demand curve tallies with most normal experience.

The demand curve *DD* assumes that all factors which might have an influence on amount demanded other than price are held constant. Such influences include incomes, the prices of other competing products, sociological changes in tastes, consumer needs, credit availability in the

Chart 4.1   The demand curve

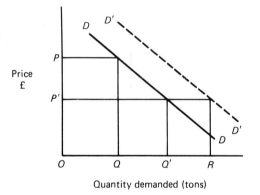

case of consumer goods, quality, expectations about future prices or supply, or the manufacturer's advertising programmes. A change in any of these conditions would involve a bodily shift in the whole demand curve. Thus a general rise in incomes through say an income-tax cut, might raise the demand curve to *D'D'*, with demand rising from *OQ'* to *OR* at the price of *P'*. It is very important to separate a movement along a given demand curve from a shift in the curve.

Since all other conditions are given, the demand curve is essentially static, representing the functional relationship between price and volume at a given time. Only one price and output exist in practice and all other points on the demand curve are hypothetical. This means that the economist's demand curve has a particular meaning. A chart relating observed prices and amounts demanded over a period of time would not strictly be a demand curve because the 'other conditions' would have altered. Such a time series would include movements along any one curve and shifts in the curve, and to treat it as a true demand curve might be misleading. Nonetheless such historical information is often all that companies have from which to infer the shape of the demand curves for their products. They do not have the full range of information on which the economist's demand curve is based. Moreover, it is misleading to imply that observed demand curves are clearly defined. Normally it would be more correct to talk of a demand 'band' around the line *DD* in Chart 4.1. Even with all other conditions fixed there would merely be a tendency for the observed prices and quantities demanded to cluster around the demand curve.

At this stage it is worth distinguishing between several different types of demand curve. The discussion so far has been of the demand for individual products, yet in most normal market conditions the demand curve facing each firm will differ from this total-commodity or industry-demand curve. Only where production is in the hands of a total monopoly will the two curves be the same. In all other cases the products of each firm will be competing with similar products made by other firms, and this will influence the shape of *their* demand curves. The likely shape of these curves in various market conditions is discussed later in the chapter. Most firms manufacture a wide range of different products, so that they are faced by a large number of demand curves, often with widely differing characteristics. It is therefore usually misleading to talk of a firm's demand curve.

Elasticity of demand

In assessing their production and marketing strategies, firms are extremely interested in knowing how the demand for their products will respond to price changes. The responsiveness of the quantity of a good demanded to a change in its price is known as the *price elasticity of demand*. Different products vary in their responsiveness to price changes, mainly because of the availability or otherwise of acceptable substitutes. Thus demand for butter is highly responsive to a change in its price because of the availability of margarine, whilst demand for basic metals is not. The demand for fuel of all types is much less responsive to price than the demand for each particular fuel.

In what follows, the measurement of price elasticity is given a precision that can rarely be achieved in practice. For the reasons stated earlier, firms can seldom measure, or are even aware of, their demand curve. Frequently, firms do not have freedom to experiment to discover how demand changes with price, particularly as all the other conditions will also change. The actions of competitors, for example, will influence the relationship; their following a price change will have a different effect than if they hold their present prices unchanged. Nonetheless these very real difficulties can be exaggerated. Most salesmen have an intuitive feel for their markets and can often guess reasonably accurately the likely impact on demand of a price change. They can usually also predict how their competitors will react. The theory of elasticity of demand is a very useful tool for explicitly rationalising the salesman's implicit reasoning. By calculating the elasticity after closely analysing his assumptions either the salesman himself or other managers can obtain a much clearer picture of the market.

Making the usual assumptions about other factors remaining constant, price elasticity of demand is measured as:

$$\frac{\text{proportionate change in amount demanded}}{\text{proportionate change in price}}$$

Mathematically it is expressed as:

$$e = \frac{\Delta Q/Q}{\Delta P/P} = \frac{\Delta Q}{\Delta P} \times \frac{P}{Q}$$

where
$e =$ price elasticity of demand
$P =$ price
$Q =$ quantity demanded

Normally the price elasticity of demand is negative because a rise in demand is associated with a fall in price, but the sign is conventionally ignored. The best method of calculating this *arc elasticity*, over a finite shift in price and quantity demanded, is to average the prices and quantities before and after the change. Thus the calculation becomes:

$$e = \frac{Q_1 - Q_0}{Q_1 + Q_0} \div \frac{P_1 - P_0}{P_1 + P_0}$$

where
$Q_0 =$ quantity demanded before price change
$Q_1 =$ quantity demanded after price change
$P_0 =$ price charged before price change
$P_1 =$ price charged after price change

Even where the demand curve is a straight line, the elasticity of demand varies throughout its length, so that this arc elasticity gives only an approximate measure of price elasticity at any particular point on the curve. This is clearly illustrated by Chart 4.2.

A fall in price from 6p. to 5p. is associated with an increase in demand from 1 to 2. Price has fallen one-sixth, but demand has doubled. The elasticity as measured by the above formula is 3.67,

$$\text{i.e.} \quad \frac{2-1}{2+1} \div \frac{6-5}{6+5}$$

When the price falls from 2p. to 1p., however, demand only rises from 5 to 6; a halving of price goes with a 20% demand increase. The elasticity is 0.27,

$$\text{i.e.} \quad \frac{6-5}{6+5} \div \frac{2-1}{2+1}$$

Chart 4.2 Varying price elasticity of demand

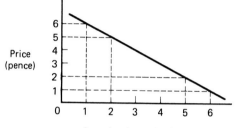

Quantity demanded (ounces)

Strictly speaking then, elasticity should be measured at particular points on the curve for infinitesimally small price changes. *Point elasticity* is measured by differential calculus as follows, with the correct sign inserted.

$$e = -\frac{\delta q}{\delta p} \times \frac{p}{q}$$

In practical terms too little is usually known about the slope and nature of the demand curve to calculate this point elasticity.

The price elasticity of demand will lie between zero and infinity, but there are five cases worth considering. An elasticity of infinity, or perfectly elastic demand, means that demand would dry up completely if prices were to rise slightly, but that firms could sell their entire output at the ruling price. Graphically the demand curve is horizontal (Chart 4.3). An elasticity of zero, or completely inelastic demand, means that however much the price is changed demand will remain constant. The demand curve is a vertical line. When the elasticity of demand is one, or unity, a proportionate change in price leads to an identical proportionate change in the quantity demanded; total revenue is unaffected by a price change. The demand curve is a rectangular hyperbola. These are the only three cases where the elasticity of demand is constant along the whole length of the demand curve.

Most products fall between these three cases. When the price elasticity is greater than one but less than infinity, demand is said to be elastic. A given proportionate change in price produces a greater proportionate change in demand; as the price changes total revenue changes by a

Chart 4.3   Elasticity of demand: the limiting cases

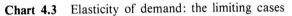
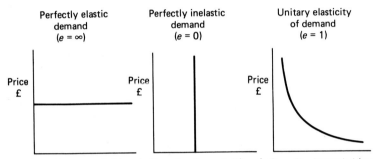

greater amount. Demand is inelastic when the price elasticity lies between one and zero; a given proportionate change in price gives a smaller proportionate change in demand, so that total revenue changes less than the price. A knowledge of the price elasticity of demand over the range in which decisions are being made is helpful in pricing; raising prices could for example reduce total revenue if demand is elastic.

The concept of elasticity can be applied to variables other than price. Two further elasticities are particularly useful in demand analysis: *income elasticity* and *cross elasticity* of demand. Income elasticity of demand is a measure of the responsiveness of the quantity demanded to a given proportionate change in income. It is defined as:

$$i = \frac{\text{proportionate change in amount demanded}}{\text{proportionate change in income}}$$

In mathematical terms the arc elasticity is:

$$i = \frac{Q_1 - Q_0}{Q_1 + Q_0} \div \frac{Y_1 - Y_0}{Y_1 + Y_0}$$

and the point elasticity for infinitesimally small income changes is:

$$i = \frac{\delta Q}{\delta Y} \times \frac{Y}{Q}$$

where i = income elasticity of demand
            Q_0 = quantity demanded before change in income
            Q_1 = quantity demanded after change in income
            Y_0 = income in base period
            Y_1 = income after change in income

Again it is not suggested that marketing management can, or indeed should, measure the income elasticity of demand for every product. It is, however, a very useful peg on which to hang important facts about the market.

In calculating the income elasticity it is assumed that all other factors such as prices are held constant. Normally the income elasticity of demand will be positive, as demand will be higher as income levels rise. At certain income levels, however, the quantity demanded of some products may fall as real income rises; the income elasticity of demand is negative. Such products are known as *inferior goods*. They are, in the main, bought by low-income households, and are replaced at least partially by better-quality products when the household's income rises. The standard example is margarine in the United Kingdom which is replaced by butter as incomes rise, other things being constant. In practice other things are not held constant, and factors such as the suspected relationship between butter consumption and heart disease and the Common Agricultural Policy are upsetting the past relationship.

An income elasticity of demand of one forms a useful dividing line between what might be regarded as luxuries and necessities. An income elasticity greater than one means that a rising share of income is spent on a product as the purchaser's income increases; the products are luxuries. An income elasticity below one means that the share of income spent falls as income rises even though the absolute amount spent also rises (unless the product is an inferior good); the goods are in some sense necessities.

The *cross elasticity of demand* measures the responsiveness of demand to a change in price of similar products, all other factors including the price of the product under study being held constant. It is defined as:

$$X = \frac{\text{proportionate change in amount of product A demanded}}{\text{proportionate change in price of product B}}$$

It is calculated as:

$$X = \frac{Q_1 - Q_0}{Q_1 + Q_0} \div \frac{C_1 - C_0}{C_1 + C_0}$$

where X = cross elasticity of demand

Q_0 = quantity of product A demanded before change in price of B
Q_1 = quantity of product A demanded after change in price of B
C_0 = price of product B before price change
C_1 = price of product B after price change

The cross elasticity of demand is a measure of the degree of substitutability of any two products. If product A and product B were perfect substitutes the cross elasticity would be infinity. Zero cross elasticity implies that the two products are independent of each other; a change in the price of one has no effect on demand for the other. In practice, most pairs of products have a finite positive cross elasticity of demand. Where two goods are in joint demand, however, their cross elasticity will be negative. A fall in price of B will stimulate demand for A. Bacon and eggs might be an example of two complementary products with a negative cross elasticity. Although management may never know the cross elasticity of demand for any two products, it is important to know what substitutes exist for the first product and how close these substitutes are. Some idea of how demand for one's own products is likely to move when a competitor changes his prices is essential.

Substitution in response to relative price movements, given similar technical characteristics, has been one of the main motors of economic growth. Much modern industry has been developed through the substitution of newer for more traditional materials. Examples are the replacement of natural by synthetic rubber, copper cables by aluminium, metals, timber and natural fibres by plastics and synthetic fibres, and coal by petroleum. In many cases the substitution has been irreversible because the new product has had technical and processing superiority over the traditional material. Natural and synthetic rubber are, however, products where the balance of advantage moves between the two. Normally the introduction of close substitutes and their capture of a large segment of the market compels the producers of the traditional material to fight back through quality improvements, grading schemes, processing changes and the like.

A change in price of any product inevitably has an effect on the purchaser's income. Normally this effect is so small as to be unimportant, but price changes caused by governments changing indirect taxes can (and are intended to) alter incomes. For example, the government might raise excise duties on drink and tobacco by 10%. These products form a significant proportion of consumer spending and demand for them is relatively price inelastic. The income available for spending on other products would therefore fall. The net effect of the tax change on consumer spending both in total, and on product groups, can only be precisely calculated by using price and income elasticities of demand.

Changes in the demand for a product in response to a price change are usually composed of an income and a substitution effect, with the latter predominant. Very occasionally, however, a product may form such a large proportion of total expenditure that price changes may have a *perverse effect*. A rise in price of the product might so reduce the income available to spend on other products that demand for the product may perversely rise in response. Instead of sloping downwards to the right, the demand curve slopes downwards to the left. It is claimed that bread was such a special type of inferior good for nineteenth-century English labourers. Although such products are unlikely to be met with in most industrial situations, their existence is mentioned here to highlight the danger of generalisations about the nature of demand.

The elasticities discussed in this section are not the only ones that can be calculated, but they are the most useful in analysing most demand situations. The elasticity concept can be applied wherever there is a need to measure the responsiveness of one variable to changes in another.

Average, marginal, and incremental revenue

The *average revenue* curve is another term for the demand curve. It shows the firm's average revenue per unit of product demanded, which is the same as the price needed to shift that amount of product. A firm's *marginal revenue* from selling a product is the change in its total revenue caused by selling one extra (marginal) unit of the product. Where the average revenue curve is downward sloping to the right, marginal revenue will be less than average revenue. The concepts of average and marginal revenue, especially the latter, are important in the traditional profit maximisation theory of pricing. Profit is maximised at that output where the firm's marginal revenue from a product is equal to its marginal cost of production. This pricing aspect of marginal revenue is discussed in Chapter V. Because it is rarely possible for a firm to calculate the shape of its average revenue curve, let alone its marginal revenue, the following paragraphs are of more theoretical than direct practical interest.

Chart 4.4 and Table 4.1 illustrate average, total, and marginal revenue for an imaginary product.

In estimating marginal revenue it is assumed that all factors other than price are held constant. In the above example the quantity demanded rises by complete units, so that marginal revenue can be read off immediately as the difference between total revenue before and after a price change. Normally, however, it would be necessary to divide the

Chart 4.4   Average and marginal revenue

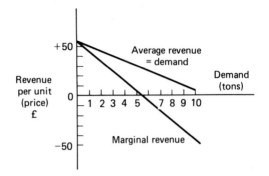

increase in total revenue by the change in quantity demanded, as marginal revenue is the change in revenue per unit demanded.

$$\text{Marginal revenue } (M) = \frac{R_1 - R_0}{D_1 - D_0}$$

Table 4.1   Total, average and marginal revenue

Quantity demanded (D)	Average revenue or price (P)	Total revenue (R) = D × P	Marginal revenue (M) = R₁ − R₀
1	50	50	
			40
2	45	90	
			30
3	40	120	
			20
4	35	140	
			10
5	30	150	
			0
6	25	150	
			−10
7	20	140	
			−20
8	15	120	
			−30
9	10	90	
			−40
10	5	50	

where R_0 and R_1 are the old and new total revenues, and D_0 and D_1 the old and new quantities demanded.

There is a close connection between marginal revenue and elasticity of demand. At any point on the demand curve:

$$e = \frac{P}{P-M} \qquad : \qquad M = P\frac{e-1}{e} \qquad : \qquad P = M\frac{e}{e-1}$$

where e = point elasticity of demand (negative sign ignored)
            P = average revenue = price
            M = marginal revenue

Provided any two variables are known the third can easily be calculated. Geometric proofs of these relationships are available in textbooks, such as *A Textbook of Economic Theory*, by Stonier and Hague, Longman. Because of the large price changes in Table 4.1, it is not possible to estimate the point elasticity of demand, so that the formulae do not work exactly on the example given.

When demand is inelastic and total revenue moves less than proportionately with price, marginal revenue is negative, as is clearly shown in Table 4.1 and Chart 4.4. Conversely, marginal revenue is always positive when demand is elastic, and is zero when the elasticity of demand is one, as when demand rises from 5 to 6 units in the example. In the unitary elasticity case, total revenue remains constant irrespective of price movements.

As already stated, management is not normally concerned with small changes in price and output, and the concept of marginal revenue, or change in total revenue per unit of output, has limited practical use. Nonetheless, as in cost analysis, examination of changes in revenue is important. *Incremental revenue*, or the change in total revenue resulting from any decision, is here the appropriate measure. Unlike marginal revenue, this is not expressed in terms of units of output. Also it has much wider applicability than the examination of price changes with other factors held constant. Incremental revenue highlights the impact of change in any variable on a firm's total revenue.

Market demand patterns

So far we have ignored the precise shape of the firm's average revenue or demand curve for particular products. It has been implicitly assumed that it slopes downwards to the right in the same way as the industry's demand curve for the product in question. Intuitively, however, one might expect demand for an individual company's products to be much more elastic than the total demand for the products in question. Each firm competes with others for a share of the market, so that it is vulnerable to a greater or lesser degree to substitution from other brands. If it unilaterally increases the price of its product it might expect to lose business to its rivals, whilst it might hope to gain market share if it lowers its relative price. Quite apart then from the nature of demand for the product, or the industry demand curve, the shape of the firm's demand curve will depend on the intensity of competition in the market for that product and on the firm's position in that market.

As is usual in economics, there are two extreme limiting cases with most products lying somewhere in between. Moreover, the extremes of complete monopoly on the one hand, and perfect or pure competition on the other, are encountered far more in theory than in practice. *Perfect competition* is the prototype market organisation of economic theory. Even though it is rarely met in practice it is often the ideal to which legislation on competitive conditions appears to aspire. As a theoretical abstraction it is both elegant and useful, but as a practical model of the market it has conceivably done more harm than good. Perfect competition assumes a completely homogeneous product sold by all firms in the industry, a large number of buyers and sellers none of whom can significantly influence the price, perfect knowledge of present and future market conditions by all prospective buyers and sellers, and no barriers to entry into the industry. Given these conditions the demand curve facing each supplier is perfectly elastic. The slightest increase from the ruling market price will cause a firm's sales to disappear entirely. Marginal and average revenue are identical. These conditions are most closely approximated in agriculture and in commodity markets, but even here they are rarely fulfilled completely. Quality differences between the output of different firms can be offset by price differentials, but there are usually many other irregularities. Often most of a commodity may be sold on long-term contracts either at fixed prices or at prices based on the commodity market which deals with marginal supply and demand. The prices in these terminal markets fluctuate widely in response to expectations. Rarely do all buyers and sellers have perfect knowledge, and usually speculators, international agencies and governments may exert a major influence on the market. Frequently large sellers having capacity available at the right time may be able to charge prices above the market levels.

Complete monopoly is also rarely encountered in practice. Where it does exist the industry's and firm's demand curves are identical. In most countries where economies of scale are so large that only one firm is justified, or other technical conditions require monopoly, the industry is usually tightly regulated by the government. Thus electricity generation and supply, gas, coal and railways, which meet these criteria, are nationalised in the UK. Because private interests might abuse the natural monopoly the State intervenes to uphold the public interest. On a more limited scale companies might manage to acquire a local monopoly in, for example, milk distribution or building materials. Often transport costs keep competitors out, provided that the monopolist does not exploit his position by charging unduly high prices. Normally, whatever the institutional arrangements made to control them, the powers of monopolies are limited by the availability of substitutes. Electricity, for example, is encouraged to compete vigorously with other fuels, however illogical and wasteful this might sometimes appear on grounds of national fuel policy.

The normal market organisation for most products is one that enables the producing firms to exert some control over the shape of their demand curve. Although demand for their products will be more elastic than industry demand, the creation of real or imagined differences will enable each producer to attract strong loyalties from a segment of the market. The types of market organisation for such differentiated products vary from *monopolistic* or *imperfect competition*, where there is a large number of sellers, to *duopoly* where there are only two producers. For many sectors of industry the most common state is *oligopoly*, where there is a relatively small number of producers.

In imperfectly competitive markets, firms can differentiate their products from those of their rivals in a large number of ways. Their aim is normally to reduce the closeness of available substitutes, thereby lowering the elasticity of demand for their output. Generally price is not altered as much as other aspects of the product, but is a limit within which firms often work. Tangible elements that can be varied are the quality of the product, the amount of technical service or after-sales service offered, the period of any guarantee and its comprehensiveness, and delivery dates. Less tangible factors might be the design of a product to appeal psychologically to a specific segment of the market, the shape and design of any packaging, and the use of gift promotions or free offers. Advertising can be used to create an awareness of a particular brand and to differentiate it from other brands. Product differentiation is particularly well developed in consumer markets. There is little to choose between competing makes of petrol of a given octane rating, for example, as far as performance characteristics are concerned, so that petrol companies have concentrated on developing consumer brand loyalty. Bread is another good example of product differentiation at work. Overall demand for bread is highly inelastic, and over many income ranges it is even an inferior good. Bakers have, however, managed in various ways to instil brand loyalty, as with Hovis wholemeal bread, or differentiate their product, as with sliced and wrapped bread. Recent innovations such as date stamping or part-baked bread have further distinguished the products of different bakeries.

Whilst most companies aim to distinguish their products from those of their competitors, the best marketing strategy may be to make the product as close a substitute of existing products as possible. The copying firm rides on the back of the demand already created for the original product. This is, for example, often the policy of supermarkets in selling their own brands in place of nationally advertised convenience foods. In the fashion industry, *haute couture* garments are widely copied. The common theme is that the copying products are usually sold at lower prices and therefore benefit from a relatively high demand elasticity for the original product.

The various methods of differentiation listed above emphasise that a product is usually not a simple unambiguous concept but has many different facets. Product differentiation is not the only method by which firms can exploit market imperfections to reduce the elasticity of demand for their products. Transport costs between factory and point of sale are often a major expense and firms may insulate themselves from most competitors by locating their plant at the point best designed to serve a particular market area.

Oligopolistic market conditions can exist both in industries where there is little product differentiation, such as heavy chemicals and cement, or where there is a great deal, such as motor cars or most consumer durables. Where products are relatively homogeneous commodities, the consumer is primarily concerned in minimising prices for goods of a given specification. Homogeneous oligopolies are most common in industries producing goods for further processing, rather than in industries directly serving the consumer.

A major characteristic of an oligopolistic market is that new firms find it very difficult to enter on a large scale. There are barriers to entry which effectively protect existing firms from increased competition. Normally the really determined firm can smash these barriers, but only at a cost. The most common barriers are where demand has grown to such a size that existing producers have been able to reap significant economies of scale. The capital needed for an economic-sized plant may be totally beyond the reach of a new entrant. Moreover, the new entrant might have to invest considerable resources in building up sufficient sales to load such a plant, unless he can obtain a large contract for a major new use. Existing firms may have the raw material sources firmly sewn up in long-term contracts. Alternatively, they may have established firm patent protection either over product characteristics or over processing methods. Such patent protection is a common entry barrier in the pharmaceutical and chemical industries. By heavy advertising, existing producers may have established strong consumer loyalty which new entrants would have to overcome. Again this involves heavy costs. Unless the new entrant is well established in other industries, its resources may be insufficient to meet these costs. Established companies might have much greater resources to beat off an attack on their markets.

If barriers were completely rigid the industrial structure would become ossified. In practice, technical change works towards lowering entry barriers. If barriers to entry are too high, and the market appears highly profitable, research and development efforts will be increased to find competing products or cheaper processes. Firms in other industries may be tempted to diversify and to carry the entry costs on their existing products. Moreover, such firms may frequently be able to introduce new products on the strength of consumer loyalty to their brand name in other fields. Patent protection is of limited duration, and there are usually competing firms overseas. Often new firms can enter by going under the existing entry barriers, by starting a new product on a small scale and then expanding. Not all challenges to existing oligopolies are successful; one spectacular failure of recent years was the attempt by a large established producer of other products to break into the UK fertiliser market. Examples of failures can, however, usually be matched with success stories in other fields.

In oligopolistic markets each seller can not only influence the price paid for his product, but in so doing will affect the demand for his competitors' products. In consequence they may be forced to retaliate, so that no one seller may be better off as a result of a price change. The pricing policies of all suppliers will be interdependent, and no single firm will be able to estimate its demand curve precisely without knowing the marketing policies of its rivals. In these circumstances traditional demand curve analysis is inadequate, and the theory of games may be more appropriate. Oligopoly, particularly in its extreme of duopoly, is a classic situation where one firm's benefit can be the other's loss. One device for explaining the position in traditional marginal terms is to assume that the demand curve for the oligopolist's product is kinked as in Chart 4.5.

Once a price OP has been set there will be strong pressures against changing it. This accords with empirical evidence of the rigidity of prices in oligopolistic markets. The firm's demand curve is therefore kinked at the existing price OP. The firm must assume that competitors will not raise their prices even when it does, unless there is an industry-wide

increase in costs so that demand will be highly elastic at prices above *OP*.
If the firm lowers its price below *OP*, however, it must assume that its
competitors will follow. This will take away the gains in total revenue
from the price cut, so that the demand curve will be inelastic at prices
below *OP*. In effect there are two demand curves centred on price *OP* as
in Chart 4.5; demand curve *D′D′* will operate below price *OP*, and curve
DD at higher prices. There will be a strong incentive for price stability.

In most oligopolistic industries prices will be fairly rigid, as the
members of the industry will have learnt that in the long term sharp price
competition usually harms all firms. Competition may nonetheless be
heavy though concentrated on the non-price attributes of the product.
Occasionally the balance of power will be disturbed and a price war may
flare up, perhaps because one firm has found a method of dramatically
reducing its costs by a process innovation, or has spare capacity it wishes
to utilise. Eventually a new equilibrium point will be reached and price

Chart 4.5   The oligopolist's kinked demand curve

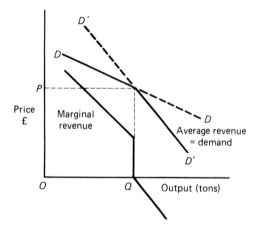

stability restored. Often this stability may be enforced by active or covert
collusion between the firms. Most individual countries prohibit restrictive
agreements between individual firms and impose stiff penalties for
transgression. The Treaty of Rome also bans restrictive agreements
which inhibit trade between EEC member states. Such legislation,
described in Chapter IX, has eliminated many formal oligopolistic price
agreements. Nonetheless many undoubtedly continue on an informal
basis, particularly between firms in different countries, perhaps disguised
as price information agreements which are usually legal. Whatever

legislative provisions are made, it is impossible to compel unwilling firms to compete on price grounds.

Oligopolistic industries were discussed by the UK Monopolies Commission in its *Report on Parallel Pricing*—July 1973. A common characteristic is price leadership, whereby one firm sets a price which is accepted by other firms in the industry. There need be no agreement for other firms to follow the price leader but they usually do. Several types of price leadership can be distinguished. Sometimes prices may be set by the strongest or dominant firm in the industry. In other cases there may be 'barometric' price leadership, whereby producers tend to follow the lead set by one company. Its cost structure may be typical of all firms, or the others may acknowledge that its marketing is particularly skilled. In some instances such price leadership may have developed from a collusive arrangement that has since been discontinued. Since the costs of firms producing similar products do tend to move together covert collusion is unnecessary for parallel pricing to exist in an industry. It is a method by which firms can overcome their kinked demand curves, by moving the kink to a different part of the curve. The Monopolies Commission report cites several industries, including petrol and bread, in which price leadership is common.

The nature of products

The previous discussion has implicitly assumed that the nature of demand is similar for all types of product. Yet several distinctions can be drawn which are particularly important for forecasting purposes. First, there is a sharp difference between *final* and *intermediate* demand, that is between goods destined for final consumption and those to be used by other firms in further processing. Demand for final consumption can be by governments or public authorities or by private consumers, whether in the producing country or overseas. Intermediate demand can similarly be by domestic or overseas firms.

Whereas goods destined for final consumption are designed to fulfil certain wants or needs directly, demand for products for further processing is *derived* from final consumption demand. Thus demand for cement, heavy chemicals or basic metals is derived from final demands for finished products, such as detergents or washing machines. Often a product may go through numerous different stages and firms before reaching the final consumer. In assessing the demand for intermediate goods it is necessary to examine the nature of the final demand.

Intermediate goods are normally purchased by far more skilled purchasers than products entering final consumption. Advertising and other promotional activity normally has little impact; branding is unimportant though the good name of the producer may carry some weight. Technical service and technical characteristics are very important, and quality differences may clinch a sale. As products are purchased for their function and fitness for purpose, buyers can be easily attracted to close substitutes. The elasticity of demand varies with the importance of the product in the final price of the item being produced. If it is a very small component, such as the fuel in a nuclear power station, its price may be unimportant. In other cases small price differences might have a major impact on the price of the final product. Frequently intermediate goods are produced to the purchaser's own specifications, as in motor-vehicle components, or are sold on tender, as with heavy electrical generating equipment.

A common characteristic of derived demand is that fluctuations in demand for the finished product have a magnified impact on the intermediate good. One reason is that firms hold stocks of the intermediate goods whether as raw materials or work in progress, whereas final consumers generally do not hold stocks. This greater cyclical variability is especially pronounced in those intermediate products used in building capital equipment. *Capital goods* have particular demand characteristics associated with the principle of capital stock adjustment discussed in Chapter VI. Demand is derived from demand for consumer goods, which grows fitfully.

Products entering final consumption do not always satisfy direct demands. Those purchased by governments are often similar to intermediate goods in that they are bought by specialist buyers with considerable knowledge of all the alternatives, and their demand is derived from the final demands of private consumers for such things as health or education. Promotional activity can, however, be very important, as in the prescribing habits of doctors.

Many products purchased by private consumers have much in common with capital goods. These are *durable goods* such as motor cars, household appliances, electrical goods, and furniture. The main characteristics of demand for consumer durables, including cars, are that they are frequently bought on credit rather than outright; they are purchased from discretionary income after basic needs have been met; their income elasticity of demand is high; purchase can be deferred; and they provide services over an extended period of time. In this last respect they are identical to capital goods used in industry. The demand for consumer durables can be subdivided into two elements, initial purchases, and replacement. When a new product is introduced, demand will be entirely from initial purchases and both price and income elasticity will be high. As more and more households purchase, the market will become gradually saturated and new sales will become increasingly harder to make without price reductions. Eventually all potential purchasers will own an appliance. In time, though, depending on the life of the product, replacement demand will develop as a 'shadow' of the original demand. Eventually the market will be dominated by replacement demand, with initial purchases related in some way to the growth of population. Typically purchasers can delay or accelerate replacement in accordance with economic conditions and the availability of credit. Thus demand tends after a period to be highly volatile. Chart 4.6, adapted from an analysis of demand for domestic appliances,

Chart 4.6   Total, initial and replacement purchases of vacuum cleaners in the UK

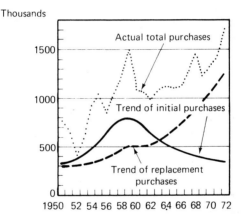

SOURCE: *National Institute Economic Review*, No. 2/73, May 1973.

shows the initial and replacement demand for vacuum cleaners in the UK.

One of the main objectives of appliance manufacturers is to introduce some major technical change which will resurrect the market when initial purchases have tailed off. The introduction of colour, for example, gave the market for television sets a completely new lease of life, as did the earlier introduction first of ITV then of BBC2, with different line standards.

Technological innovation is one method by which all manufacturers can influence demand for their products. The population of products available at any time is constantly changing as old products are forced out by substitutes. It is wrong to assume, however, that manufacturers can manipulate and influence consumer demand at will by skilful advertising and product innovation. The majority of new products launched every year meets an early and ignominious death. Only a small proportion, particularly of grocery products, ever achieves national consumer acceptance. It is possible to persuade people to try a product once, but they will only continue to purchase if it meets certain physical or psychological needs.

The dimension of time

Time is an important factor in demand analysis for many reasons. Perishable commodities, such as fresh foodstuffs and flowers, can only be sold over a limited period. No one wants to buy rotten fruit or dead flowers, and there is a premium on freshness and speed of delivery. If market traders in fruit and vegetables expect not to be able to sell their stocks by the end of the day's trading they usually reduce prices for quick sale. Refrigerators and deep-freeze stores have reduced these problems of food traders, but some products must still be sold quickly; yesterday's newspaper is of no value. In such instances producers must skilfully calculate probable demand to reduce waste. Fashion industries are other examples of where time is important; unless producers can adapt swiftly they may lose out and find large stocks of now unsaleable products on their hands.

Where products can be stored, or have a lengthy shelf life, consumers can always delay or accelerate purchases according both to underlying economic conditions and to expectations of future conditions. Expectations are in fact a key to demand for most products, particularly where a product is relatively homogeneous and speculation becomes possible. Expectations of shortages or gluts certainly influence commodity prices, whilst private consumers time their purchases in expectation of indirect tax changes. This was particularly noticeable in the UK during the first quarter of 1968 when purchase tax increases were widely forecast, and in the first quarter of 1973 before the introduction of value-added tax. The dip in UK car sales preceding the August introduction of a new model letter is a similar example of expectations working on demand. Where prices are expected to be temporary, as during sales, demand will be stimulated and the elasticity of demand may be pushed above its long-run level. Expectations about future prices and demand are just as, if not more, important at the intermediate demand level. Good examples are basic US industries such as steel, aluminium, and copper refining, which negotiate long-term wage contracts with their labour forces. In the year prior to renegotiation customers tend to stock up heavily in expectation of a long-drawn-out dispute and interruptions to supplies before signature of a new contract.

Adaptation of demand to a price change is rarely instantaneous, as buyers take time to assimilate a new price and alter their buying patterns. The time necessary for this varies with the product concerned. Housewives will react quickly to an increase of butter prices relative to margarine, but more slowly to a change in relative prices of two detergents, because the latter are bought less frequently. Where expensive equipment is needed, adaptation will be spread over a lengthy period as the old equipment becomes worn out and is replaced. Thus the impact on demand for gas of the reduction in gas prices relative to coal prices in the UK has been spread over some years. If a price increase is sufficiently large consumers will retire their old equipment before it is physically worn out. These examples suggest that, wherever a price change is considered to be permanent, the elasticity of demand will be higher in the long run than in the short run.

A useful device in considering demand is the *product life cycle*, which has widespread applicability. When a new product is introduced, initial

Chart 4.7   The product life cycle

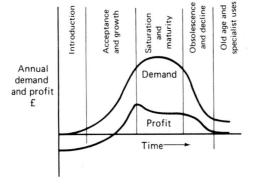

acceptance will probably be limited and demand will take off only slowly. If it is successful, however, it will become more widely known, its price will probably be reduced, both to widen the market and to meet competition from copies, and demand will grow very rapidly. Then the rate of growth will tail off as the market becomes saturated, and as substitute products with superior technical characteristics are introduced. After a time, demand will fall back and eventually be restricted either to specialist uses or to a small segment of the market. The typical curve of demand related to time will be S-shaped until saturation is reached, as in Chart 4.7. Profits will normally follow the pattern shown in the chart; losses will be made in the initial stages but the profits will grow as saturation is reached and then tail off.

The aim of management is to defer the decline of existing products by technical innovation and skilful marketing, and to have a large number of products in the introduction and acceptance stages.

Demographic and sociological influences

Population has so far been mentioned only obliquely, yet its size, sex and age distribution are very important influences on demand. For example, the progress up the age scale of those born in the post-war baby boom has led to successive bulges in demand for different types of product. Firms who ignore this demographic aspect may often find themselves running up against severe capacity bottlenecks, or else installing expensive new equipment that will only be used for a short time. Just as each product has a life cycle, so men and women make different demands over their own life spans. Many products are designed to appeal solely to a specific age group such as teenagers or babies. As people marry they have an initial heavy demand for housing, household equipment and furniture. This gives way to demand for baby goods and products such as toys and clothes for children. As the children mature, their parents' demand for holidays and leisure goods increases.

Few people are entirely rational beings who plan their purchases solely on the basis of needs, prices, and income. Fashion plays an important part in the demand for many products, and sociological and psychological factors are often highly important. Different products tend to be purchased by people at different income levels and in different occupations and social classes. Manufacturers must be quite clear which segment of the total market they plan to reach. Certain sports are predominantly working-class in nature, for example, whilst others such as hunting and riding are only available to the higher-income groups. Education standards, and income levels, are important determinants of demand. Regional and national differences, however, mean that what appeals to one group in one place may appeal to another elsewhere. Rugby-union football is a predominantly middle- and upper-class sport in England, but a working-class sport in Wales.

'Keeping up with the Jones's' is a common phenomenon in the demand for many products, particularly of a durable nature. Some products may be purchased as status symbols to impress neighbours rather than to fulfil basic needs. This is most likely where there are many types of product available, as in the automobile industry. Alternatively people may be heavily influenced by the consumption patterns of those with whom they come into contact. They may, for example, aspire to the living standards of those with higher income levels if they move to a new area. Such 'demonstration effects' may widen the market for consumer durables. As living standards rise, what were previously considered luxuries become necessities, and people's aspirations change. Growing mechanisation has increased leisure and influenced demand; changing attitudes to women's role, family size and marriage have also had an effect. In truth social impacts on demand are multifarious. Psychological motives rather than strict economic calculus determine demand for many products, and the consumer himself may not always know why he is buying. Often he may just buy on impulse, and super-markets exploit this by locating typical impulse buys in strategic places, such as near the check-out counters. Deep psychological reasons are often advanced as to why people smoke. Skilful advertisers and product designers exploit psychological and social pressures on consumers to expand the demand for their products. In essence, this section emphasises that conventional demand theory may be inadequate fully to explain demand; the social interactions between people are very important.

Forecasting demand

Enumeration of the many influences on demand shows that its analysis and forecasting require great skill. Adequate treatment of forecasting methods is completely outside the scope of this book. They vary widely according to the type of product or industry under consideration. A few general comments are nonetheless in order. Once the demand characteristics of the product have been defined firms have a wide choice of differing techniques. They can rely on sample surveys and questionnaires into buying intentions, or market research amongst their main customers if they are producing intermediate products. Alternatively, or in addition, they can merely project past trends, using either a simple statistical technique or a detailed econometric model. The appropriate technique will vary with the period of the forecast; the shorter it is, the more acceptable will be simple trend projection. Long-term forecasts require far more detailed examination of all determinants of demand and complex models. However well a statistical model fits past experience, it rarely works when projected forward unless backed up by skilled judgment of all market factors. The manager's intuitive hunch is still important.

One important point about demand forecasts is that they can rarely be divorced from the economic circumstances of the time in which they are made. The present and immediate past heavily colour most managers' views of the future, whatever historical experience suggests about basic trends. Thus demand forecasts frequently move in an optimism–pessimism cycle depending on the present state of demand. This may be unscientific and may be against all the attributes of demand analysis discussed in this chapter, but it appears to be a regrettable characteristic of human nature. Individual managers whose effectiveness may substantially depend on successful demand forecasting must therefore balance their subjective judgments (aided by basic economic concepts of demand analysis) with wider macro-economic factors of the type discussed in Chapter VI.

V

PRICE DETERMINATION

Introduction

In discussing demand in the previous chapter it was assumed that prices were in some sense given for the individual firm. This simplifying assumption is now dropped, and the present chapter discusses how prices are determined, first in theory and then in practice. Pricing is an area where behaviour apparently diverges markedly from the norms laid down by economic theory. Frantic attempts are often made to provide theoretical justification for widespread practices which may seem irrational. Economists can be imprisoned by their own simplifying assumptions and fail to recognise the wide diversity of objectives of modern industry and the complexity of large companies. The basic theory assumes that profit maximisation, whether today or in the long run, is the guiding principle of management. It is maximisation of total profits rather than of profit margins or returns on capital that is meant in this context. In practice, profit maximisation is only one objective among many, as Chapter I has recognised. The relative importance of each objective helps determine a firm's approach to pricing policy.

The analysis of costs and demand in Chapters III and IV has emphasised the wide range of cost structures and market conditions faced by most firms. In particular, Chapter IV has shown that price is only one dimension of a product package and may often not be the most important. Yet traditional economic theory accords a key role to price and often gives too little attention to other aspects such as quality, packaging, or technical service. The theory assumes that firms have far more information about demand conditions and their competitors' costs than they usually possess. It ignores the tendency for most producers to sell a very wide range of different products with differing cost structures, often in entirely different markets. In such circumstances relatively simple pricing formulae become essential. Finally, the various stages through which products pass before reaching the consumer are unacknowledged. Only rarely does a producer sell direct to the final consumer without going through a series of middlemen, and this complicates pricing.

Despite these and many other qualifications, a knowledge of the basic theory is essential.

The supply curve

Just as it is possible to formulate a demand curve relating price to quantity demanded, so too it is possible to draw up a supply curve relating price to the quantity that producers are willing to produce and sell. Normally the supply curve for a product rises upwards and to the right as in Chart 5.1.

Chart 5.1   The supply curve

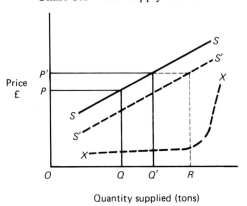

Quantity supplied (tons)

The supply curve SS assumes that all the factors other than price which might influence the amount supplied are held constant. As price rises from OP to OP' producers are prepared to devote higher cost equipment to the product, or to use less efficient resources, and the quantity supplied rises from OQ to OQ'. New producers, formerly uncompetitive at price OP, might be attracted into the industry. Apart from movements along the supply curve SS in response to price changes, other factors might affect supply and cause a bodily shift of the curve. Thus a technical change, such as an improved process, or a new fertiliser, might bring forward a much greater output at price OP' and OR might be supplied on curve $S'S'$.

Whilst the normal tendency is for the supply curve to slope upwards to the right, there are perverse cases. For example, over a certain price range farmers might devote more effort to growing more crops, but when prices have risen markedly they might decide to take more leisure rather than work so hard. In these circumstances the curve would then bend back on itself, if prices continue to rise. Such a supply curve operates in the South African gold-mining industry. Increases in the free market price actually cause a drop in output as producers mine lower-grade ore and also reduce production to increase the life of their mines.

As with demand, the responsiveness of supply to price changes can be calculated as an elasticity. This will normally be positive, although the 'perverse' cases discussed have negative elasticities. The supply of most raw materials tends to be highly inelastic in the short term with respect to price. Once a crop has been sown it is impossible to raise supply until the new crop is planted, so that short-term demand and price variations have no immediate impact on supply. Longer term, high prices will prompt producers to extend their cultivated acreage or to open new mines, and supply will be more elastic. In some cases it takes many years to expand capacity, as with new mines or crops with a lengthy maturing period such as coffee and rubber. In contrast to raw materials, the supply of manufactured products can move more easily in response to price changes in the short term and supply is usually fairly elastic.

Expectations about future price changes probably have a greater impact on the supply of many products than on demand. This is particularly so with raw materials which can be stored. Producers may delay selling in the hope of obtaining higher prices. A sufficient number doing this will in itself drive up prices. Again, such hoarding is less probable with manufactured goods, except in black-market situations. Often expectations about future price movements can lead to perverse supply curves, particularly in markets such as stocks and shares, currencies, or commodities, where speculation occurs on a large scale. A small price fall may cause many holders to rush to sell in expectation of further declines, so that supply rises. Similarly, if holders believe that a price increase merely heralds further rises, supply might dry up altogether instead of increasing.

In the last resort the shape of the supply curve is explained by the cost functions of the firms in the industry. In Chapter III it has been suggested that variable and marginal costs are constant over wide ranges of output. Since in the short run firms will sell more as long as they can cover variable costs and make some contribution to fixed costs, the supply curve for many manufactured products will be very elastic over most normal outputs until the firms involved reach full-capacity working. It will then become highly inelastic in the short run; and may correspond to the curve XX in Chart 5.1. In the longer run, when firms can enter or leave the industry or alter their capacity the supply curve will take on a more normal shape. If any number of firms can produce with identical cost curves the long-run supply curve will be perfectly elastic. More usually it will be less than perfectly elastic because entry is rarely free and new entrants will probably face higher costs.

Supply and demand

In competitive markets such as those for many commodities, shares, or foreign exchange, or even in manufacturing industries where there are many buyers and sellers, the equilibrium price will be that price which clears the market. It will bring into balance the amount that potential sellers are willing to sell and the amount that potential purchasers are prepared to buy. This equilibrium price will be at the intersection of demand and supply curves, as in Chart 5.2.

The equilibrium price will be *OP* with quantity *OQ* bought and sold. Provided other things remain equal, any lower price will lead to an excess of demand over supply, and a higher price will cause excess supply. Thus, if price were *OX* then only *OY* would be demanded, but *OZ* supplied; price would fall until supply and demand balanced. In general

Chart 5.2　Output and price in competitive markets

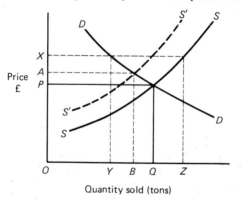

an increase in demand, with constant supply, will raise price and increase the quantity purchased, and an increase in supply, with demand constant, will lower price and increase the quantity sold. If one of the underlying 'other things' were to change, such as poor weather affecting the harvest, or a rise in income increasing demand, the supply and demand curves would shift and a new equilibrium price would emerge. Thus a poor harvest might shift supply to *S'S'* and the new price would be *OA* with quantity *OB*. The proviso that other things are equal is important. Price and quantity observations made over time rarely give a true picture of supply and demand curves, because the underlying conditions usually change.

Whereas the interaction of demand and supply leads to an equilibrium price, the equilibrium need not necessarily be stable. In many agricultural markets, price can fluctuate around the equilibrium level, leading to what is known as a cobweb cycle. If, for some reason such as a crop failure, the quantity supplied falls short of the equilibrium level, the price will rise. Each producer would see the higher price and decide to produce more in the next harvest period, but then total supply might easily exceed demand, which might anyway have been constrained by the high prices of the previous period. The price would drop sharply and producers would cut back their output in the subsequent period. There would be a persistent tendency to overshoot around the equilibrium. The stability of the cobweb would depend on the relative elasticities of supply and demand. If the oscillations around the equilibrium point were fairly regular, clever speculators might intervene in the market, buying when the price fell and selling when it rose. Such speculation would help even out the price and quantity movements.

The interaction of supply and demand in competitive markets to produce an equilibrium is Adam Smith's famous 'hidden hand'. Today it only influences commodity and stock markets. Although, theoretically, foreign-exchange rates move in accordance with supply and demand, most governments usually constrain the rate changes and intervene in the market. Indeed, whilst free markets exist for most commodities they sometimes only deal with marginal supplies, with most sales on long-term contracts at fixed prices. Sugar is one example of a managed market coexisting with a competitive terminal market. Both producers and consumers prefer stable prices without the dramatic fluctuations that can characterise primary products. With other commodities, such as tin or at periods cocoa and coffee, prices are controlled within wide limits by international agreement. Even in these latter cases individual producers or consumers must accept the going market prices.

Marginal analysis and pricing

Assuming that a firm's objective is to maximise its profits, then its rational price and output will be where marginal revenue is equal to marginal cost. This is most easily seen in the perfect-competition case shown in Chart 5.3, but the principle applies equally in all market conditions.

It is assumed that the average total-cost curve in Chart 5.3 includes some 'normal' profit sufficient to reward capital and provide some incentive to the firm to remain in business (the opportunity cost of capital). Each firm has no ability to influence demand, and in Chapter IV we have seen that in such circumstances the price is given, and that the firm's demand curve is perfectly elastic. The cost curves shown are those of economic theory. The optimal output, given the price *OP*, is *OQ*,

Chart 5.3   Price and output under perfect competition

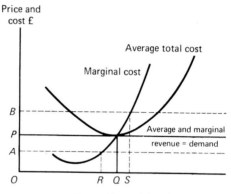

which is the industry's long-run equilibrium. A price below *OP*, at for example *OA*, would mean that the firm's most profitable output would be *OR*, but at this output it would not be covering its costs, and would therefore be forced out of business in the longer term. A price of *OB*, with output *OS*, would give the firm substantial 'excess' profits in the short term which would eventually attract new entrants into the industry, drawing the price back to *OP*. For the individual firm any output below *OQ* with price *OP* would be sub-optimal, as an increase in output would raise revenue more than costs, whilst output greater than *OQ* would raise costs more than revenue.

Although the perfect-competition case most easily shows the basic principles, we have seen that it is seldom met in practice, but is a theoretical ideal. The more usual case of imperfect competition, whether it be monopoly or many firms selling differentiated products, is shown in Chart 5.4. The chart also shows the more typical constant marginal cost structure over wide output ranges described in Chapter III.

In such cases the firm has some power to influence its demand curve by differentiating its product in some respect from those of its competitors. The marginal revenue curve is below the average revenue or demand curve. The profit-optimising price will be at that output OQ where the marginal cost and marginal revenue curves intersect (E). The price will be OP. As we have seen, the firm can within limits alter both the elasticity (slope) of its revenue curves, and by advertising shift them about. A very heavy and effective campaign, for example, might move the average and marginal revenue curves from DD and MM to $D'D'$ and $M'M'$ respectively, giving a new optimal position. Although price is unchanged at the new point of intersection between marginal cost and the new marginal revenue curve ($M'M'$), output rises from OQ to OR to give

Chart 5.4   Price and output under imperfect competition and monopoly

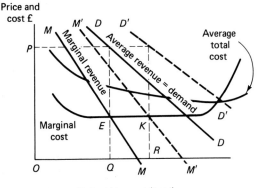

Output/demand (tons)

maximum profits. The firm could then utilise its plant more effectively. This example accords with the general tendency for companies to fix prices for their products and allow market forces to determine their output.

Given the cost and demand situation shown in Chart 5.4, each firm in the industry will be making excess profits, and there will be a tendency to attract new entrants. The equilibrium price and output for each firm would be where its average revenue curve is tangential to its average total-cost curve (including 'normal profits'). Market imperfections and barriers to entry of varying severity will however normally allow firms to retain some of their excess profits without attracting new entrants.

At the extreme of total monopoly, with insurmountable barriers to entry, the monopolist will be able to earn substantial 'excess profits' with impunity, constrained only by fears of public intervention if he becomes too greedy. Also, no product is without any substitutes in the long run, and customers and competitors will actively pursue substitute materials or processes if the monopolist charges exorbitant prices in the short run.

The theory suggests that the profit-optimising price and output in imperfectly competitive markets will tend to lead to excess capacity, even if excess profits have been eliminated. Each firm will produce less than if competition were perfect, as is brought out in Chart 5.5.

Chart 5.5   Price and output under perfect and imperfect competition

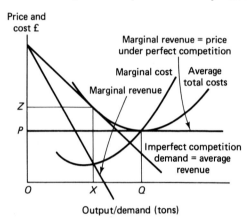

Output/demand (tons)

For convenience the chart shows conventional U-shaped cost curves. In perfectly competitive conditions the long-run equilibrium output is *OQ* at price *OP* but in imperfectly competitive markets the long run equilibrium is the lower output *OX* at the higher price *OZ*. This is the theoretical basis for all anti-monopoly legislation, and for the politicians' pursuit of the ideal of perfect competition.

The main advantages of the marginal approach to pricing policy are that it incorporates many of the salient features of the real world and gives a totally objective guide to rational behaviour. Given its crucial assumption that the firm aims to maximise profits, it shows exactly how that objective can be realised. It abstracts from the welter of detail and highlights that firms usually need to take account of market forces, and that both demand and costs influence pricing and output decisions. Firms will need to revise these decisions whenever demand conditions alter or costs change, whether as a result of forces external to the firm or of internal changes. As we shall see later, a marginal approach is the most suitable for many pricing decisions.

In practical circumstances, however, most pricing and output decisions are infinitely more complex than the theory suggests. Firms seldom know their precise demand and marginal-revenue schedules, nor in many cases their exact cost structures. The theory assumes a certain world in which managers are blessed with considerable knowledge about their environment, yet the main characteristic of the real world is uncertainty. Coping with this uncertainty and reaching decisions on the basis of very imperfect knowledge is one of the main tasks of management. Moreover, managers do not deal in the infinitesimally small changes in output implied by marginal analysis.

As we have seen, most firms produce a wide range of different goods of varying qualities, rather than the single identifiable product of the theory. All too frequently the cost structures of a range of products are closely interlinked, or the demand for one varies in a complex way with that for several others. Decisions on the price and output of one product may influence the costs of, and demand for, others.

The theory also ignores the complex organisational structure and motives of most firms. The one-man family business is not important for the mass of pricing decisions in modern manufacturing industry. Profit maximisation, as Chapter I has shown, is rarely the sole objective of most firms. Apart from whether profit maximisation involves total profits or the rate of return on capital, many firms appear anxious to increase their market share or their rate of growth. Different people within the organisation have different motives which impinge on the final pricing decision. Even internal political jockeying for position may often play a part. Most managers are conditioned to a greater or lesser extent by the values and aspirations of the society in which they live. They have obligations to the community which temper their profit-maximising behaviour. Often these obligations override the pursuit of long-run profit maximisation.

This introduces another basic objection to the theory. As normally expounded it may make ritual gestures to the longer term, but it is basically static. It is insufficiently dynamic and fails to distinguish fully the impact of short-run profit-maximising price decisions on longer-run profits. The prices charged today may signally influence tomorrow's demand curve and prices, but it is difficult to incorporate this into the theory.

Most firms can influence not only price but also their output, but the theory assumes that fixing either one determines the other. Moreover, marginal analysis is not really applicable to the special problems of pricing in oligopolistic markets. These have already been described in Chapter IV (Chart 4.5 and accompanying text). In such markets one of the most important determinants of price is the probable behaviour of competitors rather than the firm's own costs. Whatever the price and output indicated by equating marginal cost and marginal revenue, the oligopolist must take account of the likely impact of his decisions on his competitors and of their probable reactions. The price and output the oligopolist sets determine the shape of his marginal revenue curves.

Pricing formulae

The difficulties discussed above, plus empirical investigations into how firms actually fix prices, have led to the exposition of various widely used pricing formulae. These nearly all revolve round the concept of 'full or normal cost pricing'. Cost-plus pricing is another term for the same process. A firm should fix prices at a level which covers total costs, including an appropriate allocation of overheads and other fixed costs, plus a predetermined profit mark-up designed to yield a target return on capital employed. The mark-up, in the simplest forms, may be fixed as a rigid percentage to apply to costs, or it may be flexible, varying with market conditions. The phenomenon of 'full cost pricing' was first described by Hall and Hitch in a 1939 study of business men's behaviour, and the underlying theory developed by the late Professor P. W. S. Andrews (both reprinted in *Oxford Studies in the Price Mechanism*, by T. Wilson and P. W. S. Andrews, Oxford; Clarendon Press, 1951). Many subsequent empirical investigations have disclosed similar behaviour and there are almost as many variants of the full-cost approach as there are companies. A few examples will, however, be sufficient illustration.

A former vice-president of General Motors has described how car prices were fixed in the early 1920s.[1] A basic price was derived on the assumption that production would be on a standard volume, which might be 80% of plant capacity. Average costs would be calculated on the basis of this standard volume and a profit margin added sufficient to achieve the desired return on capital. The basic price would change with permanent changes in raw material and labour costs but not with volume fluctuations. In the book trade, pricing is even simpler;[2] the costs of manufacture (setting up type, proof reading, editing, etc., paper, ink, and labour time) are multiplied by a factor of about $3\frac{1}{2}$ and the resultant rounded up to a conventional price. A study of the clothing industry shows similar but more complex methods;[3] once the specifications of a garment are known a cost sheet is prepared with detailed estimates of all the separate direct labour costs to be incurred. The estimated total direct labour costs are grossed up by a percentage to cover overheads, based on

---

[1] Quoted in G. Maxcy and A. Silbertson, *The Motor Industry*, Allen & Unwin, 1959.
[2] R. Blackwell, The pricing of books, *Journal of Industrial Economics*, 1953–54.
[3] N. Balkin, Prices in the clothing industry, *Journal of Industrial Economics*, 1956–57.

the ratio between total overheads and total direct labour costs shown in the previous year's accounts. To the ensuing costs of production are added material costs plus a small percentage addition for waste, and further percentages to cover discounts, commissions and profit. The final figure is rounded to a convenient price.

The costs of production of mass-produced durable goods sold from stock are commonly estimated before a product goes into production. This is the most common situation. Posted prices are fixed for some period in advance, and the price and estimated sales are determined in advance. Although firms accept that sales forecasts are likely to prove false they will be prepared to accept a considerable margin of error and to maintain their prices during the planning period. Apart from passing on large, unavoidable cost increases they will hold prices but vary product specifications, production techniques, selling effort or even output. In one case of television receivers[1] costs are usually determined by using the standard costs of the various operations and materials for the previous financial year. Materials are taken into stock at standard predetermined costs, and the cost of direct labour is taken at standard rates and applied to standard times per operation, thereby giving a standard direct-labour cost per component. Overheads are taken as a standard percentage based on normal output load, and indirect expenses are allocated as closely as possible. The price received by the manufacturer is the retail price less discounts. To cover these, plus the firm's general overheads for administration, selling, research and customer service, a multiplier based on past experience is applied to the preliminary factory cost estimates. This multiplier is sufficient to show a reasonable return on capital with normal capacity output.

Not all manufacturing operations are of this type. Many capital equipment firms quote on detailed specifications for particular orders. Frequently such quotations are on tender and they have no firm idea, apart from general knowledge of the trade and past experience, of the strength of the competition. Costs plus a reasonable percentage mark-up for profit are in such circumstances the only reliable pricing guide, with the mark-up varying according to the firm's need to obtain the contract. If firms fail to take full account of probable costs when putting in tenders they are liable to suffer heavy losses. This is especially the case in periods of rapid inflation and in situations where there is no firm past experience on which to base cost estimates. The Rolls-Royce bankruptcy in 1971 was a clear case of inadequate appreciation of likely costs of production. Firms can often insulate themselves from the consequences of such inadequacy,

[1] F. A. Friday, Some thoughts on the pricing of television receivers, *Journal of Industrial Economics*, 1954–55.

if market conditions allow, by including appropriate escalation clauses. They tender for the job itself, as in the production of the Concorde airliner, rather than for a given item at a predetermined price.

Even these examples illustrate some of the difficulties in the full-cost approach to pricing. The cost involved is based either on past accounting costs, adjusted or not for expected inflationary movements, or standard costs at some 'normal' level of output. The costs used are average direct costs, whereas marginal theory stresses that marginal costs are what are relevant. Overheads are often allocated by some arbitrary formula which fails to take account of the opportunity costs of production of each product. The percentage mark-up is again usually based on past conditions, whereas future costs are what are relevant. In the simpler cases, the mark-up is rigidly fixed, but this can cause odd distortions even on the method's own terms. For example, an unforeseen jump in demand may force a firm to buy-in part of its component needs at higher prices than its own production. A constant mark-up on raw materials would mean increasing prices which might unnecessarily reduce the long-run demand.

The main weaknesses of the full-cost approach are on the demand side. At their most rigid, the formulae ignore all the market forces operating on the firm and fail to reflect the strength of competition. Against this criticism it is often argued that firms do not know the shape of their demand curves, particularly where they are pricing a new product, and that full-cost pricing eliminates the need for such knowledge. Moreover, in cases where marginal costs are constant over a wide output range, full-cost pricing may not be inconsistent with marginalism. It is also contended that pricing on the basis of cost will result in a long-run equilibrium and keep out new competitors; in the long run, prices tend to equal costs of production plus a normal profit margin even in marginal theory.

Most empirical investigations, including those quoted, stress that the price derived by the chosen formula is not necessarily that finally charged, but that some account, however subjective, is taken of market conditions, except in the crudest cases. In most cases the margin is flexible and is varied in accordance with the competition. Even though they may not know their exact demand curves, firms are well aware of the state of the market. Their average direct costs often set a lower limit to prices and they will not be able to get a higher price for their product than other firms will charge. To be competitive they must stay within a certain price range. Thus the full-cost theory does presuppose some standard outside the business. The General Motors' vice-president said that reduced prices were desirable to stimulate demand in periods when sales were low, but that these prices could not be below the base price unless the resulting loss of profits could be recouped through higher prices when demand was high. There was, however, a danger of higher prices at times of high volume attracting new entrants. In the clothing example, prices might differ from the costed price to clear stocks, to retain or attract new customers, to maintain long production runs or because of temporary fluctuations in demand. With television receivers the computed price would not be adopted if it were wildly out of line with competitors' prices. Other studies have disclosed very similar behaviour; cost-plus formulae provide the initial prices which are then adjusted for market conditions.

A common variant of the full-cost approach is 'backward-cost' or 'going-rate pricing'. The firm aims to produce to a price determined either by market forces or by some convention. Such a policy may be sensible where the cost structure is highly complex and it is impossible to allocate costs rationally to an individual product. It may also be essential for the smaller firms in an oligopolistic industry who have to take the price as set by a dominant market leader. Firms operating in conditions of perfect or nearly perfect competition are unable to influence the price, but must accept it as given. If they are to produce efficiently they must keep their direct costs within the market price less a mark-up for overheads and profit. Backward-cost pricing is also common in markets for many branded goods. For example, a 1946 Board of Trade Working Party on Boots and Shoes spoke of costing by elimination, which presupposes a shoe made to sell within a certain price range. The costing would start off with the selling price and then proceed by a continuous deduction of each succeeding item of cost of materials and labour to eliminate the price. Each stage would be allowed a given budget.

In many industries, consumers have come to accept conventional prices, as in cigarettes or confectionery; large multiple retailers also wish to sell at a few standard prices. Frequent price changes are inconvenient not only to customers and retailers but also to manufacturers, and wherever possible price stability is preferred. In such instances producers must tightly control costs to ensure adequate profits. Small changes in cost are accommodated through changing either the quality of the product or its size, as with cigarettes.

Some empirical investigations of firms' pricing policies have already been cited. The more famous studies of pricing behaviour apart from the Hall and Hitch work are James Earley's study of 110 firms for the American Management Association. Marginal Policies of 'Excellently Managed' Companies, *American Economic Review*, March 1956, The Brookings Institute's 1958 work, *Pricing in Big Business* by A. D. H.

Kaplin, J. B. Dirlam, and R. F. Lanzillotti (Brookings Institute Washington DC, 1958), and W. W. Haynes' 1962 examination *Pricing Decisions in Small Business* (Lexington; University of Kentucky Press, 1962). The reports of the UK Monopolies Commission and the studies of the now defunct Prices and Incomes Board also contain a considerable amount of information about pricing behaviour. A UK Study is A. S. Mackintosh's *Development of Firms* (Cambridge University Press, 1963), which is based on a sample of 36 firms in the Birmingham area. The *Journal of Industrial Economics* is a rich source of studies of pricing behaviour in particular industries, including those discussed earlier.

One difficulty is to disentangle what firms say they do from what they actually do in practice. They may often rationalise their behaviour incorrectly, or they may be unaware of economic theories their interlocutors are trying to prove or disprove, and their answers, particularly to oral questions, may be unconsciously slanted. Most of the studies show that firms rarely behave fully in accordance with the dictates of marginal theory, although the better managed ones do take account of market conditions to a greater or lesser extent. The full-cost formulae are often convenient reference points from which to shade prices or other aspects of the product package to counter competitive forces and obtain satisfactory profits. In large organisations formulae are a convenient way of delegating complex pricing decisions to lower levels of management. It is impossible to generalise adequately about the adjustments made in individual circumstances to the formulae, through variable mark-ups for example, beyond saying that firms do usually take account both of their costs and of demand conditions when fixing prices and/or output. Rarely if at all, however, is full marginal analysis carried out.

The contribution concept in pricing

Although formulae approaches to pricing based on some variant of average costs are very widely used, the previous section has implied that they are not necessarily the best method. In particular they are liable to be too inflexible and may prevent the business from taking full advantage of all market opportunities. Although marginal analysis may be far too complex for most business situations, we have shown that it does produce a profit-maximising solution if rigorously applied. Obviously it needs tempering to take account of objectives other than profit maximisation and simplifying so that it can be widely adopted. In previous chapters it has been suggested that the marginalism of economic theory can, in the business context, be redefined as 'incrementalism'. A decision will be profitable if it adds more to total revenues than to total costs, or reduces total revenue less than total costs. The key factor is the contribution made to the firm's total profit as a result of a decision, and anything which raises this contribution, suitably defined, should be pursued.

The key here is 'suitably defined'. In particular, management must have a sufficiently long-time perspective and have regard to the longer-term implications of a decision. Sharp price reductions to clear stocks may raise immediate revenue more than costs, but may harm a company's reputation for quality in the longer term and reduce profits. Alternatively, raising prices at the top of the cycle when demand is very strong may boost profits but simultaneously force customers to develop alternative sources of supply in the longer term and attract new competition, whether from domestic firms or from importers. In short, pricing decisions should take full account of longer-term implications, with future costs and revenues discounted back. The above examples also show that the opportunity cost concept is highly relevant to pricing decisions.

Concentration on incremental costs and revenues means that pricing policy should in general be based on the expected changes in costs incurred, rather than on past average costs. Arbitrary allocations of overheads that will be incurred regardless of the decision can lead to incorrect decisions. This does not of course mean that overhead costs can be ignored in the totality of the firm's business. Obviously, if it fails to cover all its costs it will very soon find itself bankrupted. It means rather that costs completely irrelevant to the decision in question should not be considered. A decision whether or not to raise or lower prices in the short term would require a study of completely different costs than a decision on long-run prices for a new product line. In the former case only the direct variable costs are relevant, whereas large chunks of indirect expense are involved in the second.

In both decisions the interconnections between the various activities must be fully explored. If, for example, a change in the price of one product affects the demand and costs of an allied product sold by the firm this must be taken into account. The implications of the joint products in the case of costs, and complementary or competitive products in the case of demand, must be carefully examined. Wherever possible, each product group should be treated on its own merits as its cost structure and demand characteristics are likely to differ from those of other product groups within the firm.

Incremental analysis requires firms to pay close attention to competitive conditions in the market for each product. Although full knowledge of demand curves and elasticities may be lacking or impossibly expensive to obtain, managers should develop a close understanding of their markets. Quite often this knowledge may be subjective or intuitive, but it is nonetheless valuable for that. The strength of competing firms in all markets, the availability and technical characteristics of possible substitutes, and the market conditions facing customers, are all important facets of the required knowledge.

In practice most large firms do study the impact of their decisions on incremental costs and revenues, even though they may use simplifying formulae to assist their decision making. An important point is that large firms often sell thousands of different products and the costs of obtaining detailed cost and demand information about each could easily outweigh the benefits to be obtained from a more sophisticated pricing method. Senior management must delegate, and this requires some simple guidelines. Also pricing is but one area of decision making and management must be able to devote sufficient attention to all the others. Beyond saying that pricing policy must be flexible in the face of shifting demand, changing competitive and market conditions, stock levels, capacity, and cost trends, there are no hard and fast rules for every business situation. Concentration on incremental changes in costs and revenues, within the constraints of limited time and management resources, of imperfect knowledge, and of changing managerial objectives, is the best general guide.

Pricing objectives and strategies

The limitations of profit maximisation, even in the long term, as the cornerstone of pricing behaviour have already been amply discussed and a wide range of other possible management objectives listed. Equity, fairness, and other ethical considerations beyond the economic calculus of profit and loss often play a major part. The threat or reality of government control can also exert an influence, even when firms are allowed full freedom to fix prices as they wish and are not constrained by price controls. Restrictive-practices legislation in the UK outlaws collusive pricing unless it can pass through rigidly defined gateways (see Chapter IX), resale price maintenance is prohibited, the possibility of investigations by the Monopolies Commission can be a deterrent to always fixing prices that the market will bear, and pricing in some industries such as pharmaceuticals or iron and steel is restrained in varying methods by government regulations. In the United States a much greater range of pricing practices is specifically outlawed than in the United Kingdom.

So far the complexity of the markets for most products has been ignored. In many cases there is a lengthy distributive chain between the manufacturer and the final consumer, and each stage expects to achieve a reasonable return. Manufacturers must so price their products as to appeal to the final buyer and sufficiently reward the distributors. The rationale of discount houses is to cut out the middlemen and pass their rewards on to customers through lower prices. Manufacturers not only sell products in a wide variety of different outlets, but also in many geographical markets. Their pricing policies must take account of these differences. Again they produce goods which are at different stages in their life cycle, as described in Chapter IV. They must aim to set their prices so as to prolong the profitable life of each product and to ensure that demand is sufficient. The continuing trade-off between price and other aspects of the product is another important factor which firms always have to bear in mind. Stable prices do not always denote a lack of competition; it may merely have been channelled into other areas such as technical content, quality, or even packaging or the psychological appeal of a product. The remainder of this chapter examines certain types of pricing policy frequently encountered in practice which are designed to meet some of the situations outlined above.

Price discrimination

Price discrimination occurs where a firm sets different prices for the same or very similar products in different markets. It presupposes some imperfection in the total market for the product so that the elasticity of demand differs in different segments, and it is difficult for customers to transfer the product from one market to another. Faced with demand curves of different elasticities in the separate markets, the firm has different marginal revenue curves, but one common marginal cost curve (subject to different transport and selling expenses). Marginal analysis implies that profits will be maximised when total marginal revenue is equated with marginal cost, and the marginal revenues in each market are the same. Chart 5.6 shows how this ensures that the price charged is higher in the market with the less elastic demand.

The left-hand chart shows the overall company marginal cost and marginal revenue curve, the latter being the sum of the marginal revenue curves in the two separate markets shown in the right-hand charts. Total output will be set where the company marginal revenue and marginal cost curves coincide at $Q_1 + Q_2$. The marginal cost OX set by this

Chart 5.6   Price discrimination

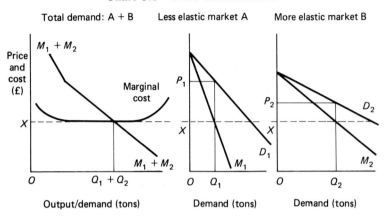

Total demand: A + B   Less elastic market A   More elastic market B

intersection is the point at which price and quantity will be fixed in the
sub-markets to the right of the chart. In the less elastic market A, the
price will be OP_1, with sales of OQ_1, and in the more elastic market B the
price will be OP_2, with sales of OQ_2. A good example is provided by the
motor-components industry. The market for initial equipment is
extremely keen, with the motor manufacturers anxious to cut costs to the
bone. There is intense competition between suppliers, so that the market
for initial equipment such as tyres, sparking plugs and batteries, is
extremely elastic (market B). Once a car has a given type of equipment,
however, there is a strong incentive for the owner to buy the same
equipment when the original wears out. Also car owners have much less
technical knowledge about the various alternatives than the car
producers, and their bargaining power is much weaker. In many
instances the component suppliers, often working through the car
manufacturers, have a near-monopoly. The replacement market is
consequently similar to market A in being much less elastic, and prices of
replacement equipment are much higher than the initial installations.

   Price discrimination is often outlawed as an unfair business practice in
the United States, but it is legal in the United Kingdom. It can take many
forms but one of the most common is the practice of charging lower
prices in export markets, where competition is frequently fiercer than in a
protected home market. Such price discrimination is often attacked as an
unfair trading practice by the importing country. Indeed the GATT
provides for duties against such dumping which causes material injury to
domestic producers (see Chapter VIII). As the detailed example shows,
segmentation of markets does not have to be geographical to encourage
price discrimination. Other examples of price discrimination are:

freight carriers' practices of charging for freight not solely according to weight, space taken or distance travelled but also according to its value; the giving of quantity discounts to large buyers over and above those warranted by the lower costs incurred in supplying them; charging lower fares or admission prices to particular groups of people such as children or old age pensioners; selling different brands of very similar products appealing to different income groups at different prices; price differentiation between the domestic and industrial markets for fuels such as coal. These examples can be multiplied by many others, but in each case the general principle is the same. Total profits can be increased if the market can be divided into smaller segments and each segment charged what the traffic will bear. What the traffic will bear does not always correspond to the costs of supply.

Basing-point prices

Many manufacturing companies charge identical prices irrespective of the distance of the customer from the plant. Transport costs are averaged out over the entire output, so that in effect customers near the factory are subsidising those situated considerable distances away. Where transport costs are low relative to the final price of the product the subsidy element may be very small and the administrative difficulties caused by charging transport separately may be considerable. In certain basic industries, however, a different pricing system known as basing-point pricing is adopted. Indeed it is now compulsory in the UK under the ECSC[1] rules for coal and iron and steel products. By contrast, such pricing systems are often illegal in the United States.

Briefly, the sales territory is divided into a series of zones each with a basing point such as a factory at which prices are set. Customers must pay the transport charges from the basing point. The theory is that no customer is subsidised and that such a pricing system will therefore encourage the most sensible and lowest-cost location of industry. The basing-point pricing system is used in the UK cement industry, as was disclosed during an examination of the Cement Makers Federation before the Restrictive Practices Court *(Restrictive Trade Practices Court Report on Cement Makers Federation 1961)*. The Cement Makers Federation fixed prices and terms for the sale of cement by its members. The fixed prices had as their basis a 'base price', which was the price to be paid for cement deliveries within a five-mile radius from the works where they were made. Concentric circles of radii increasing by successive five miles delimited zones within which the price was increased by specific amounts as cement was delivered further away from the

---
[1] European Coal and Steel Community.

works. In the cement case the price increases became progressively less the further away cement was delivered, so that there was a transport subsidy to the more distant customers. The price structure, it was argued, encouraged makers to sell to customers nearest to their works, and to site their works in areas where demand was greatest.

Pricing and the product life cycle

The concept of a product life cycle has already been discussed in Chapter IV, when it was stated that firms must always aim to have a balanced portfolio of products in various stages of their life cycle. A key question in this regard is the appropriate pricing policy to ensure that the long-run profits from each product are maximised. In the initial stages when a product is first introduced, perhaps in a test marketing area, the firm can either charge a very high price or, alternatively, a low price. The distinction has been described in Joel Dean's *Managerial Economics*, Prentice Hall, 1951, as a (high) *skimming price*, or a (low) *penetration price*. The former, often with very heavy advertising appropriations, is most suitable when the short-run demand is judged to be fairly inelastic, and a high price now is not expected to have any serious adverse effects on longer-term sales. This is more likely to be so with a product sharply differentiated from anything else in the same line already on the market, with novelty products, and with completely new products such as ball-point pens in their initial stages. In the introductory stages of a product, price is unlikely to deter adventurous consumers who might be attracted by the product's exclusiveness or snob appeal. Moreover a high price is relatively safe because the firm can always gradually lower the price if it has misjudged the market, whereas it is nowhere near as easy to raise prices. Selling at a high initial price will enable the firm to cover its high initial launching and development costs. Where the innovator is not protected by a patent position or high entry barriers, a low penetration price may be more appropriate as a means of shutting out rival producers offering close substitutes. Low prices may rapidly increase the product's market, which would be particularly important if the production process offered substantial economies of scale. Often branded grocery products are introduced at low initial prices, through cut-price offers, to gain consumer acceptance of the product. Once sufficient users are attracted to buy the product regularly the special offers are quietly dropped. The innovator is here buying consumer loyalty, and is turning a high short-run price elasticity of demand into a more inelastic demand in the longer run.

The pricing strategy changes once a product has gained widespread acceptance and is reaching saturation point. Probably competitors will have introduced similar products, or the innovator may have managed to stave off such competition by lowering prices markedly at the right stage and keeping rivals out. Normally, however, consumer loyalty to the innovating brand will weaken, as was the case with Biro ball-point pens. In the grocery field there will probably be a switch from the nationally branded product to the supermarket's own brands, and the originator may be unable to charge premium prices. In the case of durable goods, saturation is indicated when new initial purchases are overtaken by replacement demand. Skilful product innovation can, as we have seen already in Chapter IV, greatly delay this point. The danger (or benefit) when a product has entered maturity is of one firm starting off a price war, followed by the main rivals, to the ultimate benefit of no one except consumers. More usually competition will be on the non-price attributes of the product, with give-away promotions and so on. One of the most difficult questions for all firms, which is rarely tackled properly, is knowing when to pull out of a product or market. Too frequently sentiment or vested interests delay the phasing out of a product, and resources are committed for too long to products with no future.

Pricing with a variable load factor

Public utilities such as electricity and gas supply, and public transport undertakings such as bus services or underground railways, face the problem of variable demand in a particularly acute form. Demand moves not only in seasonal peaks and troughs, but also with pronounced regular weekly or daily fluctuations. Thus demand for transport is especially high during the morning and evening week-day rush hours, but tails off in the rest of the day and at week-ends. The operating companies need to provide sufficient capacity to meet the peak load even though it will probably be grossly under-utilised outside peak hours. If they do not, the service will greatly deteriorate in peak hours (voltage reductions by electricity suppliers or over-crowding in buses with long delays). The pricing problem is to price so as to shift some peak demand into non-peak hours and also, as far as possible, to make prices reflect relevant costs. In particular, prices should be higher at peak periods than in off-peak times to help cover the costs of the additional capacity. The rate for electricity supplied during the night time is cheaper than the daily rate for example, some bus companies now charge higher fares during peak periods than off-peak, and telephone calls are cheaper outside times of peak business demand.

Certain non-price methods of load shifting are possible. These include special off-peak offers for rail travel, or heavy promotional spending on appliances using off-peak electricity, or gas. Whilst the former is a rational use of resources in that it enables the existing capital stock to be used more intensively, the latter improves the load factor of the utilities at the expense of increasing their total claims on resources. In the United States, for example, the electricity companies' plugging of summer air-conditioning to offset the winter central-heating peak greatly exacerbated the United States short-term energy problems.

The peak–off-peak problem, though most acute in public utilities, exists in large sectors of industry. For example, central-heating firms and double-glazing installers face a much higher demand in winter than in summer. Special discount offers are made to push demand into the summer months. Suppliers of non-durable seasonal products such as ice cream, turkeys, or Christmas trees do not have the ability to shift demand through pricing policy. They must either rely on heavy advertising, as with the turkey producers' attempts to iron out the seasonal demand, or widen their product range to include products with different peaking characteristics.

Where the price mechanism is appropriate, fixing the correct peak and off-peak charges is complex, partly because differential prices will shift some of the demand and thereby alter the relevant costs. The aim is to equate price with marginal costs in two periods. At off-peak times the marginal cost is merely the marginal operating cost, such as the marginal direct-running costs of trains and their support facilities. In peak periods, however, it is the marginal direct-running costs plus some measure of the cost of additional capacity needed to meet an extra unit of peak demand. Full analysis of peak-load pricing is beyond the scope of this book, but Chart 5.7 indicates a solution to the problem.

The off-peak and peak demand curves are added to show how much consumers will pay for one unit of off-peak plus one unit of peak service (e.g. a kilowatt hour or a passenger mile). This gives the total demand curve *(XX)*. The supplier should fix his capacity at the point where this demand curve *XX* intersects the overall marginal cost of peak plus off-peak supply *(YY)*. The marginal cost of off-peak supply is the marginal direct-running cost, and that of peak supply the marginal direct-running cost plus the marginal capacity cost, so that the total marginal cost is twice the marginal direct-running cost plus marginal capacity cost. The appropriate prices OP_p OP_o are indicated by the intersection of this capacity *OB* with the peak and off-peak demand curves. Capacity will be fully utilised in each period. The prices set will boost demand outside the peak and flatten it at peak periods.

Chart 5.7   Peak load pricing

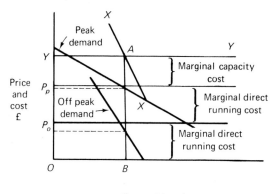

Demand (tons)

Retail pricing practices

A number of pricing practices are common in the retail trade, most of which have already been mentioned. These include the practice of multiple retailers to set conventional prices which remain fixed for long periods and to order goods to fit those prices. Whilst this releases the energies of stores staff, suppliers still have the complex problem of controlling quality and costs to provide acceptable goods at those prices. The pricing problem is essentially shifted back to the producer.

Often multiple stores set prices just below round numbers. This ensures that sales staff have to enter the sales on the till in order to give change, thereby making it more difficult to pocket notes. Odd-number prices are also said to appeal psychologically to customers, particularly where change is given. For example, £4.99 sounds much less than £5. The scope for such odd-number pricing policies has been diminished in recent years in the UK by rapid inflation, the abolition of the guinea, and the awkwardness of the decimal coinage with its half pence disliked both by stores and customers. Rather than shade prices, other retailers may prefer to settle for the even £5 rather than £4.99 to give an appearance of quality and to appeal to the customer's snob instincts.

A common phenomenon, particularly in supermarkets, is the loss leader, a product sold below cost in order to attract customers into the store and boost sales of other products. Sugar has frequently been used in this respect, though special-offer promotions apply to a wide range of groceries. A profit below customary on the one product, or even a loss, is expected to raise the store's total profit. The most effective loss leaders are products whose standard prices are widely known, which are purchased regularly, whose quality is fixed irrespective of price, and for which demand is relatively inelastic.

VI

THE FIRM IN THE NATIONAL ECONOMY

The aims of economic policy

Previous chapters have been primarily concerned with those economic influences acting within, or directly on, individual firms. This chapter, and the remainder, deal with the wider aspects of the economic environment, with macro-economics as opposed to micro-economics. An ideal starting point for considering this wider economic world is the national income and the national accounts. First though, a brief digression is useful on the economic objectives pursued by governments and to which individual firms must adapt. All post-war governments have pursued certain objectives with varying emphasis and success. Often there is some confusion between objectives and means, and there are usually conflicts of varying severity between some of the objectives. Inevitably a compromise is reached, but the elements of this compromise vary according to circumstances and the political complexion of the government. Some objectives, such as the maintenance of a fixed and stable exchange rate, have been ditched in the 1970's. The main aims on which all parties are agreed at least in theory are the maintenance of a high and stable level of employment, with the concomitant obligation to low unemployment, the avoidance of serious domestic inflation, and the fostering of conditions 'in which the nation can, if it so wills, realise its full potentialities for growth in terms of production and living standards' (Cmnd 9725. 1956). A subsidiary objective, even with floating exchange rates, is the avoidance of large long-term balance-of-payments deficits; at the very least there must be approximate equilibrium, or other objectives become unattainable. The improvement of the economy's regional balance, the contribution of at least 1% of GNP to the development needs of the third world, the promotion of greater economic equality, and the sharpening of personal incentives are further broad economic objectives which would not necessarily command universal support, but which are pursued by at least one of the main political parties.

Achievement of these objectives has become increasingly difficult; neither full employment nor low inflation has been realised in recent years.

The national income

Just as a company's operations in the course of the year can be traced in its annual accounts, so can those of a national economy. A country's national accounts build up in a form of double-entry bookkeeping. They are central to any analysis of the economic situation, and most economic forecasts and national planning exercises are expressed through a national accounts framework. An understanding of the national income and its composition is, therefore, indispensable for any thorough discussion of economic growth, inflation, or unemployment.

The national income is not just the income of the government or public authorities. In essence, it is an estimate of all the incomes accruing to factors of production such as land, labour and capital during a given period. It is not simply the total of all incomes earned, as it includes only the incomes of residents derived directly from the current production of goods and services. It does not include incomes arising from transfer payments. At the outset it is important to realise that there is no unique definition of national income. The comprehensiveness of the estimates is limited by convenience and convention, although there are generally accepted international standards. In practice, coverage is mainly restricted to those incomes which arise from economic activity, and to those goods and services which are exchanged for money. Some allowance is, however, made for the value to owner occupiers of the housing they enjoy; an annual rent is 'imputed' based on rateable values. This is done partly because of the great importance of owner occupation, but also because it competes with other forms of housing. Logically, there is no reason why a rent should not also be imputed to consumer durables and private motor cars, but practical difficulties prevent this, and such private investment goods are regarded as totally consumed in the year of purchase. Because national income measures only economic activities, no allowance is made for the value to society of voluntary or even involuntary unpaid work, such as that performed by housewives, or do-it-yourself enthusiasts. The values placed on goods and services are monetary values often determined in imperfect markets. Even when they are adjusted to constant prices, they do not provide precise measures of changes either in welfare or in productivity, although the broad trends disclosed are usually unchallengeable. In view of the growing debate over the 'quality of life' and the environment, one must be clear at the outset that the national income was never intended to measure the overall standard of living. Many of the attacks on national income statistics are fundamentally misconceived. One should attack not the concepts, but some of the uses to which they are put.

Annual statistics of national income for the United Kingdom are published each autumn in *National Income and Expenditure*, colloquially known as the Blue Book. Quarterly figures are published regularly in *Economic Trends*, with a long run of consistent estimates in the October issue, and in summary form in the *Monthly Digest of Statistics*. Most countries have similar detailed publications. The regularly issued United Nations' *Yearbook of National Accounts Statistics* and the OECD's *National Accounts of OECD Countries* are useful sources of comparative figures. The EEC Statistical Office also publishes a *National Accounts Yearbook*.

The National Income is most usually defined as the *Gross National Product* (GNP), or *Gross Domestic Product* (GDP). The latter is the total value of the goods and services produced by the country. It can be measured by totalling either all the *incomes* received for their production, or the *expenditure* on their purchase, or the *outputs* of the various industries. The sources for the income and output measures are broadly identical, but they differ substantially in coverage, reliability, and timing from those used for the expenditure estimates. There is, therefore, usually a *statistical discrepancy* between the three measures, which conventionally is shown as part of the income and output estimates. Table 6.1 shows the three ways of looking at the national income, and gives estimates for the various aggregates in 1976.

A full description of the UK accounts is given in *National Accounts Statistics: Sources and Methods*, HMSO Studies in Official Statistics No. 13, 1968, supplemented by the notes in the Blue Book. In brief, however, the national income on the expenditure side measures the total payments by final buyers of goods and services, either for current consumption or for investment. This means that all intermediate purchases, such as steel by a car manufacturer, or wood by a furniture manufacturer, are netted out. The details of the expenditure side of the accounts, shown in the first column of Table 6.1, are discussed more fully in the next section. Consumption, however, includes both purchases by households and other private individuals *(consumers' expenditure)* and by central government departments and local authorities *(general government final consumption)*. Investment, or 'adding to wealth', is the net increase in the stock of tangible net assets in the course of the year. It includes both fixed assets, such as buildings, vehicles, plant and machinery, and current

Table 6.1 Three ways of looking at the national income—1976 (£ million)

Expenditure

Consumers' expenditure	73 656
General government final consumption	26 562
Gross domestic fixed capital formation	23 427
Stock building	359
Total Domestic Expenditure at market prices	124 004
Exports of goods and services	34 837
Total Final Expenditure at market prices	158 841
Less Imports of goods and services	−36 564
Gross Domestic Product at market prices:	122 277
Less Taxes on expenditure	−16 660
Factor Cost Adjustment Subsidies	3 463
Gross Domestic Product at factor cost	109 080
Property Income from abroad	8 609
Less Property Income paid abroad	−7 430
Gross National Product at factor cost	110 259
Less Capital consumption	−13 583
National Income (Net National Product at factor cost)	96 676

Note: Gross National Product at Market prices: 123 456

Income

Income from employment	78 639
Income from self-employment	10 208
Gross trading profits of companies	12 445
Gross trading surplus of public corporations	4 460
Gross trading surplus of government enterprises	120
Rent	7 771
Imputed charge for consumption of non-trading capital	1 012
Total Domestic Income	114 655
Less Stock appreciation	−6 557
Residual error	982
-------------------------------------	109 080
-------------------------------------	8 609
-------------------------------------	−7 430
-------------------------------------	110 259
-------------------------------------	−13 583
-------------------------------------	96 676

Output

Agriculture, forestry and fishing	3 116
Mining and quarrying (a)	2 458
Manufacturing (a)	30 641
Construction	7 793
Gas, electricity, water (a)	3 905
Transport	6 624
Communication	3 691
Distributive Trades	10 379
Public Administration and defence	8 458
Ownership of dwellings	6 723
Insurance, banking, finance and business services	7 717
Public Health and educational services	8 055
Other services	13 417
Total Domestic output	112 750
Residual error	982
Adjustment for Financial services	−4 072
-------------------------------------	109 080
-------------------------------------	8 609
-------------------------------------	−7 430
-------------------------------------	110 259
-------------------------------------	−13 583
-------------------------------------	96 676

(a) Note: Energy industries 5 110

SOURCE: *National Income and Expenditure 1966–76.* Central Statistical Office. HMSO.

assets such as stocks. The former investment is known as *gross domestic fixed capital formation*, and the latter as the *value of the physical increase in stocks and work in progress*. A proportion of the output of British industry is sent overseas in the form of *exports of goods and services*, and this must be added to these domestic demands to show *total final expenditure*. Some of this spending, particularly by private consumers, will, however, be on *imports of goods and services*, which must be deducted as they do not boost UK incomes, but are part of the incomes of foreign countries. This gives the *gross domestic product*.

The income side of the accounts includes wages and salaries of employees, incomes from self-employment, rents, trading profits of companies, and the trading surpluses of the nationalised industries and other public sector bodies and an imputed charge for the consumption of non trading capital (the estimated rent on property occupied and owned by general government and private non profit making bodies which was included in rent in earlier years). These *total domestic incomes* are adjusted slightly to equate to the gross domestic product calculated from the expenditure route. Apart from the residual error already mentioned, the main deduction is *stock appreciation*. Gross profits include the increase in the price of goods held in stock during the year, and this must be deducted as it has no direct connection with changes in output. Incomes such as interest and dividends, pensions and social-security benefits are not included. They are merely transfers between income recipients and are not rewards to factors of production.

Another method of looking at total incomes is to regard them as the sum of the outputs of all the industries or productive enterprises in the country. Output in this context is value added, which eliminates any double counting. It is the difference between the value of total sales and the cost of all materials and services purchased, whether from UK sources or from abroad. The third column of Table 6.1 shows the value added in the broad industrial sectors. A complicating factor is the net interest received by financial companies, which was subtracted from their value added prior to the 1973 Blue Book. This is no longer appropriate and their contribution to GDP is now shown gross, with a separate adjustment for financial services.

Income from employment accounts for slightly over 69% of total domestic incomes. Its share has tended to rise in the post-war decades. In 1950 it took 60% of domestic incomes, in 1960 it accounted for 66%, in 1970 for 68% and in 1976 for 69%. The share of rent has also tended to increase, whilst self-employment incomes and company trading profits have fallen relatively. The industrial composition of output has also changed, with a rising proportion going to the service sectors. For example, manufacturing industry accounted for 35% of income in 1961, but for 31% in 1971, for 28% in 1974, and for 27% by 1976.

So far we have discussed only the top half of Table 6.1. The lower section shows how the main measures of national income are linked together. The *gross domestic product* (GDP) measures the total value of goods and services produced within the country. It can be measured either at the prices which final buyers must pay for these goods and services, that is at *market prices*, or it can be measured at the prices received by producers, that is at *factor cost*. The latter is the more useful measure for international comparisons. In the UK accounts the expenditure estimates are calculated at market prices and the income and output measures at factor cost. The difference between the two measures is the *factor cost adjustment*. To convert the prices received by producers to those paid by buyers, it is necessary to subtract subsidies and add on all indirect taxes. Subsidies have diminished considerably in importance in post-war years with the phasing out of food subsidies, rising council house rents and insistence on the viability of nationalised industries, but indirect taxes have become more important. The main ones are value-added tax and excise duties on alcoholic drink and tobacco.

If Britain were a totally closed economy with no dealings with the outside world, the GDP would be adequate by itself. In practice the UK has made extensive investments overseas from which it derives substantial profits, interest and dividends. Conversely, foreigners have invested in the UK, and especially in the North Sea in recent years, and there is an outflow of property income. The net property income accruing to UK residents is added to the GDP to obtain a more comprehensive measure in the *Gross National Product* (GNP). Table 6.1 shows that the difference between GDP and GNP is relatively small, as the large flows of property income in both directions are very similar.

So far all incomes and expenditures have been measured gross. No allowance has been made for the fact that a significant proportion of fixed investment is merely to replace worn-out plant and equipment. Moreover, the profits shown are before making any allowance for depreciation. Even in company accounts the calculation of depreciation is an arbitrary affair, usually owing more to the requirements of the tax system than to economic logic. It is that much harder to calculate the national *depreciation* or *capital consumption*, and the estimates made are rather arbitrary. For this reason most discussion of national income is based on the gross rather than the net estimates. Nonetheless, as Table 6.1 shows, the *net national product* is calculated, and it is this magnitude that is, strictly speaking, *the national income*. In 1976 capital consumption accounted for about 12% of the GNP and for 58% of gross investment. Thus less than half of each pound invested increased the capital stock.

Within the overall estimates of GNP, there are numerous more detailed analyses. One of the most useful is that relating to personal incomes, which is shown in Table 6.2.

In the UK national accounts the personal sector is taken to include all unincorporated businesses and also non-profit-making enterprises. This explains the inclusion of company contributions to charities. Whereas transfer payments are netted out when considering the total

Table 6.2 Calculation of personal incomes and expenditure 1976 (£ million)

Income from employment (as Table 6.1)	78639
Income from self-employment (as Table 6.1)	10208
Rent, dividends, and net interest	10451
Current transfers to charities from companies	42
National insurance benefits and other current grants from public authorities	12822
Imputed charge for capital consumption of private non-profit-making bodies	192
Total Personal Income	**112354**
Less UK taxes on income (inc. addition to tax reserves)	18049
Less National Insurance, etc., contributions	8426
Less Transfers abroad (net)	65
Total Personal Disposable Income	**85814**
Consumers' expenditure (as Table 6.1)	73656
Savings before depreciation and stock appreciation	12158

SOURCE: *National Income and Expenditure 1966–76*, Central Statistical Office, HMSO.

national income, they are an important part of many personal incomes (e.g. of retirement pensioners), and are therefore shown. Employment incomes are the main source of personal income—70% in 1976. A significant percentage of personal incomes is automatically deducted for taxes, and social-security contributions. The remainder is the *disposable income* which the recipients can spend or save as they wish. In 1976 disposable incomes accounted for 76.4% of total personal incomes and consumers' expenditure took 85.8% of these disposable incomes. The remaining 14.4% of disposable incomes was saved, and this percentage is the *savings ratio* to which we return later on. It has risen substantially during the 1970s, from 10.1% in 1972 for example.

Changes in the value of national income over a period not only include *volume* or *real* changes, but also the effects of price rises. For many purposes, and particularly in discussions of national economic policy, it is more helpful to separate out the effects of price and volume changes. The main aggregates are, therefore, recalculated at *constant prices*, and it is these that are referred to in any discussions of economic growth. The various components of GDP are separately adjusted or *deflated* by appropriate price index numbers. Separate constant-price estimates are made in this manner of the GDP built up from expenditure and income data. Also estimates of output at constant prices are built up from indicators such as the index of industrial production weighted according to their contributions to GDP. Because of timing and coverage differences these three measures of real GDP often display markedly different trends. This is, to put it mildly, confusing for economic policy, and a widely used device is to take the average of the three estimates as the best indicator of real movements. Although the real GDP is frequently used as an index of improvement in standards of living, it is important to bear in mind the major qualifications made earlier. It is an indicator but is by no means self-sufficient; the composition and distribution of changes in real GDP and other non-economic factors are also very important.

Chart 6.1 shows the trend since 1960 of the UK's GDP at constant prices (average estimate), and also how the GDP price deflator has moved. The GDP has shown a marked cyclical pattern which is clearly brought out by the annual percentage changes shown in the lower part of the chart. During the 1960s the UK recorded an average rate of growth of real GNP of 2.9% per annum. All countries have recorded significantly slower growth rates during the 1970s than in the 1960s. In both decades, though, Britain's rate of growth has been well below the average of other major industrial countries as Table 6.3 clearly demonstrates.

International comparisons, even of growth rates, are hazardous because of statistical differences in definition and coverage and also because of more fundamental disparities in economic structure, base levels and values. The differences between the countries in the table are sufficiently marked, however, to demonstrate that the UK's GDP has persistently grown relatively slowly. One consequence has been a relative decline in the UK's per capita GDP, which is often used as a very crude measure of living standards. Table 6.4 shows the figures for a recent year for major industrial countries.

National currencies have been converted into dollars at the ruling official exchange rates, which might be a very poor guide to relative

Chart 6.1   The growth of GDP in the UK 1960–76

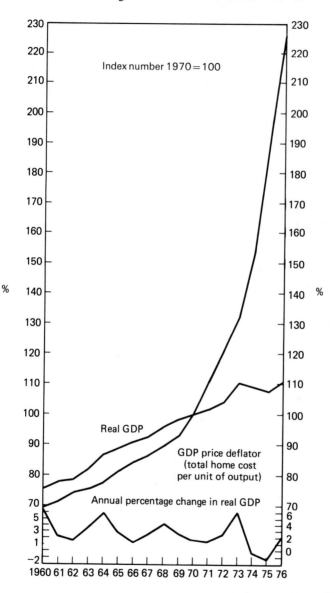

Index number 1970 = 100

Real GDP

GDP price deflator
(total home cost
per unit of output)

Annual percentage change in real GDP

1960 61 62 63 64 65 66 67 68 69 70 71 72 73 74 75 76

SOURCE: *UK National Income and Expenditure 1966–76*, HMSO.

ECONOMICS FOR MANAGERS

Table 6.3 Comparative rates of growth of real GDP, 1960s and 1970s (per cent per annum at constant prices)

	1959–60 to 1970–71	1970–71 to 1975–76
United Kingdom	2.9	1.9
Canada	4.9	4.4
United States	3.9	2.5
Japan	11.1	5.2
Germany	4.9	2.0
France	5.8	3.6
Italy	5.5	2.5
Netherlands	5.3	3.0

SOURCE: *OECD Economic Outlook*, July 1973, Main Economic Indicator, August 1977.

purchasing power, particularly during periods of currency unrest. Also statistical coverage problems are even more important for comparisons of levels than they are for trends. Finally such comparisons ignore all the non-measurable elements in living standards, regarding which the UK tends to score relatively well. In brief, such comparisons are worth very little indeed; the table has been included here mainly to emphasise the warnings which are usually ignored in general discussion.

Table 6.4 Per Capita GDP 1976 (Dollars at 1976 Exchange Rates)

United Kingdom	3 840	Germany	7 370
United States	7 855	France	6 545
Canada	8 185	Italy	2 915
Japan	4 905	Netherlands	6 410

SOURCE: *OECD Main Economic Indicators*, August 1977.

Economic growth

The above comparisons of growth rates lead automatically to a consideration of the determinants of economic growth before a more detailed examination of aggregate demand. Essentially this is a distinction between long-run and short-term problems. In the short term the main aim of government policy is to ensure that aggregate demand keeps in line with aggregate supply, whereas the long-term problem is to enable domestic supply to rise sufficiently rapidly to prevent either serious balance of payments problems or inflation.

In the short term it may be possible to raise total output merely by using existing capacity more intensively; for example, by reducing unemployment or operating idle machines. This typically occurs during the initial phases of an economic recovery, and enables a rapid expansion of output fostered by a sharp increase in aggregate demand. Once resources are fully employed, however, stable growth of output can only occur in line with the growth of *productive potential*. The growth of aggregate demand no longer becomes the dominant influence on the rate of expansion. The growth of productive potential is the rate at which output can grow without any change in the pressure of demand either on capital or labour, or any other productive resources. This growth can crudely be subdivided into that resulting from an increase in the labour force and that accruing from rising productivity (i.e. output per head) in its widest sense. Productivity grows in a variety of ways, but perhaps the most important are through the provision of more capital equipment per worker, and the use of more advanced techniques. In other words, from an increase in the quantity and quality of capital as a result of greater investment and research and development. Indeed, investment is usually regarded as the key to economic growth. Normally, however, too much emphasis has been laid on the absolute value of investment, and far too little on the direction and quality. A nation may invest large sums in unproductive prestige projects with no impact on economic growth. The other main possibility is not to regard the existing economic structure and methods of organisation as given but to seek means of using existing resources of labour and capital more efficiently.

The supply of labour depends mainly on demographic factors such as the size, sex, and age distribution of the population. Social pressures such as the acceptability of married women going out to work, the age of retirement, and the required length of schooling also have an impact. Furthermore, the number of hours worked can vary both per day, or shift, and according to the length of holidays. Many European countries depend heavily on large net inward migration from Mediterranean countries to balance the demand for, and supply of, labour. Germany, for example, has over 1½ million *gastarbeiter*, or foreign workers, a much smaller number than in the early 1970s before the oil crisis and 1974–75 world recession. Since the population of working age grows very slowly in the UK, and large inward migration is no longer politically acceptable, growth of the labour force cannot be a major factor in economic growth. There is, however, some scope for a more intensive employment of the existing labour force, which partly explains the UK's persistent emphasis on regional policy. Historical reliance on coal and iron-ore deposits has led to large concentrations of industrial population away from those industrial centres which now make most economic sense. This has occurred despite the substantial mobility of labour between jobs in post-war Britain. Labour tends, at the margin, to be less mobile than industry. The coexistence of substantial under-utilised infrastructure in the less well-off areas, with, frequently, heavy congestion in those areas most favoured by industry, means that regional policies designed to attract industry to areas less well-off have been regarded as economically justified. One estimate in the mid-1960s was that a carefully conceived regional policy could raise the effective labour force by 50 000 per annum. Thus regional policy has economic as well as social and environmental justifications, although the precise weapons of such a policy are subject to sharp political debate. Regional policies are discussed in Chapter IX.

Post-war British policy has been directed to improving the quality and mobility of the labour force as a means of promoting economic growth. Extensions to higher education, retraining schemes, and redundancy payments are all regarded as important in this context. More recently, though, with the rise of unemployment to well over 1 million, official emphasis has shifted to the creation of jobs.

The growth of productive potential is not totally independent of the pressure of demand, even though it is convenient to regard it as such in the short run. A persistently high pressure of demand can raise both the supply of labour, and also its productivity in a variety of ways. Indeed, one of the main causes of high economic growth may well be high economic growth itself; countries can enter what is called a 'virtuous circle', whereby rapidly rising demand leads to heavy investment in advanced equipment, which greatly boosts output per man, and provides the necessary facilities for further growth. It is important to emphasise, however, that too high a pressure of demand may not be an unmixed blessing if it means that even relatively inefficient firms can earn acceptable profits in a sellers' market.

The growth of productive potential is measured by fitting trend curves to past data. It is normally calculated between periods of approximately equal pressure of demand, as measured by the ratio between unfilled vacancies and unemployment. Such a trend growth rate is, of course, merely an expression of what has happened in the past, and extrapolation into the future can give only a first approximation to the likely growth of productive potential. All the likely influences on output must be taken into account before a reasonable projection can be made.

Aggregate demand

Regulation of the pressure of demand is the main means by which governments achieve their short-term economic objectives. Classical economic theory tended to assume that the 'invisible hand' would automatically ensure that, apart from temporary crises, demand would balance supply. Since Keynes' teachings of the later 1930s, however, it has been realised that there is no such automatic regulator and that demand can be out of step with supply over long periods.

This chapter has already discussed the measurement of national income, output and expenditure, in an accounting sense. It is now necessary to discuss the relevance of these concepts to the management of the economy. Given that in the short term total capacity sets a potential ceiling, the level of domestic output is set by the level of aggregate expenditure. To recap, total demand (Y) is composed of the following elements:

(a) Consumers' expenditure (C)
(b) Final consumption of general government (G)
(c) Investment, in both stocks and fixed assets (I)
(d) Exports of goods and services (X)

Thus $Y \equiv C + G + I + X$ (1)

In this equation Y, or total demand, is the Total Final Expenditure of Table 6.1.

By definition total expenditure equals total income (output) from productive activities within the economy plus purchases from abroad. Over the economy as a whole this becomes:

(a) Consumers' expenditure (C)
(b) Savings (S)
(c) Receipts from taxation (T)
(d) Imports of goods and services (M)

Thus $Y \equiv C + S + T + M$ (2)
Therefore $C + S + T + M \equiv C + G + I + X$ (3)

In terms of these equations the gross domestic product at market prices (GDP) is:

$GDP \equiv Y - M$ (4)

Subtracting C from both sides of equation (3),

$S + T + M \equiv G + I + X$ (5)

This is the more accurate formulation of the simple expression that savings equal investment. Admittedly the latter is so where the government's budget is balanced $(T \equiv G)$, and there is a balance of payments equilibrium $(M \equiv X)$, but this rarely occurs in practice.

The main point about savings and investment is that they are generally carried out for different reasons by different people. Most investment in fixed assets is made either by the government, or by companies. Both these sectors save, but a significant proportion of saving is carried out by private individuals. There is, therefore, no automatic tendency for investment and saving to take place at the same rate. Although equation (5) above must inevitably pertain, as an accounting identity, intentions may not be precisely fulfilled. Technically, the *ex post* outturn may not accord with the *ex ante* intentions. If the government's fiscal and monetary policies are incorrect, the economy is liable to move out of balance, either with aggregate demand falling short of potential supply (planned savings exceeding planned investment) and leading to idle capacity and unemployment, or with excess demand and inflationary pressure (desired investment greater than desired savings).

Where it is necessary to alter the pressure of demand the government can theoretically act on C, G, I, or X. Both practical and policy considerations intervene, however, to limit the choice. First, international agreements on export subsidies and taxes, the impossibility of exerting any major influence on demand for exports, and the need to preserve balance of payments equilibrium, combine to prevent frequent attempts to alter exports as a short-term economic regulator. Variations in exchange rates under a regime of floating rates are an indirect and often unreliable exception to this general rule. Secondly, investment in fixed assets, and even stocks, is the mainspring of long-term economic growth which governments generally support. More practically, investment is not quickly responsive to policy weapons; it is usually impracticable as well as wasteful to leave expensive investments half finished, and most capital projects have a fairly long gestation period. This means that, in the short term, governments tend to act on C and G. Even the latter is not usually quickly responsive to 'fine tuning'; as with large oil tankers, it takes a long while to change direction, and even longer to stop or reverse unless the government is willing to take dramatic action. Usually this only occurs when economic pressures have mounted to create a crisis. Public procurement of goods and services on current account rose very rapidly in the late 1960s and early 1970s, partly as a conscious policy, and partly through a breakdown of effective controls, especially on local government expenditure. The reorganisation of Local Government in 1973 greatly boosted the latter. During the mid 1970s the government was forced to take increasingly severe steps to tame public spending and tailor it to available resources. Future spending plans on capital and current accounts were slashed, forecasting and control systems improved, and a system of cash limits on spending was introduced to prevent the problem recurring. This was an exceptional period, however, complicated by the structural problems caused by steep energy price increases, and by recession. The main thrust of short-run regulation of demand normally falls on private consumers, whether through measures to influence voluntary savings, to alter tax levels, or to impose direct controls.

Once the government has set its targets for growth of GDP, and the implied level of unemployment during the year, it compares these with forecasts of prospective trends on unchanged policies. The Treasury regularly makes detailed national income forecasts three times a year, with more sketchy up-dating in between. If a gap exists between the target and prospective levels of activity, the government will take the appropriate action.

Obviously the type of action taken would depend on the nature of the gap. Direct action on a particular sector might be more effective than general measures to change demand pressures. For example, not all unemployment is amenable to demand management. Aside from seasonal and other temporary variations, such as changes in school-leaving practices, unemployment might be '*structural*' in nature. It might result from the failure of a large firm in a particular area, or the pressure of intensive foreign competition on one industry. Prior to Keynes' work, the annual government budget was designed simply to raise sufficient revenue to enable the government to meet its commitments. Indeed, the form and presentation of the budget still bears witness to this role. Today it is accepted that the government may use the budget to control demand by lowering or increasing taxes as necessary. Whereas the main problem when Keynes was writing was persistent general unemployment, this has never been a serious long-term post-war problem. Rather, persistent excess demand has been the main weakness. During the 1970s, it has appeared that the traditional weapons for management of economic demand have lost much of their effectiveness, but it is first necessary to discuss their underlying rationale before pointing out recent weaknesses.

The multiplier

In essence the multiplier hypothesis is that a unit of spending power injected into the economy will raise incomes by substantially more. The initial unit will be partly saved and partly spent by the recipient, and his spending will form someone else's income. In turn, part will be saved and the remainder spent. The simplest formulation of the multiplier is in terms of consumption *(C)* and savings *(S)*, where national income *(Y)* is divided solely between consumption *(C)* and investment *(I)*. The relationship between consumption and income is called the *propensity to consume*, and that between saving and income the *propensity to save*. The average propensity to consume is $C \div Y$, and the marginal propensity $\Delta C \div \Delta Y$.

$$\text{Since } Y \equiv C + S \equiv C + I$$

The marginal propensity to save (and by definition to invest) is $1 - $ marginal propensity to consume. The multiplier is the reciprocal of this sum, namely:

$$\frac{1}{1 - \text{marginal propensity to consume}}$$

For example, if the marginal propensity to consume in respect of each extra £1 of income is 0.9, then the multiplier $= 1/1 - 0.9 = 10$. Each £1 injected into the economy would, in theory, eventually raise final demand by £10.

In practice the real economy is far more complex than this simple model suggests. In the UK the typical value of the multiplier is around 3, because there are far more 'leakages' than personal savings. They include taxes, both direct and indirect, savings by companies and other bodies, and imports of goods and services. The chain reaction from the initial income change still takes place, but its impact is far more muted than in the simple model, and dies down more quickly. The importance of the multiplier is that quite small changes can potentially have a large impact on final demand.

Consumers' expenditure

The concept of the propensity to consume is derived from Keynes, who suggested that the level of consumption is largely determined by current personal income. This is supported by cross-sectional budget studies such as the *Family Expenditure Survey*; the higher a household's income, the greater its expenditure, as Chart 6.2 shows.

As their income rises individuals increase their consumption, but not by as much as their increase in income. In other words, their marginal propensity to consume is likely to be positive and less than unity. Keynes also believed that it was likely to be relatively stable over the short run, and this view has also coloured most government attempts to regulate demand. In practice the marginal propensity to consume has fluctuated markedly in the UK, and has in some years exceeded unity; factors other than current income have been important. Other important influences have been the availability of credit either from hire-purchase companies or the banks, the level of accumulated wealth, the dynamics of replacement demand for consumer durables and, most important, expectations about future incomes. Expectations about the future have conditioned the impact of the other factors; in periods when expectations

Chart 6.2   Household income and expenditure in 1975

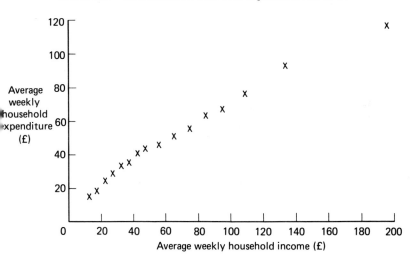

SOURCE: *Family Expenditure Survey Report for 1975*, HMSO.

are for a large rise in income there will be a greater recourse to credit, and a willingness temporarily to dip into savings, and the reverse holds when the outlook seems pessimistic. In the 1974–75 recession, savings ratios rose sharply in all industrial countries even though rapid inflation denuded the real value of those savings; the security motive was then very strong. Also declining stock market values had eroded the value of consumers' assets, and savings were increased to restore assets to more desirable levels. Chart 6.3 shows in the form of a scatter diagram the relationship since 1962 between percentage changes in disposable personal income and consumers' expenditure.

Building on Keynes' work, other economists have developed more refined theories of consumer behaviour incorporating the role of expectations. One theory distinguishes between permanent and transitory income; it takes time for consumers to adopt to a new income level and regard it as permanent, and they will initially treat the increase, particularly where it is large, almost as a windfall. This theory also implies that a form of ratchet effect operates on consumption. If there is a temporary fall in income, consumers will take a long while to adjust and the initial impact will be felt mainly by savings. Another view is that consumers try to spread the income they expect to earn while they are working over their whole life span; they save heavily during their period of maximum income to finance future consumption during their retirement.

Although consumers' expenditure is a relatively complex function, governments have usually been able to steer demand in the desired direction, by a judicious mixture of controls on hire-purchase and other forms of consumer credit, and qualitative restrictions on bank credit, taxes on income, or analogous changes in social-security contributions,

Chart 6.3   Percentage changes in disposable incomes and consumer expenditure 1962–76

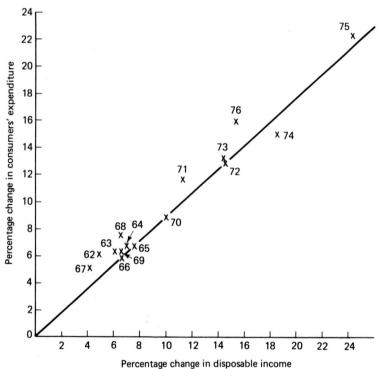

SOURCE: *National Income and Expenditure, 1966–76*, HMSO.

and variations in indirect tax rates. At times, and particularly during the heavy inflation of the 1970s, expectations were so important that many of the traditional weapons lost much of their effect. Possible reasons are advanced in a later section.

Investment and the accelerator

In many ways it is more difficult to explain variations in investment than in consumers' spending, though expectations again play a dominant role. Investment, whether in housing, fixed productive assets, or even inventories, represents the deferment of current spending in expectation of a future stream of income. It will only be carried out if the expected proceeds, suitably discounted, exceed the likely cost. This implies that the key factors influencing the level of investment are likely to be the cost and availability of funds, the degree of utilisation of existing capacity, and present and forecast profits. A common theory of investment is the accelerator principle, which relates the size of the capital stock to the output produced from it; an increase in output requires an increase in capital stock (investment) to produce it. The ratio between the output increase and investment is the accelerator. Such a simple theory abstracts too much from the real world, assuming that firms react immediately to increased demand by investing more, and that capacity is always fully utilised. In practice, new investment, in Britain at least, is usually delayed as long as possible; firms usually expect a rise in demand to be transitory rather than permanent and rely on overtime working and lengthened delivery dates rather than new plant. The stop–go history of the British economy has tended to support the apparent correctness of their view. Nonetheless, the accelerator principle, suitably refined, can be used to predict investment in some sectors, and particularly in stocks and work in progress. This refinement in the capital stock adjustment principle postulates a relationship between desired capital and output. If output rises rapidly above the expected level, desired capital will rise above actual capital and firms will make plans to invest, after a varying time-lag. Investment will vary directly with output and indirectly with existing investment. When applied to investment with a short life, such as stocks of raw materials, and finished goods, the theory also provides for a run-down in investment. If actual output lags behind expected output then the desired capital stock will be too high, and there will be a run-down of stocks.

Classical theory held that investment responded to changes in the rate of interest. A rising rate would adversely affect the cost/benefits equation, whilst conversely a decline would improve it. In practice any relationship is likely to be asymmetrical. In Keynes' phrase, lowering interest rates in the depths of an investment recession is like 'pushing on a string'; no firm will invest unless it is assured of adequate future profits. Confidence and animal spirits are all important. High interest rates have some impact, particularly on stockbuilding and investment in houses, where high mortgage rates choke off borrowers and also raise construction costs, but elsewhere are likely to be matched by expectations of high profits. In Britain the large amount of self-financing from retained earnings diminishes the importance of interest rates. In contrast, Japanese industry relies mainly on bank finance, and variations in interest rates have tended to have a pronounced impact on investment in fixed equipment, as well as stocks, at least prior to the 1974–5 recession.

More important than its cost is the availability of finance. This is partly, but not entirely, dependent on the actual and expected level of profits. Ease of bank and trade credit, the severity of the tax system, and arrangements for government-financed investment incentives are also important. In the spring of 1971, for example, a very tight liquidity squeeze on companies led to a sharp cutback in investment plans. In 1974 rapid inflation, particularly in raw material prices, greatly increased companies' cash requirements to finance stocks and, by tightly squeezing their liquidity, contributed to capital spending cutbacks. Variations in investment incentives can influence the timing of investment though not necessarily the planned total amount. Germany has frequently used this device, and the UK found it effective in 1968–69. Control of private investment as a means of regulating total activity is always hamstrung, however, by the great difficulty of stimulating firms to invest during recessions. Use of public investment, whether in dwellings, roads or other public works, or even nationalised industries, is possible, but the long gestation period of most public projects makes changes in course difficult. The UK government's cutbacks of public investment in recent years have been mainly in response to the UK's structural problems, rather than as short-term demand regulators. Other industrial countries though, such as Germany, France and Japan, relied heavily on public works programmes to drag them out of the 1975 recession.

Cyclical fluctuations

Despite sophisticated economic forecasting techniques and a battery of fiscal and monetary devices for regulating demand, no major economy has managed to secure stable growth of demand. All countries have experienced fluctuations in activity of varying degrees of severity, although none has experienced the major booms and slumps that characterised the inter-war years. The 1974–75 recession was certainly deeper than any previous post-war downturn, but even that was relatively mild for most industries compared with the 1930s depression. Chart 6.1 has already shown the post-war cycle in the UK, and Chart 6.4 gives a comparative picture for a number of advanced economies. Unlike Chart 6.1 this does not show annual percentage changes in GDP, but deviations of industrial production from trend.

Although the timing of the cycle often varies between countries there is sufficient correspondence to suggest close interdependence between the main economies. The growth of world trade, the reduction of tariff and other trade barriers, the spread of international business, and the greater ease of transport and communications have bound the economic links between countries more tightly. A phenomenon of recent years has been the much faster growth of trade between industrial countries than of total trade. When a large country such as the USA, which still accounts for over half the industrial output of the developed world, enters a recessionary phase, the repercussions are felt by its suppliers. Exporting firms' expectations of continued growth in sales to the US are frustrated by the US slowdown, and this sets off adjustment processes which spread the cycle. This is but one possible mechanism; in the early 1970s international monetary disturbances accentuated domestic fluctuations, and the fivefold rise in oil prices of 1973–74 greatly contributed to the severity of the 1974–75 recession by imposing structural changes on a normal business cycle downturn.

Most theories on the genesis of business cycles rely on the interaction between the multiplier and some capital stock adjustment mechanism, and all stress the importance of expectations. The originating sector may be stockbuilding, fixed investment, or demand for consumer durable goods, which behaves in the same manner as other investment. Sometimes the initial cycle may be induced by the government over-reacting to events.

Economic forecasting is still more of an art than a science, and most forecasts are subject to a large, but usually unstated, margin of error. This is particularly true of balance-of-payments forecasts which are the difference between two large magnitudes. Forecasting errors may lead to faulty policy decisions, particularly when governments are attempting to 'fine tune' the economy. Attempts to run the UK economy on too narrow a margin of foreign-exchange reserves and to avoid any change in the sterling parity during the 1950s, and most of the 1960s, meant that governments had to pay very close regard to the balance-of-payments position. Whenever the economy was in danger of overheating, imports were sucked in, and the lack of reserves meant that the government had to restrict demand. Too often measures were too late and the economy overshot into high unemployment, which was politically unacceptable. Insufficient knowledge of time-lags led to over reaction again and a form of stop–go cycle existed. Another factor has been the interrelationship between economic management and political events, especially the timing of elections. It is not entirely accidental that in 1972 vigorous measures to stimulate demand were introduced almost simultaneously in the USA, Japan, and Germany, each of which faced major elections. In Britain, too, there has been a tendency to ensure that elections have coincided with periods of buoyant demand. Similar reflationary measures were introduced in many countries in 1976, but fear of persistent inflation prevented a recurrence of the 1972 excesses.

Charts 6.1 and 6.4 have shown how total output has moved cyclically whilst Chart 6.5 shows the cyclical behaviour of the main components of demand in the UK in recent years. For this chart, consumers' spending on durable goods has been separated from other consumer spending, and public sector investment from total investment. The absolute changes in stockbuilding and the foreign balance are shown with annual percentage fluctuations for the other elements.

Inflation

Inflation is politically and socially one of the most serious economic problems to have emerged in the post-war years. The main symptom is a persistent and general tendency for rising prices and costs, unaccompanied by similar rises in per capita output. In other words it is an unstable state of excess demand, with the volume of purchasing power outpacing the supply of goods and services; in consequence prices rise to fill the gap. This description of inflation says nothing about its causes, which can change over time. Lax monetary authorities may allow the money supply to grow more rapidly than is required to support the desired level of real spending. Such monetary inflations occurred during Tudor times with the opening up of Spain's new reserves of precious metals in the Americas, and have also been common when governments have resorted to the printing presses to finance major wars. Several individual countries, including the UK, greatly boosted their spending during the early 1970s in expectation of continued growth of output. When this failed to materialise because of the 1974–75 recession, tax revenues lagged behind government spending and the rising public sector deficits contributed to inflationary pressures. When the money supply gets completely out of hand a state of *hyperinflation* can develop, and the value of money can depreciate to a tiny fraction of its former value. Such

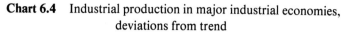

Chart 6.4 Industrial production in major industrial economies, deviations from trend

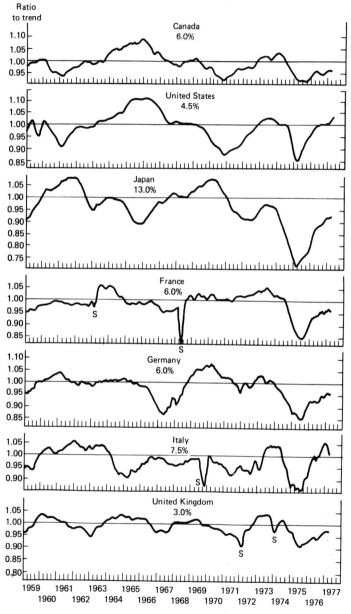

SOURCE: *OECD Main Economic Indicators*, August 1977.

hyperinflations occurred in Germany in 1923 and in Greece after the Second World War. The only cure has been total currency reform.

Inflation has normally been much more gentle, as in the 3–4% per annum average price rises of Britain during the 1950s and most of the 1960s. Even this rate was high compared with the relative price stability then enjoyed in the USA. Many economists, ignoring the social consequences for those on fixed incomes such as pensioners, have argued that such mild inflation might be beneficial. It reduces the real burden of debts incurred in depreciated currency, and assists entrepreneurial firms in making profits. The initiating excess demand might be totally unrelated to the money supply, but might result from a sudden investment boom or a surge of demand from abroad. There might also be some influence acting to depress supply, such as a rise in the school-leaving age, or persistent labour troubles reducing the output of a major industry.

Frequently somewhat artificial distinctions are drawn between *demand-pull* and *cost-push* inflation. Proponents of the latter claim that trade unions have become so powerful that they are able to use their monopoly power to bid up wages. Higher wages are in turn passed on by complaisant employers who are unwilling to disrupt production schedules by courting labour unrest and strikes. In other words, this is an institutional explanation for inflation. It is argued that it can occur even without a state of excess demand. Another variant of genuine cost-push inflation for a national economy might be sharp increases in imported raw material prices caused by worldwide excess demand. The demand-pull school argues that inflationary pressure can only reach the labour market after it has appeared in the market for final output. It is the ability of sellers to raise prices that leads either to the unions exploiting the situation by pressing high wage claims or to the employers themselves bidding up wages to attract the labour they need. Close examination of the two approaches suggests that they are not inconsistent with each other.

The traditional cure for inflation has been to aim at eliminating excess demand, whether by rigidly controlling the money supply, or by various fiscal means. During the 1960s it was believed, on the basis of work done by Professor Phillips, that there is a trade-off between the level and rate of change of unemployment and the rate of inflation of money wages. Unemployment was used as an indicator of the pressure of demand.

Furthermore, there was some level of unemployment, in the 3–4% range, that would ensure an acceptable level of inflation. Typically unemployment fluctuated in the $1\frac{1}{2}$–2% range, so that such a policy would have meant the creation of a large margin of excess capacity. It was argued that this would have reduced the bargaining strength of the

Chart 6.5   Cyclical changes in the main components of demand in the
UK 1967–76

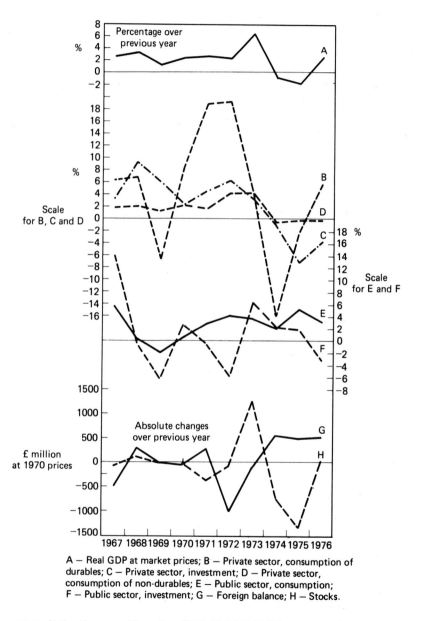

A – Real GDP at market prices; B – Private sector, consumption of
durables; C – Private sector, investment; D – Private sector,
consumption of non-durables; E – Public sector, consumption;
F – Public sector, investment; G – Foreign balance; H – Stocks.

SOURCE: *National Income and Expenditure 1966–76*, C.S.O., HMSO.

unions, and cost-push pressures, as well as tackling demand inflation. Moreover, the policy would have stimulated competition and strengthened the balance of payments. The adverse social impact of such unemployment with its markedly uneven regional spread was ignored. Also firms would have had to operate below full-capacity output, which would have raised unit costs in capital intensive sectors as their overheads were spread over a smaller output, and even contributed to inflation in the short term. The effects of domestic deflation on confidence and business investment would also have been deleterious.

Although the proposals appeared to be a classic case of academic economists being out of touch with industry, there is no doubt that the UK economy was run at too high a pressure of demand in most of the post-war period. The 1970s have, however, exploded the relevance of the 'Phillips curve' for practical policy especially in the UK. In recent years most economies have experienced unemployment well above average coexisting with exceptionally high rates of inflation. The trade-off between unemployment and inflation has worsened considerably. Although a policy of savage demand deflation, if continued long enough, undoubtedly could reduce the rate of inflation, the political cost is considered far too great in most developed economies.

One of the defects of the mechanistic Phillips-curve approach was that it ignored the important element of expectations. Individuals in their daily affairs, trade unions, and companies grow accustomed to the existing rate of inflation and adapt their behaviour accordingly. They expect that rate to continue. If there is a sudden rise in the rate, induced perhaps by an exchange-rate change, their expectations will be frustrated and they will in time over-compensate. Also, they will soon base their behaviour on the new and higher inflation rate; it will become institutionalised. During the 1970s international monetary disturbances and OPEC's oil price rises have provided external stimuli working to raise expectations.

Another important aspect of the accelerating inflation of the 1970s has been its impact on traditional fiscal weapons of demand management. Again the role of expectations is important. Under a progressive tax system with a marginal rate above the average rate, workers will have to demand progressively more to maintain their real take-home pay. For example, if they expect price rises of 10% per annum, and a productivity gain of 3% per annum, they may put in for a 13% per annum pay rise. With a 34% marginal tax rate, however, and graduated national insurance contributions of $5\frac{3}{4}\%$ on average weekly earnings, the rise in their net take-home pay will be substantially less than 13%. The actual rise will depend on their personal tax positions, but for a married man with two children, earning near the average weekly wage, and merely receiving the statutory tax allowances, a 13% rise in gross salary will mean a rise in net take-home pay of rather less than $11\frac{1}{2}$%. Their expectations would be partly frustrated, and there would be strong pressure for even higher nominal wage increases. The traditional policy for countering inflation has been a rise in tax rates. Not only would a rise in the inflation rate from 8% to, say, 12% prompt a higher wage demand, but the increase in taxes to deal with it would accentuate wage demands even further. Workers are concerned with take-home pay rather than nominal pay, yet it is the latter that enters employers' costs. Increases in indirect taxes would provide no relief because they would immediately be reflected in higher prices which in turn would prompt higher wage claims.

The realisation of this possibility of tax-push inflation, and the impossibility of reducing inflation by modest demand cuts, were major reasons for the resurgence of direct controls in the form of prices and incomes policies in the 1970s. These were attempts to alter the institutional climate in which prices and wages are fixed and to compel employers and unions to take the public interest in reduced inflation into account when fixing prices and wages. To be fully effective a prices and incomes policy should be accompanied by appropriate monetary and fiscal policies; it is not a substitute but an additional weapon. The success of a policy should not be judged, as it usually is, by comparing the actual outturn with its stated aims (policy makers are always far too optimistic) but with what would have happened in its absence. On this basis the various attempts at such policies in the UK since 1945, from Sir Stafford Cripps' onwards, have had limited success. Three important points are that for maximum effect a policy must be voluntary and be supported by all parties, second that it must not be too rigid and attempt to achieve too much and thirdly that it has a limited useful life. Absolute prohibitions on price and wage increases, whilst they might be suitable for short-term emergency situations, are untenable over lengthy periods. In view of the frequent changes in policy in both the UK and USA in search of an ideal, this is not the place to describe policies in any detail. Their main elements, however, are the imposition of guidelines on permissible wage increases, linked in some manner to national productivity, and also the limitation of allowable price increases. A new approach in Britain in 1974–77 was the development of the so called Social Contract whereby the trade unions offered wage restraint in exchange for a wide range of social and economic policies. This incomes policy did successfully reduce wage pressures especially in 1976–77, but at the expense of narrowed differentials and labour market distortions which will plague wage negotiations for many years.

To the extent that they seriously interfere with the market, price and wage policies tend to distort the allocative efficiency of the pricing system. Keeping prices too low might force many goods off the market and create shortages, as occurred during the US price freezes of 1971 and 1973. In the latter there are examples of price restraint exacerbating rather than moderating inflationary pressures. Also, if restrictions are too severe, ingenious but less efficient means of circumventing them are usually found. One tendency is an increase in labour mobility as workers move to other firms to secure higher pay. Nonetheless, this reduced efficiency is not likely to be large compared with existing restrictions on the market and would be far outweighed by the benefits of lower inflation.

Rapid inflation creates serious planning and accounting difficulties for companies. Profits, for example, are measured in current values, but the productive assets are usually valued at historic costs, which may be substantially below replacement costs. Profit rates based on conventional accounts may, therefore, give a misleading view of a firm's true worth and, as mentioned in Chapter III, there is growing pressure for some form of 'inflation accounting', which adjusts for price and cost changes. Whereas, with moderate inflation, it is reasonable to assume that cost increases can be recouped from price rises, this assumption is no longer valid when inflation accelerates, particularly for firms in an open economy such as that of the UK. Not only does this mean that managers must carefully evaluate likely future cost and price trends, but also that rapid inflation intensifies the search for efficiency and means of reducing costs.

Environmental considerations

Industrial firms in the UK have always had to have regard to their impact on the environment since the establishment of the Alkali Inspectorate in the nineteenth century. Public concern for various aspects of pollution, of course, predates this by a considerable time with laws to control the consumption of coal being enacted in the Middle Ages. Nonetheless, public interest in, and awareness of, the environmental impact of industrial activities has recently risen sharply. There is a continuing public debate on the most appropriate means of, for example, controlling vehicle exhaust emissions, or industrial stack gases. Economics has a definite role to play in this debate, both in analysing the *status quo* and in putting forward appropriate remedies to deal with pollution.

The main reason that the environment tends to be misused and polluted, unless special measures are taken, is that each individual's incentives induce him to use it more heavily and protect it less than is socially desirable. It is pointless for one commuter to leave his car behind and travel by train, because this makes no noticeable impact on congestion. Not throwing away one small piece of paper in a field scarcely reduces the litter problem. Only collective means of control have any value; these can either be through regulation, or through economic inducements. The difficulty with government regulations is that there is usually inadequate information on which to base them, they are very crude and blunt weapons, there are usually problems of enforcement, and the burdens fall haphazardly. The main types of regulation are blanket restrictions or the prescription of specific measures. Both are usually inefficient. In contrast, economic inducements such as charges, taxes, or even subsidies leave the maximum discretion to the individual and are substitutes for market prices. Used correctly, they bring home to users the costs they would otherwise disregard. Each user alters his behaviour to minimise the costs to him of the charge or tax, which has altered his marginal cost curve. Thus the response to a charge will vary according to the ease or difficulty to the user of reducing the pollution, and maximum economic efficiency will be retained. In practice, of course, it is very difficult to fix the most appropriate charge to ensure that throughout the economy the additional costs of pollution control balance the additional benefits gained from pollution abatement; but this remains the ideal. Few people are seriously concerned with turning all rivers into 'swimming pools for fish' by abolishing all pollution, as the costs would be too great, but merely with restricting it to acceptable levels. If society changes its view of 'acceptable' an increase in charges would cause further reductions in pollution.

Cost—benefit analysis

The failure of private costs and benefits always to reflect social costs and benefits is the rationale behind cost—benefit analysis. Its basic aim is to supplement the more usual financial calculations of returns on large capital projects such as roads and airports with measurements of their economic benefits and costs to consumers and society as a whole. Whilst a private firm's primary legal responsibility is to maximise profits for shareholders, the public sector must select projects that give the greatest net benefit to society. This means taking account of all the 'external' costs and benefits which would not normally enter a private investment decision, such as the impact of noise, road congestion, traffic accidents or a clean environment. These 'externalities' do not produce revenues to the body carrying out the investment, neither do they directly impose costs. The correct prices in computing social costs and benefits are nearly always market prices, which usually adequately reflect opportunity costs.

There are, however, important exceptions. Thus, if a project uses unemployed labour the appropriate cost of that labour to society would not be its wages, as it would otherwise remain unemployed; its opportunity cost would be its unemployment benefits. Conversely use of collective goods such as water or air may be free, but may carry a social opportunity cost. Use of water to cool a power station may reduce the pollution absorbing capacity of that water, or it may directly create future shortages requiring investment in alternative supplies. A refinement to the use of market prices is to use resource costs—i.e. after taking taxes, subsidies, and other transfers away from market prices to show the real cost of resources.

Whilst costs and benefits can fairly easily be assigned to material factors, the intangible factors such as despoliation of a beautiful view by pylons, or the non-monetary factors such as road accidents, present difficulties. In cost–benefit analysis attempts are made to create shadow prices for such factors so that they can be evaluated in monetary terms to obtain an overall cost–benefit equation. Sometimes it is possible to assess such shadow prices by questionnaires asking people what they are willing to pay for, say, solitude. Many costs and benefits relate to particular groups of people rather than to the community as a whole. This raises the question of whether costs and benefits should be 'weighted' to reflect their importance to various sections of the community. Many costs and benefits are likely to be spread over time and, as in all investment projects, must be brought to present values by an appropriate discount rate. The latter is subject to much debate; it is not so important when choosing between alternative projects as when assessing whether a project should continue or not. The normal rate chosen is 10%, which is judged near to the opportunity cost of capital in the private sector.

Well-known examples of projects in which cost–benefit analysis was used are the M1 motorway, the Victoria line, and the Third London Airport. The Report of the Roskill Commission on the latter is a clear illustration of the uses and limitations of such analysis, particularly where the valuation of a large number of intangibles is involved. After an exhaustive study of various sites, the Roskill Commission finally chose Cublington. Very strong and effective local resistance led to the site being overruled on political grounds in favour of the offshore Maplin site which had been discounted as the least favourable on cost–benefit grounds. However skilful and thorough a cost–benefit study, the final decision always lies with politicians who are usually swayed by non-economic factors. The irony was Maplin was abandoned in turn, in 1974, when it was decided that a third London airport was no longer needed at that time.

VII

MONEY AND FINANCE

What is money?

Money is one of civilised man's earliest and most effective inventions. Without it tribes either had to be entirely self-sufficient, go to war periodically to obtain goods they could not provide themselves, or engage in complicated and time-consuming barter transactions. Money was the essential lubricant for the growth of trade and living standards. Initially it consisted of man's most treasured possessions, with durability and intrinsic beauty as additional attributes. This inevitably meant the precious metals, gold and silver. The growing sophistication and complexity of economic life, the lack of sufficient gold and silver to meet demand, and the inconvenience and insecurity of possessing and carrying large amounts of metal prompted the development of new forms of money. In recent years, the dramatic innovations in communications have led to the creation of new forms of money, or near-money.

Money includes any widely accepted medium of exchange, and its general acceptability as payment for goods and services is its primary attribute. Secondly it is used as a unit of account for evaluating the relative worth of different products. Whereas it is impossible to add apples and oranges directly in any meaningful sense, the sum of their values does have a meaning. Use of money values enables the direct comparison of dissimilar items. The third attribute of money is as a store of value, as a convenient means of holding wealth in a readily acceptable form. Whereas many things may have one or two of these three attributes only money has all three. Impressionist paintings are a wonderful store of value, for example, but are useless as a medium of exchange. Weight or length are often a unit of account but hardly a store of value. When money ceases, for whatever reason, to be widely acceptable it rapidly loses its value.

The supply of money originally consisted solely of precious metals, with tokens of baser metals for the lower denominated coins. Gradually goldsmiths, the predecessors of today's banks, began to issue notes in exchange for gold kept for safety in their vaults, and these notes became acceptable as money. Initially these notes were fully backed by gold, but goldsmiths soon realised that all depositors were unlikely to withdraw their gold at the same time. They could profitably issue more notes than they had gold in their vaults, provided they maintained a safe ratio between gold deposits and their notes. Modern banking was born. Today notes and coin are acceptable even though they are no longer backed by gold. Although pound notes carry the legend 'I promise to pay the Bearer on Demand the Sum of One Pound', all that the bearer now gets is another pound note. Many bankers still hanker after the days when there was some backing for the currency as it imposes a strong discipline on governments. They are unable to resort to the printing press to finance growth.

With the spread of banking and the use of cheques to settle bills, current accounts with banks have acquired all the attributes of money. Even deposit accounts, which are theoretically slightly less liquid, are often counted as money because the holder of a deposit account may be able to draw a cheque on his current account even when he has insufficient funds there to meet it. Also it is often easy to switch funds at short notice between current and deposit accounts, so that in many respects they are interchangeable. British banks have traditionally paid interest on deposit accounts but not on current accounts. In future years, as the use of credit cards, which are not even backed by bank deposits, becomes more widespread, some means of incorporating these into definitions of the money supply may become necessary. At present they are excluded.

The various definitions of the money stock used in the UK are shown in Table 7.1.

The two definitions employed most frequently are the narrow M_1 and the much broader M_3. The other definition shown, M_2, has little operational significance and is not even shown in regularly published statistics. For most monetary control purposes the authorities lay greatest stress on the widest definition M_3. The table shows, however, that the various definitions can occasionally move in different directions and this complicates both the operation and interpretation of monetary policy. Between July 1976 and July 1977 the size of M_1 rose by 11.8% whilst M_3 sterling increased just 7.2% and total M_3 8.6%. Earlier in the 1970s the divergence was more marked; between September 1972 and September 1973, for example, M_1 increased by 8.7% whilst M_3 rose by just over 28%. The reasons for the divergence are tied up with the detailed operation of monetary policy and are properly outside the scope of this book. In brief, however, the interest-rate situation in 1973 was such that many companies found it profitable to draw on unused overdraft facilities and invest in certificates of deposit bearing higher interest rates. Thus sterling deposit accounts rose by over 46% in the year. The movement of funds from one centre to another, or from one type of deposit to another, to take advantage of different interest rates, is known as *arbitrage*.

Table 7.1   UK money stock (£ million)

	21 July 1976	20 July 1977
Notes and coins in circulation with public	6 269	6 957
+ UK private sector's sterling sight deposits		
Non interest bearing	10 288	11 343
Interest bearing	2 207	2 791
− 60% of Transit items	923	1 146
= M_1 Money Stock	17 841	19 945 (+ 11.8%)
+ UK private sector sterling time deposits	19 660	20 020
= M_2 Money Stock	37 501	39 965
+ UK public sector sterling sight deposits	926	1 113
+ UK public sector sterling time deposits	201	335
= M_3 Sterling Money Stock	38 628	41 413 (+ 7.2%)
+ UK residents deposits in other currencies	3 324	4 179
= M_3 Money Stock	41 952	45 592 (+ 8.6%)

SOURCE: *Financial Statistics*, August 1977, HMSO.

Theories of money

Lord Keynes distinguished three main motives for holding money, which together determine the demand. First people and companies hold money to pay their everyday expenses and meet known bills. This is the *transactions motive*. They will usually hold rather more than is necessary for everyday expenses in order to meet unforeseen contingencies and sudden unplanned expenses. It is often expensive and time-consuming to liquidate investments in shares or stocks, or borrow to meet such emergencies. This is the *precautionary motive*. The stock of money held for these two reasons will tend to move in step with the total value of people's transactions, which, on a national level, means the money national income. The relationship between the money required and incomes will depend on custom and habit, the institutional framework, and the social and financial position of those concerned. Unless prices are rising rapidly, the amount held for these motives will, in the short term, tend to maintain a relatively stable relationship with incomes.

The third reason for holding money is the *speculative motive*. Those with surplus incomes above current needs, and holders of wealth, will tend to keep a portion of their assets in liquid form, even though this involves a loss of the interest it would otherwise have earned. Possession of money balances will enable active investors to react flexibly to developing opportunities. Whilst many investors are primarily concerned with long-term capital values and are not too concerned about short-term changes, there are a significant number, particularly amongst the institutions, who do manage their portfolios actively and are responsive to changing circumstances in the short run. If the going rate of interest is expected to rise in the near future, the loss of interest involved in holding money might be more than outweighed by the likely capital loss involved in holding securities, and also offset by the gain from buying securities at a lower price. There will tend to be more money held for the speculative motive, when the short-term outlook is for an upward trend in interest rates, than in reverse circumstances. The main influences on this speculative demand for money are interest rates and expected movements therein. When there is a general desire to hold money, *liquidity preference* is said to be high. Since, it is argued, the demand for money for the transactions and precautionary motive is stable in the short run, variations in interest rates will affect money balances held for the speculative motive, and thus change people's liquidity preference.

Under this simple formulation the demand for money will tend to react relatively passively to developments in the economy. Interest rates, it was argued, have only a marginal effect on people's decisions to invest, except in houses and other construction, and perhaps in inventories. Falling interest rates do increase security prices and capital values. This makes holders of securities feel richer and slightly more willing to invest. Nonetheless, at the bottom of a depression, when confidence is lacking and there is abundant spare capacity, an increase in money supply would have little impact either on the price level or on real activity. Lowering interest rates would be like 'pushing on a string'. At the same time Keynes most emphatically did not adopt the views of some of his more extreme followers that money and monetary policy are irrelevant. The main economic disease in post-war years has not been recession and surplus capacity but over-full employment and inflation. In these circumstances the extreme Keynesian view of money becomes invalid. Here economists and politicians were too long confused by conventional views of what constituted high interest rates (today they would be considered relatively low), and by attitude surveys of industry asking hypothetical questions about the likely impact of interest-rate changes. Expectations of continued price inflation offset the effects on activity of increases in nominal interest rates, at least until the late 1960s.

The oldest theory of money is the *quantity theory*, which in its crudest form merely stated that an increase in money supply would bring forth an equivalent percentage rise in prices. The theory was refined in Fisher's identity of exchange in the 1920s as:

$$MV \equiv PT$$

where M = Quantity of Money, suitably defined
V = Velocity of circulation (the average number of times each monetary unit is turned over in a period)
P = The general price level
T = Total monetary transactions in the period

As this equation stands it is tautological. The expression PT on the right-hand side is another means of expressing the term on the left-hand side, and both are approximately equivalent to money national income. Nonetheless the extreme monetarists argue that the equation does have operational significance. The velocity of circulation is believed to be conditioned by social customs and institutional habits, and to be fairly stable. Except in periods of considerable excess capacity the rate of growth of total transactions is limited to the growth of the labour force and productivity, neither of which depart radically from their trend rates over the longer term. This means that a sharp rise in M will automatically involve an expansion in the general price level.

Critics of this extreme view point out that such a quantity theory lays far too much stress on the supply of money and ignores the demand. Since the theory ignores the role of interest rates it is an inadequate theory of money. Moreover, the terms in the equation are not independent, but a change in any one may influence the others. Governments may, for example, allow the money supply to react passively to an upsurge in economic activity. The theory also operates at too high a level of abstraction; for example, the general price level conceals widely divergent movements in individual markets. Also, as expressed the theory refers to a totally closed economy with no safety valve of the balance of payments. It is also argued that the velocity of circulation is not stable, a view for which Chart 7.1 provides some support. Whilst relatively stable between 1964 and 1969, the velocity of circulation has subsequently moved all over the place—a reflection of the inflation of the 1970s.·

The main exponent of the monetarist position is Professor Milton Friedman. He argues that changes in the money supply are the main determinant of economic activity and that fiscal measures only work through the money supply. The lags between changes in money supply

Chart 7.1   Velocity of circulation

Ratio of GNP at current market price at annual rates to average M_3 money stock outstanding Quarterly, seasonally adjusted

SOURCE: *Economic Trends, Annual Supplement, 1975, Financial Statistics,* August 1977.

and in economic activity are, however, fairly lengthy and uncertain, so that 'fine tuning' of the economy is impossible. Governments should aim at a stable rate of growth of the money supply consistent with relative price stability and full employment and should not attempt dramatic short-run swings in policy.

In practice the truth lies, as always, between the two extremes; both money and fiscal policy matter, and both can have effects for good or ill. Governments must ensure that their monetary and fiscal policies do not work in opposite directions, as it so often appears that they do. Also governments should work to a longer time-scale than has been usual, and aim to keep both the money supply and the overall budget fairly closely within long-term guidelines. Monetarist policies have gained widespread support in the 1970s with the emergence of seemingly intractable inflation, coincident with heavy unemployment. Following a United States lead many governments have published targets for the growth of money supply to which they will adhere, even at a cost of fluctuating money markets and interest rates. In the UK such targets have been given further backing by a system of 'cash limits' to restrain public sector spending. This prevents government departments claiming large supplementary budgets to cover unforeseen expenses (due perhaps to large wage increases). Such limits also provide some control over local authority spending, hitherto apparently immune to central government pressures.

An objection to the use of monetary policy closely associated with the Radcliffe Committee, which reported in the late 1950s (*Report of the Committee on the Working of the Monetary System 1959,* HMSO Cmnd 827), is that the money supply is not uniquely defined and that it is impossible to control something so elastic. The complexity and ingenuity of the London money markets ensure that a demand for funds will always be met even if one source is blocked up. It is not money itself that matters but the total liquidity of the economy. We have already seen how difficult it is to define money, but there is a wide range of *near-money* assets, which have some of money's attributes, even though not readily spendable. These liquid assets would include deposits with local authorities, building societies, finance houses, and other financial institutions, Treasury Bills and even short-term government bonds. When denied credit, frustrated borrowers can liquidate such assets or even obtain funds from outside the banking system, through extended trade credit for example. With the abandonment of quantitative controls, a greater readiness to disturb gilt-edged prices, and the institution of a competitive climate in banking, such objections have lost much force.

The banks and credit creation

Before enumerating the various monetary weapons open to the Government, and its agent the Bank of England, to reduce the rate of growth of the money supply and to change interest rates, it is necessary to discuss how the banking system can effectively create new money.

Originally for reasons of commercial prudence, but more recently because compelled by official direction, banks keep a certain proportion of their assets either as cash or in very liquid form such as Treasury Bills. The balance sheet of a London clearing bank might typically appear as in Table 7.2; the figures are merely illustrative. The London clearing banks are the commercial banks with widespread branch networks dealing with the general public, who clear their cheques in London.

Let us assume that the bank must keep 15% of its total assets in liquid or near liquid form, as in the table. Such assets earn little or no interest. As they are the least profitable items in the bank's portfolio it will normally wish to reduce them to a minimum and have as much of its assets as possible in the form of lucrative advances to customers (65% in the illustration). If deposits were to rise by £100 million, the initial impact would be on the bank's liquid assets which would rise to £250 million so that the reserve ratio would become about $22\frac{1}{2}$% (250 ÷ 1 100), far

Table 7.2   A typical bank balance sheet (£ million)

Liabilities		Assets		%
Current accounts	500	Coin, notes and balances with		
		Bank of England	30	3
Deposit accounts	450	Money at call and short notice	70	7
Other	50	Treasury bills, other bills and credit	50	5
TOTAL LIABILITIES	1 000	Total liquid assets	150	15
		Investments in government stocks, etc.	200	20
		Advances and loans	650	65
		TOTAL ASSETS	1 000	100

above the acceptable 15%. On the basis of the extra £100 million the bank will be able to expand its advances until the 15% ratio is restored. Extension of overdrafts will involve offsetting the creation of new current-account deposits. The new equilibrium balance sheet will become:

Table 7.3   The new bank balance sheet (£ million)

Liabilities		Assets	
Current accounts	1 167	Total liquid assets	250
Deposit accounts	450	Investments	200
Other accounts	50	Advances	1 217
TOTAL LIABILITIES	1 667	TOTAL ASSETS.	1 667

Liquid assets of £250 million are restored to 15% of the total assets of £1 667 million, but the initial injection of £100 million has allowed a £567 million rise in advances and a £667 million rise in total deposits. The proportionate increase is equivalent to the reciprocal of the required liquid assets ratio.

Even though advances may soon be drawn down, they will become new deposits in other banks, so that the multiplier effect of the initial rise will spread throughout the banking system. As always there will be substantial leakages in an open economy, whether overseas or to other financial institutions. The broad principle remains, however, that an injection of new money into the system allows a much greater rise in the total money supply. The same is true in reverse; a reduction in the money supply will require banks either to sell investments to restore their liquid assets ratios or to make a cumulative reduction in their advances. This is the simple theory underlying monetary policy, although its practical operation, as outlined in the next section, is inevitably far more complex.

The National Debt

Prior to September 1971, monetary policy was operated through a complex collection of direct controls on hire purchase and other consumer credit, directives from the Bank of England to the Clearing Banks setting quantitative restrictions on their lending for particular purposes such as property finance, manipulation of interest rates and Open Market operations, which will be described more fully below. Cartel arrangements between the banks greatly restricted competition and facilitated a standardised and conventional tariff of interest rates. The Bank of England was heavily concerned with managing the National Debt and ensuring the smooth financing on attractive terms of the government's large annual borrowing requirement. This in turn meant that reliance on interest-rate changes to regulate the money supply was limited; too sudden or dramatic changes in interest rates were thought to inhibit sales of securities. Also there was a need to limit the annual interest payments on the National Debt, and this restricted the authorities' ability to raise interest rates.

Management of the National Debt remains a crucial part of the Bank of England's functions and an essential component of monetary control. The National Debt represents the accumulated value of annual net borrowings by the government. The main reason for its growth since its institution in the late seventeenth century was the need to finance major wars, particularly the two world wars of this century. The resources needed were greater than the nation's taxable capacity. Since 1945 the nationalisation of major industries, and growing state involvement in economic activity, have led to continued heavy annual borrowing to finance capital expenditure. Also, deficit financing has become an acceptable means of influencing the level of economic activity. Table 7.4 shows the composition of the National Debt at the end of March 1976 both by holder and by type of liability.

The ownership of the debt is widely distributed. Most financial institutions include some percentage of government stock in their asset portfolio. Overseas holdings, both by governments and private bodies, make up nearly one-seventh of the total. Official holdings account for nearly one-quarter of the total; these are stocks held within the Bank of England and government departments, partly for controlling the monetary system. The government's aim is to ensure that as much of the debt as possible is either in the form of non-marketable securities, or is long term. This explains continued emphasis in budgets on National Savings and on new means of promoting them. Treasury Bills are used to finance the government's spending needs in the short term. They are issued in varying amounts, normally for ninety days, at varying interest rates, whereas longer-term stocks usually have a fixed coupon rate of interest. The government is continually *funding* the debt when possible by issuing new longer-term stocks, both to replace maturing stocks and to lengthen the average maturity of debt outstanding.

Table 7.4   The National Debt, 31 March 1976 (£ millions nominal)

By holder		*By liability*	
UK official holdings	13 634	National Savings securities	4 334
Public bodies	54	Other non-marketable debt	3 278
Banking sector	5 090	Treasury bills	10 849
Insurance companies	6 953	Govt stocks up to 5 years to run	13 753
Building societies	2 396	Govt stocks 5–15 years to run	6 500
Other financial institutions	4 714	Govt stocks over 15 years to run	11 946
Private trusts and funds	10 192	Undated govt stocks	3 381
Overseas holders	6 333		
Other holders	4 675		
TOTAL DEBT	54 041	TOTAL DEBT	54 041

SOURCE: *Bank of England Quarterly Bulletin*, December 1976.

Although definitional problems prevent precise comparison with other countries, it appears that the UK carries a substantially higher burden of debt than other industrial countries. Excluding official holdings and IMF notes, the national debt equals roughly 50% of the UK's Gross National Product, for example, compared with under 30% in the United States and 20% in Germany. Debt servicing is expensive, accounting for around 4% of the GNP, and this explains the past tendency towards cheap money. Whilst interest paid on the debt to national holders merely represents a transfer payment through the tax system, that paid to overseas holders is a substantial drain on national resources. In another light, the national debt has fallen considerably relative to GNP from three times the GNP at the end of the second world war to today's 50%; the real burden of the debt has fallen.

Methods of monetary control

By selling or purchasing government stocks on the open market, that is through the stock exchange, the Bank of England can influence the level of deposits of the commercial banks. The buyers or sellers of stocks will almost certainly be customers of the banks. They will run down or increase their bank deposits depending on whether they are buyers or sellers of stocks. Changes in their bank deposits will not be offset by reverse changes elsewhere in the commercial banking system but within the Bank of England. The commercial banks will therefore find that their reserve-assets ratios have departed from the desired levels and they will either have to contract or be able to expand their advances. It is through such *open-market operations* that the Bank of England is able to influence the size of the money supply. Inevitably the Bank may have to change the price offered or required for government securities in order to buy or sell them, which means a change in interest rates.

Under the regime of Competition and Credit Control adopted in September 1971, all cartel arrangements on interest rates were abolished and banks were allowed to compete for customers. All deposit banks are now required to maintain given *reserve assets ratios* of at least $12\frac{1}{2}$% of total *eligible liabilities*. In essence, total eligible liabilities equal all sterling deposit liabilities less deposits with an original maturity of over two years, with adjustments for various items in transit and inter-bank transactions. Reserve assets include cash balances held at the Bank of England, Treasury Bills, first-class commercial and local-authority bills, money at call with the discount market, and government stock with one year or less to maturity. Cash in tills and refinanceable credits, included in the earlier cash ratios, are excluded. The banks have to return details of their reserve-assets ratio to the Bank of England every month. The Bank has power to vary the size of the required reserve ratio.

The use of reserve-assets ratios as the prime method of control has greatly increased the flexibility of the banking system, and also complicated the means of creating bank credit outlined earlier. Whilst the banks' ability to create credit is determined by their ability to obtain reserve assets, the methods of obtaining such assets are now more complex than in the past. They can, for example, switch their investment portfolios from stocks with several years to maturity to shorter-dated stocks with less than one year to run, thereby boosting their reserve assets. The sale of securities by the banks is eased by the existence of the *Discount Market*. The discount houses are wholesale dealers in Treasury and other bills and in short-dated government stocks, and act as intermediaries between the banks and the Bank of England. One of the Bank's main functions is as *lender of last resort*. If the banking sector as a whole is suffering from a liquidity shortage, the discount houses may then borrow from the Bank against the security of their stocks of bills, but only at a price. The banks can also issue negotiable *certificates of deposit* by offering high yields, and use the proceeds to increase their money at call. Certificates of deposit (CDs) are widely used by commercial companies with short-term cash surpluses. The market in sterling CDs was established in 1968, although dollar CDs had been introduced several years earlier. It developed because bank customers were increasingly borrowing on a medium-term basis and the banks needed to match the maturity of deposits more closely with loans. Another method for the banks to alter their reserve assets ratios is for them to borrow in the wholesale *inter-bank market*, which does not receive Bank of England support in the last resort. Also inter-bank deposits do not count as reserve assets, whereas money at call with the discount houses does. The inter-bank market deals with deposits on short notice between the banks. It was used mainly by the non-clearing banks prior to the September 1971 change in credit regulations. Before this only the clearing banks were required to observe reserve ratios, but all banks must now meet them, as, to varying degrees, must other financial institutions.

Apart from reserve ratio requirements, the second arm of the regulatory system is the Bank of England's ability to call for *special deposits*. These are funds deposited by the banks at the Bank of England, which do not count as part of the banks' reserve-assets ratios. They are expressed as a uniform percentage of the total eligible liabilities of all banks and, with modifications, of finance houses. A call for special deposits is a means of rapidly reducing the liquidity of the whole banking system, and thereby forcing it to cut back on its lending. The liquidity of the system varies seasonally, being lowest when taxes are paid for instance. Also the banks rarely lend as much as their reserve-assets ratios would theoretically allow. Special deposits can bite more effectively when liquidity is low for seasonal reasons.

In December 1973 the Bank of England introduced a new form of special deposits designed to limit the growth of the money supply within defined targets. Banks and finance houses had to deposit up to 50% of the growth in their interest-bearing resources (the interest-bearing element of their eligible liabilities) above a defined rate at the Bank of England in non-interest-bearing deposits. The growth was calculated on a three-month moving average basis above a given base. These deposits could be repaid if the growth of an institution's interest-bearing resources fell back to the specified rate. The proportion to be deposited with the Bank was progressive, with 5% in respect of an excess of 1% or less over the defined growth, 25% for 1 to 3% over, and 50% thereafter. This so called 'corset' of supplementary special deposits was suspended at the end of February 1975. It was reintroduced, though, as part of the package of measures accompanying the IMF loan announcement on 18

November 1976. Its life on that occasion was relatively brief; the UK's dramatically altered financial outlook enabled the 'corset' to be loosened in August 1977.

The fourth prong of the system is the Bank of England's Minimum Lending Rate which replaced the old Bank Rate in October 1972. This is the rate at which the Bank will provide funds to the discount market as lender of last resort. It is intended as a penal rate which will force the discount market, and through it the entire banking system, to raise interest rates.

Normally the minimum lending rate is calculated on the basis of the Treasury Bill rate paid at the weekly tender on Fridays, rounded up to the nearest $\frac{1}{4}$%, plus $\frac{1}{2}$%. In exceptional circumstances, however, the Bank retains the right to change the rate whenever it wishes without regard to the formula. In November 1973 the rate was raised by $1\frac{3}{4}$ percentage points above the formula rate to signal a new credit squeeze. Again the Minimum Lending Rate was artificially fixed in late 1976 and early 1977 as part of a crisis package.

The weekly Treasury Bill tender is the means by which the Bank raises short-term finance for the government. The main participants are the discount houses who normally obtain a sizeable proportion of the weekly allotments. The price they offer determines short-term interest rates. The Bank can influence this price by varying the amount of Bills offered. Also, it can alter the ratio of bills and longer-term stocks used to finance government spending, and can operate daily in the market, as outlined above, buying and selling stocks to influence yields on gilt-edge stocks and hence the general level of rates, and to alter the general liquidity of the banking system. The Bank does not always force the discount houses to borrow funds at the penal rate; it can provide funds 'at the window' by buying government stocks if the market is short of liquidity and the Bank does not wish to tighten it further.

Although quantitative restrictions and guidelines were nominally renounced under Competition and Credit Control there was an escape clause for the Bank to fall back on them in exceptional circumstances. The money market conditions of 1973, with rapid inflation and spiralling interest rates, in fact caused the Bank to urge the commercial banks to restrain lending for property investment, and to limit lending for arbitrage. Moreover, controls on hire-purchase lending and credit sales were reimposed in December 1973, on both the minimum deposit and length of repayment of loan.

Under the clearing banks' interest-rate cartel abolished in 1971, most deposit and lending rates were directly linked to Bank Rate, which became the lynchpin of the whole system. Depositors might be paid several percentage points less than Bank Rate and borrowers charged more. The excess would depend on a borrower's credit rating, with 'blue chip' first-class industrial borrowers paying a premium of 1% and private individuals paying an excess of $4\frac{1}{2}$ to 5%. The abolition of Bank Rate, and the freeing of competition, severed this link. Each bank is free to set its own base rate, which is obviously linked to the general level of rates, but also depends on the bank's policy and specific circumstances. Borrowing and lending rates are linked to these base rates. In general, the base rates of all banks tend to move in concert, but banks can and do step out of line. Again the Bank of England has retained reserve power to direct the banks to change their rates, as on 13 November 1973, when they were told to raise them in step with the MLR. Also the banks were in 1973 directed to hold down interest paid on deposit accounts under £10 000 to limit competition with the building societies.

The corollary of the Bank of England's change in methods of operation in 1971 was a much greater willingness to see sharp changes in interest rates and in security prices. The Bank dropped its previous strongly-held desire to smooth out fluctuations, to keep the cost of debt service to a minimum and to ensure the maximum marketability of government stocks. Interest rates, now much more readily influenced by the supply and demand for money, have been pushed to new heights.

An adverse side effect of Competition and Credit Control and the Bank of England's withdrawal from active market intervention, was the rapid development of the secondary or fringe banks. These banks had borrowed short wherever they could obtain funds, but had lent long, mainly in the property market, the classic recipe for financial disaster. Their competition had helped bid up interest rates on short term funds. Huge pyramids of paper assets were quickly built up on very shaky equity bases. The collapse of the property market brought the rickety structure close to a major financial disaster in 1974–75 only averted by swift Bank of England intervention and the formation of a rescue fund to which the clearing banks contributed. The clearing banks themselves had lent on a large scale to the secondary banks. Few institutions were allowed to collapse and most were shored up by a massive injection of funds. Henceforth there was more emphasis on credit control and less on competition.

The money markets

The traditional London markets of the banks and discount houses, plus some of the newer markets such as the inter-bank market and certificates of deposit, have been described above. In addition, there are a number of other parallel markets which both compete with the traditional markets for funds and are additional sources of finance. The main ones are inter-company deposits, finance houses, and local-authority deposits. Since the mid-1950s, local authorities have been unable to obtain all the finance they require from the official Public Works Loan Board, and have therefore had recourse to the money markets. A large market in local-authority deposits has developed, which is integrated closely with the inter-bank market. Funds from this are often deposited with local authorities and interest rates in the two markets are closely linked. The finance houses, which are the main source of credit for consumer hire-purchase transactions, obtain funds through the issue of bills acceptable to the banks and also through short-term deposits. The inter-company market developed during the credit squeeze of the late 1960s when bank lending was tightly controlled by lending ceilings. Companies which temporarily had surplus funds lent to firms which needed cash. The market in inter-company deposits is relatively small, mainly because credit from the banks became freely available in the early 1970s, but also because the legal status of inter-company lending is not entirely clear. Another major money market in London is that in eurocurrency deposits which is described in more detail in a later section.

The interrelationships between the various short-term money markets are outlined diagrammatically in Chart 7.2.

In this diagram the blocks represent firms and institutions and the circles represent various types of credit instrument. The unbroken lines show the direction of flow of deposits—by companies in local authorities, for example—and the broken lines represent negotiable instruments of debt—a flow of deposits in the opposite direction. Thus the banks issue negotiable certificates of deposit which are bought by companies, and these raise the companies' bank deposits.

The monetary institutions

Over the years a wide variety of institutions has grown up in London, catering for different financial needs, and responding to changing circumstances. Changes in methods of official regulation have influenced trends, as for example with the growth of inter-company deposits. The role of the discount market has already been described. It is an institution unique to London; the central banks of other countries in their role as lenders of last resort deal direct with the commercial banks. A relatively recent function of the discount houses is as a secondary market for certificates of deposit. The commercial banks too have already been discussed. Their main functions are to act as bankers for most private individuals, through their wide branch networks, and as the main

Chart 7.2　The primary London money markets

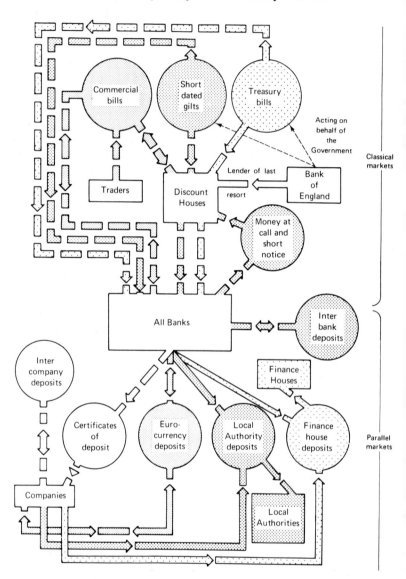

SOURCE: Based on chart in *Barclay's Bank Review*, November 1972.

channels of cash through the economic system. Apart from the Scottish banks, which still have the right to issue their own notes and other privileges, there are four main clearing banks—Barclays, Lloyds, Midland, and National Westminster. They have grown steadily by merger throughout the century.

Quite apart from these, there is a wide variety of other banks in London. First there are the *merchant banks* or *accepting houses*, whose original main role was to 'accept' commercial or financial bills of exchange. By signing such bills these houses made them into negotiable instruments. Although the use of bills to finance trade, particularly domestically, has considerably declined, they are still used in international trade. The accepting houses, by signing a bill, become responsible for its payment on maturity, and earn commission as the difference between the amount they give the issuer of a bill and the latter's face value. Apart from this original role, the merchant banks cover most aspects of company finance, and deal in the foreign-exchange and bullion markets. Most new issues of securities, company flotations, takeovers and mergers are managed by one or other of the merchant banks.

The internationalisation of business and the UK's lack of exchange controls on non-resident dealings in foreign securities had attracted a large number of *overseas banks* to set up branches in London. These banks are heavily engaged in the eurocurrency markets and in financing trade. They were greatly encouraged to set up in London both by the persistent outflow of dollars during the years when the United States was running a large balance-of-payments deficit, and by the introduction in the USA of regulations governing the allowable level of interest rates and foreign borrowing.

Under the 1971 credit regulations, these banks became subject to the same reserve-ratio and special-deposit requirements as the clearing banks. Hitherto they were exempt from most of the official controls over bank lending and from the requirement to provide special deposits. In consequence, they had certain competitive advantages over the clearing banks which the latter were forced to offset by setting up subsidiaries unshackled by the restrictions governing their parents.

The role of the *finance houses*, as stated above, is the financing of hire purchase and other instalment credit, mainly to private customers but also, in certain fields, to companies. Relatively short-term deposits, up to twelve months, are their main liability. During most of the post-war period, controls of varying intensity were imposed on the terms and conditions of hire-purchase contracts as an economic weapon. Such controls were highly effective in damping down demand in the short term as an emergency measure, but their effectiveness rapidly wore off the longer they were applied. Also, they bore very heavily on the motor and consumer-durable industries and distorted these industries' growth prospects. All such controls were finally abolished in July 1971, partly in response to the recommendations of the Crowther Committee on Consumer Credit which reported in March 1971 (Cmnd 4596 HMSO). The finance houses are now subject to reserve-asset ratios similar to those of the banks, but only 10% rather than $12\frac{1}{2}\%$, and to calls for special deposits. The requirement for them to keep reserve assets in a fairly liquid form has affected the finance houses because they previously kept few of their assets liquid; the return they could earn on such liquid funds was relatively low. In practice the authorities were unable to forswear intervention in hire purchase for long; controls in hire purchase lending were reimposed in December 1973 as part of that month's emergency economic package.

The finance houses obtain their deposits from companies, banks and other financial institutions as well as wealthy private individuals. The *building societies*, in contrast, obtain the bulk of their deposits from private individuals, and they are one of the main channels for individual savings, with extensive branch networks. Their role is to finance the purchase of houses, whether new or secondhand, mainly by owner occupiers. Their main liabilities are deposits withdrawable on fairly short notice, so that their interest rates must be competitive with other money rates such as those offered on bank deposit accounts. Roughly four-fifths of the societies' assets are long-term mortgages repayable in regular monthly instalments. Whilst the nominal term of these mortgages exceeds twenty years, many are repaid early and their average life is about ten years. To a certain extent this is illusory, however; new mortgages are taken out to replace those repaid early as people move house. Interest on building society deposits is paid net of income tax, and interest on mortgages attracts tax relief, making the real cost less than the nominal cost. Lower-income earners paying little tax can qualify for a government-financed option mortgage scheme. The societies must hold at least $7\frac{1}{2}\%$ of their assets in liquid form, but their usual liquid-assets ratios are much higher. The societies defend them as a hedge against sudden withdrawals, but they are strongly criticised as limiting the societies' lending power.

Although building societies are non-profit-making they have heavy administrative expenses, which must be supported by the margin between the interest earned on mortgages and that paid on deposits. Their need to retain and attract deposits when the general level of interest rates rises means that the societies are compelled to raise their mortgage rates if the general level of interest rates moves up. Normally they prefer stability, and aim to hold rates steady. When rates do rise they affect existing as well as new mortgages, and many borrowers have in the past elected to extend the life of their mortgages rather than increase their monthly repayment. When the general level of interest falls steeply, as in 1977, the building societies face tremendous pressure to reduce their lending and borrowing rates. This pressure is almost as strong from competing borrowers of funds as from house owners and politicians. Building-society rates follow the market in steps as infrequently as possible. The full workings of the Competition and Credit Control regime in 1973 wreaked havoc on the traditional building-society attitudes because it made interest rates far more volatile. Not only was the government forced at one stage to subsidise mortgage rates, but also later on to restrict the banks' freedom to offer higher interest rates to small savers, as it was claimed that the banks were competing too effectively with the societies for deposits. One of the problems of the building societies is the alternative mortgage feast and famine which inevitably reacts on the housing market and on new housebuilding. It seems that the societies will be compelled to introduce some type of reserve scheme to even out the flow of money over the cycle. The freeing of other money markets has paradoxically increased the desirability of greater control of building-society finance.

Table 7.5 Relative size of UK financial institutions by size of total assets–liabilities (£ million end 1976)

London clearing banks	35 032
Scottish clearing banks	4 197
Northern Ireland banks	1 113
Accepting houses	7 191
Other British banks	23 232
Overseas banks: Japanese	16 502
Overseas banks: American	48 024
Overseas banks: other	31 802
Consortium Banks	8 030
Discount houses: total assets	2 677
Finance houses: selected assets	1 698
Building societies: total book value of assets	28 131
Unit trusts: total funds, market value	2 543
Investment trusts: total holding, market value	5 958
Insurance companies: holdings, book values	36 737
Superannuation funds: local authorities holdings, market value	2 328
Superannuation funds: long term and general funds, other public sector holdings, market value	5 617
Superannuation funds: private sector holdings, market value	8 947

SOURCE: *Financial Statistics*, August 1977, HMSO.

The other financial institutions which deal direct with the general public are perhaps more important in the secondary securities markets than in providing new funds to finance current economic activity. They include the *insurance companies* and *pension funds*, and *investment* and *unit trusts*. These are all major investors in stock-exchange securities, whether fixed-interest or equity shares; and are also very important holders of government debt. To a certain extent they also provide new finance, particularly for smaller and unquoted companies.

Table 7.5 shows the relative size of the main financial institutions. The figures shown for the banking sector refer to total deposits, which are the banks' main liabilities. In the case of the overseas banks the greater part of these deposits is denominated in foreign currency rather than sterling, and their main business is in the eurocurrency markets. Wherever possible the assets are shown at market value, but this is not published for every type of financial institution. All that the table is intended to convey is a general impression of relative size. The figures are not directly additive as the assets of one financial institution may well be the liabilities of another.

The eurocurrency market

The eurocurrency market is so named because it is concentrated in European countries, with London as its centre. In essence it is a market in freely convertible currency, and eurocurrency can be broadly defined as a deposit made in a bank outside the country of origin of the currency. Thus a eurodollar, which forms the major part of the market, is an ordinary US dollar initially held on deposit in the United States by a non-resident of the United States through a non-American bank. Euro-currencies may be subsequently accepted or loaned out through redeposits in other banks, whether in the USA or overseas. Dollars account for roughly 70% of the foreign currency liabilities of banks in the main European centres, although the dollar is gradually losing ground to other currencies such as the Deutschmark, which accounts for one-fifth of the total compared with one-twentieth in the mid 1960s. London is the largest centre with about 40% of total eurocurrency business. The most rapid growth though has been in offshore tax havens.

Unlike national currencies, eurocurrencies are relatively free from restrictions. The market originally developed in the early 1960s when the US monetary authorities restricted the ability of US banks to raise funds locally. Regulation Q of the US Federal Reserve prevented US banks from paying interest on deposits of 30 days or less and limited the interest rates they could pay on domestic deposits. The US banks were placed at a disadvantage in attracting funds and they turned elsewhere. London became the centre for the mobile short-term funds discouraged from depositing money in the USA, and US banks set up branches in London to tap the growing pool of non-resident dollars. The size of the eurodollar pool increased in step with growing US balance of payments deficits, and grew as US residents shifted funds in search of high interest rates. The main sources of eurocurrencies today are central banks holding large amounts of foreign exchange in their reserves, transnational companies, investment institutions, and individuals. The greatest shock to the system was the influx of oil exporting countries' funds after the 1973–74 increase in oil prices. These funds, the counterpart of massive balance of payments surpluses, have largely been invested on a revolving short-term basis. At the end of March 1977 the gross foreign currency liabilities of UK banks—the London share of the eurocurrency market—were $207 billion. At the end of 1976 the total eurocurrency market was almost $550 billion, more than double the end 1973 total of about $250 billion.

The eurocurrency market provides a large pool of highly mobile short-term funds which can move without much reference to national monetary policies, in search of high interest rates. Particularly during the currency upsets of 1971–73 central bankers have complained bitterly about the lack of controls over the market, but no feasible controls have been suggested. At times individual countries have introduced measures affecting the market, as with the UK's ban on short-term eurodollar borrowing in 1971 to reduce the inflow of speculative funds, and the US authorities' 1969 imposition of reserve requirements on US banks' eurodollar borrowings.

For many companies the eurodollar market is a useful source of capital, not available in their domestic markets. UK firms wanting to invest outside the sterling area were able, for example, to raise money in the eurodollar market when funds were unavailable at the official rate from the Bank of England. During 1973 and again in 1975–76 the Bank of England encouraged large eurodollar borrowings by UK companies and nationalised industries to bolster up the UK reserves and prevent a depreciation of the UK's floating exchange rate. Because the market acts as a vehicle of gigantic private capital flows, many governments have tried to insulate their economies from its effects. Both Germany and Switzerland, for example, have at times imposed tight restrictions on foreign borrowings, including large compulsory deposits with the Central Bank, and negative interest rates.

Whilst most eurocurrency operations were initially of a very short-term nature, mainly from one day to one year but going up to five years, a subsequent market developed in *eurobonds*. These issues, usually denominated in a currency other than that of the borrower, are fixed-term up to periods of 10 years, but usually of 5–10 years' duration. The eurocurrency markets are continually adapting to new needs and steadily developing new instruments. The currency uncertainties and inflationary conditions of 1971–73, for example, encouraged the development of roll-over *eurocredits*. These have no fixed interest coupon or terms, but are regularly extended, with the interest rate fluctuating with the going market rate.

The greatest shock to the eurocurrency system has been the influx of Arab capital arising from increased oil revenue in 1974, and the need to adapt to the huge short-term capital flows resulting. Also, bank failures arising from unwise foreign exchange dealings seriously jolted both the eurocurrency and the foreign exchange markets in the early 1970s.

The IMF is searching for means of tightening controls on the eurocurrency market, but it will always remain a major capital market. Although the repeal of US restrictions might be expected to attract US banks to return home, London will probably remain the centre. The time difference between Europe and New York favours London, which also has a unique range of financial institutions and skills which can be drawn upon.

Sources of capital and finance

In order to grow in line with its financial targets, a company must obtain sufficient finance to expand its working capital in step with production and sales and to increase its fixed assets. The necessary finance is available from a wide variety of sources, and those finally adopted will depend partly on the company's size, on its objectives and targets, and on the type of industry it is in. The main choice is between the internal generation of funds, the issue of new shares, reliance on long-term debt, or the use of more volatile short-term finance.

Short-term financing is usually the way most companies initially meet their extra cash requirements, either repaying out of profits or funding their debts in a more stable form when conditions are suitable. In the nineteenth century, *bills of exchange* were one of the most common methods of finance, as has been noted above in discussing accepting houses. Today, however, bills are relatively unimportant, and have been largely superseded by more flexible credit instruments. Traditionally the banks are a major source of funds, through the provision of *overdraft facilities*. Customers are permitted at a price to draw from their current accounts in excess of their deposits up to specified limits. In many instances these overdraft facilities may be under-utilised but other companies rely on them heavily. Whilst the the UK banks are willing to grant overdrafts to tide companies over short-term cash needs they have been traditionally unwilling to grant long-term loans of fixed duration. In theory an overdraft is a revolving credit with a variable interest rate repayable on demand. In practice banks would not call in overdrafts if by so doing they prejudiced the stability of a creditworthy customer. The banks' attitudes to financing industry are changing, but cannot compare with those of the German or Japanese banks who supply the greater part of industrial capital needs in their countries.

By delaying payment to suppliers and pressing for prompt payment from customers, companies can obtain considerable funds in *trade debts*. A company with annual purchases of £10 million for example could obtain £2½ million by delaying settlement of its bills by three months. This source of finance has been extremely important in the UK in periods of credit restraint, but less used in boom periods.

The *inter-company deposits* market has already been mentioned. A much more important source of funds is *inter-company lending* between subsidiaries or large companies. A subsidiary with surplus cash can lend it temporarily to one in need of funds. Company taxes are usually assessed and collected in substantial arrears, but companies must provide for them. *Future tax provisions* are a useful source of funds for most companies.

Tax allowances, investment grants and similar investment incentives are a useful source of internal finance, particularly for capital-intensive companies with heavy investment programmes. *Depreciation* provisions are also a major generator of cash. These are funds set aside annually to cover the eventual replacement of the company's fixed assets. The economic rationale of depreciation has been discussed in Chapter III (historic and economic costs). Most companies tend not to distribute all the profit available to ordinary shareholders, but retain a proportion in the business, partly to finance investment, but also as a contingency against a future downturn in business. Profit *retentions* are boosted by periods of official dividend restraint, when companies are prevented from raising dividends. The greater the ratio of retentions to distributions the faster the company's potential rate of growth.

The major external sources of finance are loans and the issue of new shares. The balance between the two depends on the nature of the business. In general the cost of fixed-interest loan finance is much less than that of equity. This must be balanced, however, against the fluctuating nature of most business profits. Loan interest must be paid whether or not a profit is made, whereas dividends can be forgone on ordinary shares. Thus the company's and stock market's attitude to risk affects the required *gearing ratio*. Gearing ratios above some 30% (loans as a percentage of total capital employed) are relatively less common than lower ratios. Changes in the corporate tax system during the 1960s with the separation of personal and company tax altered the attitudes to fixed interest debt. It then became a more attractive source of finance.

The impact of gearing on shareholders' profits can be seen from Table 7.6, giving a simple example of two companies of the same size, each with post-tax profits of £100 000, but one with a 20% and the other a 60% gearing ratio. Shareholders in the low-geared company obtain an

Table 7.6 Impact of gearing on shareholders' yields

	20% Gearing			60% Gearing		
	Capital	Return	%	Capital	Return	%
6% Debenture Stock	200 000	12 000	6	600 000	36 000	6
£1 Ordinary Shares	800 000	88 000	11	400 000	64 000	18
Total (£)	1 000 000	100 000	10	1 000 000	100 000	10

11% return, whereas those in the 60% geared firm enjoy an 18% yield.

Most fixed-interest finance is issued in the form of *debentures*. These may either be in the form of a mortgage on certain defined fixed assets, such as a mine, or an office block, or a floating charge on the company's assets as a whole. In the latter case the debenture holders have a prior claim on the assets if the company is liquidated, whereas mortgage debenture holders only have a prior claim on the mortgage assets. Given the upward trend in interest rates during recent years prior to 1977 and the natural unwillingness of companies to saddle themselves with such rates over extended periods, *convertible debentures* became popular. For investors these combined the advantages of equity and loans. They carry a lower coupon-interest rate than ordinary debentures but may be converted into ordinary shares before a given date at a share price rather higher than that quoted when the loan is issued. The normal expectation is that this share price will be below the market rate applying when the conversion is made, giving the holder a capital gain. *Preference shares*, a minor source of finance since the 1965 tax change, also combine the attributes of loans and shares. The dividend is restricted to the rate shown on the coupon, but is a prior charge before ordinary dividends. *Ordinary shares*, or *equity*, give the holders a chance of either zero profits or large rewards depending on the success of the business. Table 7.7 shows the main sources of finance in 1975–76 of UK quoted industrial and commercial companies.

Table 7.7 Sources of Company Funds 1975–76: Industrial and Commercial Companies

	£ million 1975	1976
Undistributed income	8 643	11 779
Investment grants	96	57
Other capital transfers	346	344
Bank borrowing	418	2 494
Other loans and mortgages	482	529
UK issues of ordinary shares	966	769
UK issues of debentures and preference shares	71	22
Import credit and advance payments on exports	369	510
Capital issues overseas	10	−8
Direct investment in securities overseas	77	75
Intra-company investment by overseas companies	1 498	1 730
Total funds	12 976	18 301

SOURCE: *Financial Statistics*, August 1977, HMSO.

There are several methods by which a company may raise new money through the issue of shares or debentures. In general, new issues to the public involve large commissions to the banks and other financial institutions and are beyond the reach of small companies. Unless the company is relatively well known, there is also a risk that the issue will not be fully taken up. For these smaller concerns a *private placing* with institutions such as insurance companies is the easiest method. The company's bank merely arranges the sale of the company's shares without the intervention of the stock market. As the company grows in size the institutions may be unwilling to hold a large amount of its shares without the assurance of a ready market for them. Essentially this requires an introduction to the stock market.

The Stock Exchange, which now consists of London and the several provincial exchanges, is merely a secondary market in government securities and company bonds and shares. It provides a market for investors to buy and sell shares, thereby increasing the marketability of securities and reducing the cost of new finance. A unique feature of the London Stock Exchange is the coexistence of two types of dealer, brokers and jobbers. *Brokers* buy and sell on behalf of customers; *jobbers* are wholesalers in specialised groups of securities, trading on their own account. All dealers earn their income through commission. The number and size of London Stock Exchange transactions in 1976 were as shown in Table 7.8. Whilst the turnover was greater in public-sector securities, dealings in company securities made up the bulk of the transactions.

Table 7.8   London Stock Exchange transactions 1976

	Turnover £ million	Transactions '000
British Government securities:		
Up to 5 years to maturity	47 511	299
Over 5 years and undated	34 414	466
Irish Government securities	4 460	38
Local Authority securities	4 266	83
Overseas public sector securities	198	17
Private sector fixed interest and preference	1 424	393
Ordinary shares	14 163	3 568
Total	106 435	4 868

SOURCE: *Financial Statistics*, August 1977, HMSO.

Companies can be introduced to the stock market through a *stock-exchange placing*, whereby the company's merchant bank arranges for investors to purchase, or there can be a *public issue by prospectus*. In these instances a prospectus is issued inviting subscriptions, and the merchant bank making the issue arranges for financial institutions to underwrite it. This means that the institutions agree to buy any unsold securities to ensure that the issue is fully subscribed. A successful issue often results in a greater flow of applications than shares available and the issue has to be allotted to subscribers. Frequently small subscribers are at a marked disadvantage in such cases. In some instances the shares may not be offered direct to the public but issued to one or more institutions who then make an *offer for sale*. Another method, where there is a strong expectation that the issue will be over-subscribed and that initial dealings on the stock exchange will be at a large premium over the issue price, is to call for tenders. Debentures are issued in a similar fashion to these methods of issuing shares.

Not all new share issues are to the general public. Well-established companies anxious to raise new equity finance might prefer to make *rights issues* to existing shareholders. The latter are invited to buy one new share for so many existing shares at a price below the ruling market price. Shareholders may take up, or sell, their rights. Right issues have the effect of diluting the companies' earnings available for ordinary shareholders; profits have to be spread more thinly over more shares and this affects the share price. The hope is that profits per share will soon return to former levels because of the injection of new funds. Where companies have been building up retained profits in the form of reserves they may decide to capitalise them by *bonus issues* to shareholders. The reserves are converted into new shares distributed to existing shareholders in proportion to their existing holdings. The aim is to increase the marketability of the shares, and also to make takeover more difficult by widening the ownership of shares.

In 1976 total capital issues less redemptions of UK-quoted companies amounted to £1 080 million, of which £1 054 million was in the form of ordinary shares, £31 million as preference shares, £8 million convertible debentures, and there was a net repayment of £12 million for other types of loan capital. Four years earlier, in contrast, convertible debentures had accounted for £102 million and other types of loan capital for £231 million from total issues of £1 045 million.

VIII

WORLD TRADE AND PAYMENTS

The basic theory of trade

The advantages of trade between vastly different economies are self-evident. It appears to help both countries that Britain should import, say, Ghanaian cocoa in exchange for machinery and equipment. The advantages of large-scale trade between economies at a similar stage of development, with similar cost structures, are not so readily apparent. Yet in recent years trade has grown fastest in manufactured products between industrial countries.

The *theory of comparative advantage* developed by the British classical economists in the early nineteenth century explains the basic rationale of such trade. Just as specialisation and the division of labour within a country help raise total output in that country, so the international division of labour maximises current world output. International trade is mutually profitable, even when a country has an absolute cost advantage over its rivals in the production of all goods. Trade will take place provided there are differences in the relative efficiencies of production of different goods in the various countries. The country which is less efficient overall will still have a *comparative advantage* in the production of those goods in which it is relatively most efficient. The superior country will have a *comparative disadvantage* in making those products in which it is relatively less efficient. In these circumstances trade will raise the real incomes of both countries.

A simplified example, with only two countries and two products, clarifies the principle. Suppose the costs of making cameras and clocks, in terms of, say, a day's labour, are:

	Japan	Britain	Japan–Britain ratio
cameras	1	6	0.167
clocks	2	3	0.667

Japan, whilst having an absolute advantage in making both products, has a comparative advantage in camera production. Without trade, one day's labour obtains one camera or half a clock in Japan. In Britain it gives one-third of a clock or one-sixth of a camera. If trade now takes place the relative prices of cameras and clocks in the two countries will move to a common level. Britain will import cameras from Japan where they are relatively cheaper and export clocks. The price of cameras will fall in Britain, and the price of clocks in Japan, so that both countries will gain.

Comparative costs provide the main reason for trade, but other factors may be important. Thus, two countries with equal cost structures may still trade in response to differences in the pattern of demand. Even if Japan and Britain had identical costs in producing cameras and clocks, Britain might be snap happy, and the Japanese have a mania for telling the time; Japan would export cameras and import clocks. Secondly, the comparative-cost theory initially assumed constant returns to scale. If, however, some products are subject to increasing returns to scale over a wide output range, it would yet pay two countries with similar cost structures to specialise. Each could then install a much larger plant than its domestic market could support and enjoy lower unit costs.

Protection

The principle of comparative advantage is the theoretical justification for international free trade rather than protective tariffs. It is, however, essentially a static, rather than dynamic, argument and ignores the possibility of changing patterns of advantage over time. Whilst all countries gain from free trade, any one country might gain more by delaying free trade until a much later date. In essence this is the *infant-industry* argument for tariffs. A tariff is needed against more efficient and larger established producers to give an industry a chance to become firmly rooted. The argument is valid, but it is very difficult to estimate future comparative advantages or the amount of protection needed. Experience has shown that industries established behind protective tariffs frequently come to rely on those tariffs and never become internationally competitive. Many South American countries, such as Mexico, Brazil and Argentina, have increasingly realised that they have depended too much on very high tariffs and that industries established behind these barriers have been unable to compete internationally. Yet the small domestic market greatly limits the opportunity to raise scale and cut costs so that trade is vital for expansion.

The principle of comparative advantage and the case for free trade may also be overridden where objectives other than the maximisation of current output are being pursued. One example is the need, for strategic reasons, to ensure security of supplies of certain products. If it is expected that the supply of imports may be unstable it may be in order to encourage higher-cost domestic production. Social policy objectives, such as the need to limit unemployment or preserve the rural population, may also justify some restraints being imposed on imports.

Whatever the theoretical arguments, and despite the great post-war liberalisation, restraints on trade are the rule rather than the exception. Traditionally, *tariffs* have been the most important protective devices, but this position is being increasingly challenged by non-tariff barriers. A tariff may be *ad valorem*, in which case it is levied as a percentage of the *value* of an import, or it may be *specific*. It is then based on the *quantity* of a good, i.e. £x per kg (lb). Some tariffs combine both ad valorem and specific elements. The *nominal rate of protection* is the percentage increase in the price of an imported good resulting from the imposition of the tariff. It measures the increased cost borne by the consumer, but it is an unsatisfactory indicator of a tariff's effects on the allocation of resources. This is measured by the *effective rate of protection*, which indicates the protection afforded to individual processes in the production of goods. It is usually very difficult to calculate in practice, as it requires estimates of probable cost structures in the absence of tariffs.

Non-tariff barriers are legal or administrative obstacles to trade which increase the cost of a product in the domestic market. An exhaustive list of non-tariff barriers is impossible, but the main categories are quantitative restrictions, variable levies, subsidies to domestic production, exchange controls and export credit, export price and quantity controls, administrative practices. The main quantitative restrictions are *quotas* which prohibit imports of a product above a certain level, and *import licences* which prevent any import unsupported by a licence. The EEC's agricultural policy embodies numerous examples of *variable levies*; a customs duty brings import prices up to a target price set for the product in the domestic market. The scope offered by administrative practices for restricting imports is extensive. They include government purchasing policies, health and safety regulations, or industrial standards.

Whilst the negotiation of tariff reductions, though time-consuming, is relatively straightforward, it is very difficult to quantify the effects of non-tariff barriers. This makes negotiation on their removal extremely difficult.

During the 1950s and 1960s tariffs on trade between developed countries in industrial products were progressively reduced under the auspices of the General Agreement on Tariffs and Trade (the GATT), but liberalisation of agricultural trade and of non-tariff barriers was much more intractable. The balance of payments disequilibria of the USA and UK, world monetary disorder, and disputes between the USA, Japan, and enlarged EEC have bedevilled trade negotiations in the 1970s. Moreover, these problems have also encouraged the resurgence of protectionist sentiments, especially but not solely in the USA.

One area of disagreement between countries is in the application of *anti-dumping duties*. The theory of price discrimination underlying dumping has been covered in Chapter V; technically a product is dumped, or 'introduced into the commerce of another country at less than its normal value if the export price of the product exported from one country to another is less than the comparable price, in the ordinary course of trade, for the like product when destined for consumption in the exporting country' (GATT). In other words export prices are less than home market prices. Under the terms of the GATT Code signed in 1967, importing countries may only apply anti-dumping duties if this technical dumping causes or threatens material injury to their domestic producers. The Code sets out the detailed procedure to be followed in dealing with complaints about dumping. Britain and the EEC apply the important proviso about material injury, but the United States does not. Sometimes it levies duties merely when the export price is below the home market price of the exporter.

The importance of trade

So much for the theory underlying international trade. The remainder of this chapter discusses trade in the context of official economic policy, and of foreign-exchange rates and international monetary arrangements.

The importance of trade varies considerably according to a country's size, structure, and natural resources, but no country is the typical *closed* economy of the textbooks. No single measure adequately defines the importance of trade in a country, although its share of GNP is used most frequently. Exports of goods and services made up around 29% of the UK's 1976 GNP, whereas the US percentage was just over $9\frac{1}{2}$%, the Japanese $14\frac{1}{2}$%, the German $27\frac{1}{2}$%, and the French $18\frac{3}{4}$%. The Benelux countries were far more *open* than the UK; the Belgian ratio was 46% and the Dutch 53%. The relatively low Japanese percentage illustrates the danger of relying on a single percentage. Lacking many natural resources of its own, Japan relies almost entirely on imports to support its broad manufacturing base. Also its export industries have spearheaded Japanese development, and are Japan's most modern and technically advanced sectors.

The balance of payments

The full record of a country's dealings with the outside world is, in principle, given in its balance of payments. As Table 8.1 demonstrates, this is essentially a series of accounts designed to show a country's economic transactions with the outside world. The accounts are arranged in such a way that the total of all entries is made equal to zero; each transaction involves both a credit and a debit and is entered twice, in a manner analogous to double-entry bookkeeping. Since the two entries

Table 8.1   Summarised UK balance-of-payments accounts (£ million)

	1956	1966	1976	Row
Current account				
Exports (f.o.b.)	3377	5276	25416	1
Imports (f.o.b.)	3324	5342	28987	2
Visible trade balance	+ 53	− 66	−3571	3 = 1 − 2
Government services and transfers (net)	−175	−470	−1546	4
Private services and transfers (net)	+101	+253	+2533	5
Interest, profit and dividends	+229	+387	+1179	6
Invisible trade balance	+155	+170	+2166	7 = 4 + 5 + 6
CURRENT BALANCE	+208	+104	−1405	8 = 3 + 7
Currency flow and official financing				
Current balance	+208	+104	−1405	8
Investment and other capital transactions	−409	−578	−2814	9
Balancing item	+ 42	− 73	+ 591	10
BALANCE FOR OFFICIAL FINANCING	−159	−547	−3628	11 = 8 + 9 + 10
Gold subscription to IMF	—	− 44	—	13
Financed by:				
Net transactions with overseas monetary authorities	+201	+625	+ 984	14
Foreign currency borrowing (net)	—	—	+1791	15
Official reserves (drawings on +/addition to −)	− 42	− 34	+ 853	16

SOURCE: *UK Balance of Payments*, 1977 edition, HMSO.

made in respect of each transaction are in almost every case derived from separate sources, of varying completeness and reliability, a balancing item is included to bring the total of all entries to zero.

In the UK balance-of-payments accounts, transactions are classified in three main groups.

(a) The *current account* covers exports and imports of goods and services, investment income and transfers.

(b) *Investment and other capital transactions* covers official long-term capital transactions, investment flows both direct and portfolio into and out of the UK, changes in the monetary balances of other countries held in London, trade credit, and other capital flows.

(c) *Official financing* covers changes in the official reserves, net borrowing from the International Monetary Fund, net transactions with other overseas monetary authorities, and net foreign currency borrowing by the government and public sector under the exchange cover scheme.

Table 8.1 summarises the UK's balance-of-payments accounts for 1956, 1966, and 1976. The first important point is that the balances shown are the differences between two very large sets of credits and debits. One of the aims of economic policy is usually to prevent the emergence of a large deficit, which means acting on something which can only be forecast with a very large margin of error. Indeed the error margin is usually sufficiently large to swamp the forecast.

Row 3 of the table shows the visible trade balance as the difference between imports and exports of goods, both measured f.o.b. (free on board). This requires adjustments of coverage and valuation from the monthly trade accounts which normally show imports c.i.f., i.e. including the cost of freight and insurance. Traditionally the UK has run a deficit on visible trade (in 19 of the 22 years to 1976) which is usually offset by a large surplus on invisible trade (Row 7). This is the balance between inward and outward trade in services and transfers, plus a net inflow of receipts of interest profits, and dividends on the UK's still substantial overseas investments. In post-war years there has been a growing deficit in the government's invisible trade account, and a mounting surplus in the private sector. Row 8 gives the total current account balance which shows whether the UK has had a surplus of income over expenditure, i.e. whether it has added to or reduced its net overseas assets in the period. The jump in oil prices in 1973 greatly increased the size of the current account deficit; the deficit on oil account was £708 million in 1972, but £3 444 million in 1974. In 1976 at £3 989 million it more than accounted for the current account deficit. North Sea oil production, already a factor in 1976, is rapidly altering this picture.

The remaining rows of the table illustrate the manner in which net overseas assets have been altered. Row 9 shows the UK's net investment and other capital flows. The components of this section of the accounts are various official and private capital transactions of both a long-term and short-term nature. Official net flows are usually negative, a reflection of the UK's position as a net lender to other governments. Private investment by UK residents outside the UK traditionally exceeded the inflow of capital, but between 1971 and 1975 there was a large net inflow mainly to finance North Sea oil exploitation. By 1976 there was again a small net outflow (£2 100 million outward direct investment versus an inflow of £2 051 million). Trade credit included here is normally heavily negative, a reflection of the growing tendency to sell capital equipment on credit. The balancing item in Row 10 is usually positive, reflecting unidentified receipts, probably of a short-term capital nature, although additionally associated with time lags between the recording of the various components of the accounts. The balance for official financing of Row 11 is a measure of the country's overall balance with the outside world, and of the government's financing requirements. First, though, account is taken, in Rows 12 and 13, of special non-recurring transactions with the International Monetary Fund, which complicate the picture. The rationale of these transactions is discussed later. The total balance for official financing was positive in eight of the years between 1955 and 1976 and negative in the remaining fourteen; in the three shown it was negative. Thus it was financed partly by a decrease in the UK's official gold and foreign-exchange reserves, partly by a net increase in the UK monetary authorities' liabilities to other governments and central banks, and partly by foreign currency borrowing by the government and public corporations to finance their investment. The latter have been protected against exchange rate changes by the government—the exchange cover scheme.

Full information on the UK's balance of payments, with considerable regional detail and analysis of each item in the summary, is given in the official publication known as the Balance of Payments Pink Book, published every autumn.

The balance of payments and economic policy

Whilst the balance of payments, as a series of double-entry bookkeeping accounts, must inevitably balance in an accounting sense, it is not necessarily in equilibrium. The UK's economic policy in the post-war decades was dominated by the overwhelming need to keep the balance of payments at or near equilibrium. As long as countries adhere to a system of fixed exchange rates, a balance of payments deficit can be met only by using up reserves of gold and foreign exchange, borrowing from overseas monetary authorities, rigid exchange controls restricting residents' ability to make various types of payment overseas, or by running the domestic economy with a substantial margin of excess capacity. All these expedients were used in varying combinations and with varying degrees of success in the UK during the 1950s and 1960s. All, however, cause considerable difficulties if they are used for extended periods. Use of reserves is fine as long as a country has very large reserves on which to draw, but the UK was certainly not in this position. Foreign borrowing also runs up against foreign countries' eventual unwillingness to lend further sums. After a period, exchange controls, which are normally against international agreements, lead to increasing rigidities and distortions. Inventive dealers usually discover ways of circumventing them and they gradually lose any effectiveness. Also, controls on foreign capital expenditure may after a period place UK firms at a growing competitive disadvantage. For these reasons exchange controls can normally only be countenanced as short-term expedients, rather than permanent policy measures. The final method, of deflating the domestic economy, is based on the relationship between the level of imports and domestic activity. If the latter is curbed sufficiently, imports will eventually be checked, and the balance of payments brought into equilibrium. Domestic deflation is fine if the home economy is suffering from severe overheating, but is inefficient, let alone socially harmful, if there is already an ample margin of spare resources. It should be used only as a short-term emergency weapon rather than a permanent policy measure.

If a country's balance of payments does not balance in the economic sense over a run of years then it is in a state of 'fundamental disequilibrium'. This has been variously defined, but the most practical definition is where the average current balance is insufficient to cover the required level of external capital outflows of a non-speculative nature, and to ensure an adequate increase in reserves in line with the growth of trade, without an increase in net official indebtedness, without restrictions on trade and payments which offend against any international obligation, or without running the domestic economy with persistent margins of excess capacity. The accepted remedy for countries in fundamental disequilibrium is an alteration in their exchange rate. The above definition assumes that only countries running balance-of-payments deficits can be in fundamental disequilibrium. This is not strictly true, but merely acknowledges that a deficit country can in the last resort be compelled to put its house in order, whilst there is much less pressure on a surplus country which is amassing reserves of foreign exchange. In essence, however, surplus countries should be just as concerned to bring their accounts into balance as deficit countries. Continued large surpluses cause problems of domestic economic management; for example, inflation becomes a problem if the inflows of reserves are not effectively prevented from raising the money supply. Also a chronic surplus implies an undervalued currency, which means that workers are receiving lower real wages than they need. Concentration of reserves in the coffers of a few rich countries reduces world liquidity, which can hamper the orderly development of world trade.

Foreign exchange rates and the IMF

A country's foreign exchange rate is the price at which its own currency exchanges for that of others. It differs from other prices, however, in that governments seldom allow it to be determined solely by the interplay of supply and demand. Indeed governments were committed in the post-war decades to exchange stability, the maintenance of orderly exchange arrangements, and the avoidance of competitive exchange depreciation, through membership of the International Monetary Fund (IMF). The agreement establishing the IMF was signed at Bretton Woods, New Hampshire, USA, in 1944 with the aim of avoiding the currency disorders of the inter-war period. The system was based on a series of exchange rate parities established with the IMF. These par values became the currencies' official values. Most countries specified the value of their currency either in terms of the dollar or by reference to a certain amount of gold. The USA committed itself to maintaining the price of gold at its 1944 values of $35 per fine ounce, so that all currencies were effectively tied to gold. Most sterling area countries tied their exchange rates to sterling, whilst French colonies and former colonies fixed their rates against the French franc.

To maintain their par values, countries agreed to intervene in their own exchange markets, buying their currency when it was weak and selling it when it was strong. In most cases countries intervened in the market with US dollars. So that traders, banks and other institutions could operate effectively in exchange markets, some scope was allowed for the spot exchange rate to diverge from the official par value. A margin of 1% either side of par was agreed on, although many countries agreed on a narrower margin of 0.75%. Intervention was mandatory when the rate strayed outside the band, but was also allowed within the margin. Whilst many countries fixed their rates rigidly against their intervention currency and allowed no fluctuation around the par value, the major countries have active spot markets and also operate forward exchange markets. Forward markets enable traders to reduce the risks associated with foreign exchange dealings, and also offer a vehicle for speculation. Most monetary authorities have intervened in forward as well as spot markets.

Whilst the aim of the IMF system was exchange rate stability, the Bretton Woods signatories recognised that countries would periodically suffer balance of payments difficulties. They assumed that all countries would aim at full employment. Deflation of domestic demand through restrictive fiscal and monetary policies, if carried out sufficiently promptly, would probably be enough, it was judged, to restore equilibrium. This was true even if the deficit was caused by a country's inflation rate being greater than that of other countries. Initially the pressures of a deficit would be felt on a country's official reserves, but to supplement these the IMF was given defined lending rights. Each member could borrow from the IMF sums based on the size of their subscription or quota. The more that a country borrowed, the more closely its domestic policies were subject to IMF scrutiny. The aim of this system was to prevent recourse to trade or payments restrictions on the one hand or frequent exchange rate changes on the other.

The combination of deflation and use of reserves supplemented by IMF loans was expected to cope with most situations. No country was, however, expected to suffer severe unemployment to protect its balance of payments. A country was permitted to alter its exchange rate parity to restore equilibrium to its external accounts in conditions of 'fundamental disequilibrium'. Countries had, however, to obtain IMF permission for any change greater than 10% in their original par value. This permission would not be lightly given. The IMF was expected to have sufficient sanctions to force necessary changes on reluctant countries, and to prevent unnecessary or excessive movements. Cutting off credit would soon force a deficit country to devalue, whilst a country in chronic surplus could be brought into line by invocation of the IMF's scarce-currency clause. This permits member countries to discriminate against the trade of a surplus country if the IMF's stocks of its currency have been exhausted by the borrowings of other members. In practice the scarce-currency clause has not been invoked.

The 'adjustable peg' exchange-rate system set up at Bretton Woods never worked in its intended manner. In the post-war reconstruction phase the world economy was unbalanced in favour of the USA. Most countries maintained tight exchange controls on current as well as capital payments, and also restricted trade by tariffs, quotas and other barriers. Most major European currencies were not made convertible until 1961. More important, the internal policy measures envisaged at Bretton

Woods for adjusting external imbalances never proved very effective. Deflation of domestic demand does hold back the rate of price inflation, but there are strong institutional barriers to the downward movement of prices and costs necessary to restore a country's competitive position. Also exchange rates remained more inflexible than was intended so that when they were changed the movements were greater and more violent than was necessary. Such parity changes were preceded by periodic bouts of speculation and exchange crises. Finally, the sanctions on countries in chronic surplus, such as Germany and later Japan, were too weak to be effective, so that the full burden of adjustment tended to fall on the deficit countries. The problems were increased because these were the two countries (UK and USA) whose currencies financed the greater part of world trade and were used as reserves by other countries. Sterling was finally devalued in 1967 after years of debilitating crises, and the US dollar was effectively devalued in 1971. In the case of the USA, the difficulties were increased by the dollar's use as the basis or *numéraire* of most other currencies. The US authorities remained passive in foreign-exchange markets, only intervening on behalf of other countries. A change in the US dollar relative to other countries could only be accomplished by other countries revaluing.

Fixed versus floating exchange rates

The growing international monetary problems of the 1960s and early 1970s increased debate on the relative advantages of fixed and floating exchange rates. There was a general desire by the 1970s for greater flexibility, but disagreement on its appropriate extent. Under a regime of completely flexible exchange rates, central banks would not intervene in exchange markets and rates would find their own levels in response to supply and demand. The advantages claimed for flexible rates are that they bypass the institutional and political pressures which prevent exchange rate variations under the Bretton Woods system. Adjustments to a payments imbalance would be gradual and easily accommodated rather than sudden and destabilising. The periodic exchange crises affecting blatantly undervalued or overvalued currencies under a fixed-rate system would be eliminated. Speculators would be unable to make substantial profits through correctly anticipating dramatic rate movements. Traders would have no incentive to accelerate their payments for imports, or delay payments for exports, the so-called leads and lags which accompany every currency crisis. Flexible rates allow countries to insulate their economies from outside pressures, and run them in whatever fashion, with whatever level of inflation, they wish. A flexible exchange rate policy is a preferable alternative to distorting restraints on trade or payments. Finally it would enable an economy to operate with a much lower level of international reserves than would otherwise be necessary. The case for flexible rates does, however, depend on a sufficiently large and low-cost forward-currency market in which traders may insure against future exchange-rate movements.

So much for the advantages put forward for completely flexible exchange rates. The opponents, who in the past included most governments and traders, argue forcefully that a flexible-rate regime increases uncertainty, and greatly hinders trade and investment, even with an efficient forward market. Although forward markets enable traders to hedge against currency risks, they do so only at a cost. The uncertainty of floating rates forces manufacturers to quote higher prices than they would in stable exchange rate conditions in order to cover uncertainty, and this accentuates inflation. Moreover, much trade is of necessity conducted under long-term contracts which really need fixed exchange rates. Examples of such trade are long-term supply contracts for oil and metals, and complex capital equipment deals. Overseas investment decisions are hampered by frequent fluctuations as the investors will be unsure of the probable return on their investment in their own currency. Fixed exchange rates do place a strong discipline on governments to exercise responsibility in the conduct of their domestic economic policies. Inflation is socially and economically harmful and the straitjacket of fixed exchange rates is a powerful force for governments to keep it in check. In an open economy, heavily dependent on imported raw materials, frequent exchange rate variations react adversely on the price level and can even accentuate inflation. Moreover, a flexible exchange rate policy requires even more sophisticated economic management than a fixed-rate policy to ensure that resources are channelled to the most appropriate use. In the present state of economic knowledge the necessary sophistication is unavailable, particularly in a democracy. A counter argument for floating rates is that they render stop–go domestic economic policies less necessary and that these cause more problems to business than the uncertainties associated with floating. They may also be an essential lubricant to enable countries with chronically high inflation rates to maintain the competitiveness of their exports and preserve their manufacturing base.

In essence, the debate over fixed and floating exchange rates revolves around the role of speculators. Supporters of floating rates argue that they will be able to predict likely movements in exchange rates. They will act in such a way that the actual value of the rate diverges little from the trend, buying when a currency appears cheap and selling when it is dear.

They argue that currencies are just like other commodities. This view of the role of speculators is open to strong challenge both on the grounds that it is impossible accurately to predict the trend value of something as sensitive as an exchange rate, and on practical comparisons with other markets. Both in stock exchanges and commodity markets, speculators tend to take a very short view and reinforce price movements in a destabilising manner rather than counteract them. Also the floating-rate supporters often ignore the identity of so-called speculators. Exchange controls usually effectively prevent the existence of fully-fledged speculators; the gnomes of Zurich are in most cases as mythological as any gnome. Most so-called speculation is carried out by companies legitimately acting to protect their genuine business interests; whereas speculation means gambling on an open position, most exchange rate transactions are 'hedging' which means a closed position. They are covering a known future commitment. Company treasurers, particularly in multinational companies, are anxious to protect their funds from exchange risks, and traders wish to minimise any losses on the exchanges. On this view, any pronounced movement in the exchange rate becomes self-reinforcing as people rush to protect themselves. Experience with widely floating, if managed, rates in 1973 suggests that the market tends to overreact to underlying economic trends and that the rate on any one day may bear little relation to the economically correct rate. The market takes far too short a view of developments.

Whatever the theoretical merits of freely floating exchange rates, no government would be willing to sacrifice complete control over its sovereignty to the necessary extent. Whenever a major country has floated its currency in the post-war decades, even since 1973, its monetary authorities have tended to intervene both to smooth out short-term fluctuations and also to ensure that the rate does not stray too far from some predetermined but unannounced level. Such 'managed flexibility', or 'dirty floating', has the advantage for governments that speculation need never provoke a loss of reserves, but it suffers, for traders, from all the defects of floating rates. Moreover, it is mathematically impossible for all countries to conduct a 'managed float' simultaneously; at least one country must adopt a passive stance and allow its rate to move with the market. If it does not, some cross rates of exchange will move out of line and large profits will be made through arbitrage movements. This means holders of one currency will be able to profit by converting their funds in one centre and reconverting them in another.

Various proposals have been made for coping with the problems of exchange rate adjustment. In most cases they are designed to avoid the need for large destabilising adjustments at infrequent intervals, and to reduce the discretion afforded governments for interfering. Most involve some combination of fixed and floating rates, through some variant of what is known as the 'crawling peg'. Parities would be fixed but could move by some predetermined percentage up or down every year, depending on changes in relative competitiveness. The theoretical elegance of many of these schemes is at odds with the practical difficulties involved in their application. Whilst, in theory, they eliminate the uncertainties of freely floating rates, it is rarely possible to ensure that an economic change which is well signalled in advance occurs at the planned time. Speculators will always cause the change to occur much more quickly, unless distorting and complex controls are introduced.

Prior to the 1971 dollar crisis, IMF members had agreed that some widening of the margin within which currencies could fluctuate around their fixed parities would be beneficial. A move to this end was incorporated as a 'temporary' measure within the Smithsonian settlement which ended the crisis, at least until early 1973. From the end of 1971 most major currencies were allowed to fluctuate up to $2\frac{1}{4}$% in terms of the intervention currency (usually the US dollar) either side of their agreed par value. This gave a total $4\frac{1}{2}$% fluctuation band for each currency against the US dollar, which implied a possible maximum exchange rate fluctuation of up to 9% in cross rates between other currencies, compared with the 3–4% maximum available under the old system.

Not all countries made use of this ability to introduce wider bands, and many imposed further restraints. In particular, the members of the EEC agreed to limit the possible variation between their currencies to a maximum of $2\frac{1}{4}$% when expressed against the US dollar. This was the so-called 'snake in the tunnel'; the tunnel was the plus or minus $2\frac{1}{4}$% fluctuation around each country's parity against the US dollar, and the 'snake' was the maximum $2\frac{1}{4}$% range between each currency's quotation against the dollar. The 'snake' was flexible in that it could disappear if all member countries' currencies were at the same rate against the dollar. These EEC arrangements were the first step towards the expressed aim of absolutely rigid internal EEC exchange rates by 1980. In 1972 Britain joined the system for only a few weeks before withdrawing and allowing the pound to float. The system worked well provided one currency did not remain persistently weak or strong; if it did, it imposed strong pressures on all the others. The strength of these pressures was probably underestimated when the system was set up.

In February 1973 a renewed foreign exchange crisis caused a further 10% devaluation of the US dollar against SDRs (see later in the chapter) and most major currencies floated against the dollar. Italy left the EEC 'snake', and the snake itself left the tunnel. The remaining EEC countries plus Sweden and Norway continued their arrangements but periodic revaluations have been necessary (by Germany, Netherlands and Norway) to prevent the various currencies bursting out of the snake's skin. Most countries in the bloc have altered their par values against each other's currencies several times in order to preserve the system; Sweden though eventually quitted.

The hopes of early 1973 that the world would soon revert to fixed exchange rates were dashed by the strains caused by the 1973–74 rise in oil prices, the preceding and accompanying rapid inflation, and the 1974–75 recession. Major industrial countries were subjected to severe balance of payments pressures, which they would have been unable to surmount without flexible currencies. Once operators adjusted to the system, however, it settled down and the sharp fluctuations that characterised 1973–74 have been less prominent. Monetary authorities have operated a system of guided flexibility whereby a country's effective exchange rate versus its main trading partners is allowed to move in step with basic economic trends. Large exchange rate movements have taken their rightful place in the armoury of economic policies, and the stigma attached to devaluations in the post war decades has been largely erased. One of the features of the system is that currencies can, and do, move either up or down, rather than as in a one way street.

Reserves and the finance of world trade

The 'adjustment problem', of maintaining appropriate exchange rates, is linked with the other international monetary problem of liquidity. As in domestic affairs, international trade requires a widely accepted medium of exchange and store of value. Traditionally, gold performed this function, but it proved inadequate to its tasks almost from the start of the Bretton Woods system. Gold has extensive non-monetary uses, which makes it subject to external demand influences. Supplies of newly-mined gold are dependent on the economics of mining and on geological accident rather than on the needs of the monetary system. The distribution of gold deposits favours South Africa and the Soviet Union, which introduces strong political overtones into discussions of gold prices. The industrial uses of gold are growing rapidly and there is a large private demand for gold for hoarding in countries such as India (illegally), France, and the Middle East sheikdoms. As backing for the world's monetary system gold requires a fixed stable price, but to encourage rising supplies for industrial use its price should rise in line with costs. The consequence of a fixed price for all forms of gold, which ruled before March 1968, was that supplies were reduced except from new South African mines, and unreliable Russian sales. After March 1968 a two-tier market was created which separated the private from the official gold market. No new gold was allowed to enter official monetary reserves at the fixed price, whilst the private price was allowed to move in response to supply and demand. Table 8.2 shows how gold supply and demand has moved in the post-war decades.

The two-tier gold market was abolished in November 1973, but considerable confusion remained over the role of gold and gold prices. In practice the growth of world reserves and the finance of world trade have been only marginally dependent on gold supplies. The USA's economic strength in the immediate post-war period, with its generous aid and recovery programmes, allowed other governments to make extensive use

Table 8.2 World supply and use of gold 1946–70 (millions of US dollars at $35 an ounce; annual averages of 5-year periods)

	SUPPLY			USE	
	New production	Russian sales	Total	Private	Net official purchases
1946–50	793	—	793	393	400
1951–55	872	45	917	460	457
1956–60	1071	226	1297	715	582
1961–65	1343	410	1753	1208	545
1966–70	1427	—	1427	1817	(390)

SOURCE: *The Sequel to Bretton Woods,* L. B. Krause, Brookings Institute, 1971. *IMF International Financial Statistics,* December 1972.

Note: New Production was roughly constant from 1964 onwards. Figures in brackets denote declines.

of the dollar. Under the IMF rules the dollar was the currency against which others were valued, and other countries accumulated dollars in their reserves beyond their immediate needs. Dollar assets earned interest whereas gold earned none. The dollar was a stable store of value and became the main unit of account in world trade, being used for transactions even where the USA was not involved. Exchange controls made the use of other currencies much more difficult, and the dollar toppled sterling from its pre-war eminence. Sterling was, however, still widely used to finance trade within the sterling area, and many primary commodity prices remained quoted in sterling.

The use of dollars to finance world trade required supply to increase roughly in step with the growth of trade. During the 1950s and early 1960s the USA's large gold stocks and its concern for world economic recovery and military stability made it willing to run balance-of-payments deficits. Surplus countries were also willing to accumulate dollar assets as the counterpart to these deficits. As the 1960s progressed, however, the situation became increasingly unstable. Surplus countries gradually became worried about the growing amounts of dollars in their reserves, and the US deficits began to increase in size. It is inherently unsatisfactory to link the growth of world liquidity in a haphazard way to any single country's balance of payments. There is no guarantee that its deficit will exactly match the reserve increase required by other countries. The demands of the Vietnam war and a loss of competitive power in the late 1960s increased the US deficit to almost unmanageable proportions. Although its balance of payments is small relative to its national income, the US was losing reserves at an alarming rate and action became necessary.

The basic problem was to replace the haphazard growth of world liquidity through unplanned US trade deficits by some planned mechanism which allowed liquidity to keep pace with world trade. Too rapid a rise in liquidity would have fuelled inflation, whilst too slow an increase would have constricted trade. Numerous plans of varying complexity were proposed, most based on increasing the powers of the IMF and turning it more into a proper world central bank. A widely canvassed alternative, or accompaniment, particularly by the French, was a substantial increase in the dollar price of gold. This would, at a stroke, have raised the dollar value of existing reserves, thereby adding to the stock of liquidity. This proposal was usually opposed on the ground that it favoured countries which already had large gold reserves whereas any liquidity increase should be biased towards needy countries. Also it would aid South Africa and Russia, and this was opposed on political grounds. A more substantial objection was that continued reliance on gold is archaic and irrational, and that its use as international money should be phased out in the same way that it is no longer used for domestic trade in most major countries. The Americans in particular subscribed to this last view. As an official gold-price increase would be impossible without their agreement, little has been done apart from the small increase from $35 per fine ounce to $38 per fine ounce negotiated as part of the 1971 Smithsonian settlement and the February 1973 rise to $42.22 per fine ounce. The ending of the two-tier market in the Americans' eyes demoted gold, but in the French opinion paved the way for a rise in official prices, at least for internal EEC transactions. The financing problems raised for the oil-deficient countries, but particularly Italy, by the 1973–74 increases in oil prices caused a complete reassessment of the role of gold. Central banks are now able to enter gold in their reserves at a price based on the free market price rather than the much lower official price. Whilst the death of gold as part of the world's international reserves is regularly predicted, it resolutely refuses to lie down. The oil crisis brought it into renewed prominence after many years' comparative neglect. In 1976–77 the IMF moved further towards the international demonetisation of gold, partly through returning part of its gold stocks to member countries, but also by auctioning off its gold to contribute to a Fund for aiding Developing Countries. A large part of the gold thus sold was taken up by industrial users and investors, although some was snapped up by Central Banks.

Apart from new gold supplies and increased dollar balances, world reserves can increase in a limited fashion with the growing lending activities of the IMF. The IMF's loans can only create reserves, however, in association with simultaneous obligations on the part of debtor countries to repay loans. They are not therefore the same as 'owned' reserves but have strings attached. Increasing the IMF's ability to lend is a complicated procedure linked to the increase of national subscriptions or quotas. It is not sufficiently flexible to allow the regular expansion of world liquidity.

The changes in world liquidity in the post-war decades and also the apparent need for its controlled expansion are illustrated in the following tables and chart.

Table 8.3 Growth of world reserves and trade (per cent per annum compound growth in terms of SDRs)

	1952–69	1952–71	1971–76	Total end 1976 billion SDRs
Gold	0.9	0.3	− 0.3	35.4
SDRs	—	n/a	8.1	8.7
Reserve positions in Fund	7.7	6.5	22.8	17.7
Foreign exchange	3.8	8.4	16.4	160.3
Total reserves	2.3	4.6	12.5	222.1
Total imports	7.0	7.7	19.4	803.2

SOURCE: IMF Statistics.

Note: Since July 1974 an SDR is valued in terms of a basket of currencies. At end 1976 an SDR was equivalent to 1.161 83 US dollars.

178 ECONOMICS FOR MANAGERS

Table 8.4 Percentage composition of world reserves (end of period in terms of SDRs)

	1951	1961	1969	1971	1976
Gold	66.8	61.0	51.9	29.8	15.9
SDRs	—	—	—	4.8	3.9
Reserve positions in Fund	3.4	6.5	8.9	5.2	8.0
Foreign exchange	29.8	32.5	39.2	60.1	72.2
Total	100.0	100.0	100.0	100.0	100.0

SOURCE: *IMF Annual Report*, 1972, Table 8, and *International Financial Statistics*, July 1977, IMF.

Between 1952 and 1969 world imports grew at an average annual rate of 7.7% per annum, but world reserves grew by only 2.3% per annum. Most of this growth came from the foreign-exchange component and the gold element increased by under 1% per annum. A consequence was a marked change in the shares of gold and foreign exchange in total reserves, particularly during the 1960s. The ratio of world reserves to imports fell markedly through the period.

Chart 8.1 Ratio of world reserves to world imports 1954–76 (per cent) (reserves at year end as percentage of year's imports)

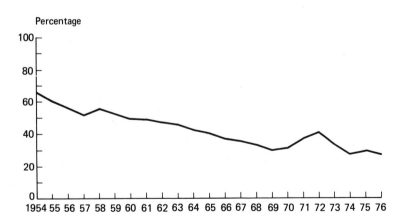

SOURCE: *IMF International Financial Statistics*, 1977 Supplement, May 1977.

Special drawing rights

Realisation of an approaching world liquidity crisis finally persuaded some unwilling IMF members to accept the creation of a new reserve asset in 1969. These assets, known as Special Drawing Rights (SDRs), were allocated to countries on the basis of their IMF quotas and form part of each country's official reserves. They are not, however, freely negotiable like the gold and foreign exchange component of reserves, but may only be used to settle legitimate balance-of-payments needs. Deficit countries may transfer SDRs through the IMF to surplus countries in exchange for convertible currencies, but will be expected to reverse these transactions when their balance of payments improve. SDRs have a gold guarantee and earn interest. The initial allocations of $10.1 billion were made in three instalments in 1970, 1971 and 1972. Further allocations required further approval which was withheld on the grounds that world liquidity grew very rapidly in the 1970–72 period as a result of the burgeoning US deficit. Basically SDRs are a formal and institutionalised type of credit facility with an unlimited duration. Their creation in 1969 was a major achievement, but they lack an automatic mechanism for growing in step with world trade. Too much political interference is involved in their operation. Also the role of gold and dollars as competing reserve assets has not been satisfactorily defined. SDRs are an acceptable reserve asset for official holders but they are not available to private bodies. The latter are basically limited to foreign exchange, which means that they manage their portfolios with regard to expected currency stability. This lays reserve currencies open to periodic confidence problems and greatly increases pressures on the reserves of the USA and UK.

Britain's balance-of-payments problems in 1974–76 and the steady downward drift in sterling's external value contributed to the phasing out of sterling. The UK government hastened the process as part of its crisis package in late 1976; arrangements were made to run down the sterling balances, foreign governments' and institutions' deposits in London, and also to inhibit the use of sterling in international trade. Although offered an opportunity to switch, though, many sterling balance holders decided to stick with the existing arrangements. During 1977, when the UK's balance of payments was on the mend and London's interest rates were high there was a large inflow of short term funds into the UK.

The final aim of most would-be monetary reformers is the creation of a general world central bank with an extended form of SDR providing the world currency. Some would link the creation of new SDRs to the provision of development aid to the developing countries. SDRs would flow into the reserves of industrial countries in exchange for much-needed goods and services. Whatever happens, the use of national currencies, such as sterling and the dollar, will be phased out in favour of some form of international money. The timing is of course highly uncertain; the international disturbances following OPEC's oil price increases temporarily clouded the issue and also altered the basic problems.

Money and multinational companies

The chronic international monetary instability of the early 1970s was partly blamed on the operations of the eurocurrency market described in Chapter VII, and on the behaviour of multinational companies. The general definition of a multinational company is a firm with operations in more than one country. This covers a very wide range of organisations with disparate structures and aims, based in different home countries and operating in varying industries. The term is popularly used for large manufacturing companies, invariably based in the USA, with very closely controlled subsidiaries overseas. It is argued that these firms can and do quickly move large liquid balances merely by lifting a telephone in an attempt to protect themselves against an expected exchange rate change. The funds at their disposal exceed those of most central banks. Their actions to protect their positions can often precipitate the very changes they are trying to protect themselves against. Their prophecies become self-fulfilling and encourage further evading action in future periods of currency unrest. Not only are the companies concerned to protect current trading income and liquid balances, it is argued, but also the value of their overseas assets in their home currency.

This is an area in which considerable emotion is generated and there is a large amount of myth. All companies engaged in international trade can take advantage of 'leads' and 'lags' to protect against currency changes, whether or not they are multinational. Such leads and lags can have a profound impact on movements of short-term funds. Merely accelerating payment for the UK's imports by one week and delaying export receipts by a similar time, for example, would cost the UK reserves some £1 000 million. Secondly, all companies can operate in the forward exchange market to protect their future profits; it is not necessary to have overseas plants. Sophisticated banking facilities and advice are available to all companies through the world's main financial centres, and the multinationals have no monopoly of financial talent. It is a myth to presuppose that large firms have abundant liquid assets which can be varied at will; any company which does maintain large cash balances over long periods is probably not making the most efficient use of its assets. The main difference between multinational and national companies is that the former have a stronger incentive to protect themselves against exchange rate instability. Some, but by no means all, also have greater opportunities. Where there are wholly owned subsidiaries trading with the parent company there is scope for moving funds by changing transfer prices. The scope is limited, however, by the watchful eyes of the tax authorities. Also such a possibility is not available to multinationals with local minority shareholdings in their subsidiaries; such companies must pay full regard to local wishes and needs.

Whilst the operations of multinational companies have undoubtedly accentuated the problems of governments in regulating exchange rates, they did not create those problems. The companies may precipitate movements in trying to protect themselves, but if the basic instability were not already there, they would not go out of their way to create it. Their business is not to gamble but to sell or manufacture goods, and they will stick to their primary business as long as the economic environment remains stable. In large part the machinations of multinationals are a scapegoat for the inability of governments to maintain adequate control over economic trends.

The oil problem

The basic philosophy of the General Agreement on Tariffs and Trade in the post-war decades is that supply of goods will adapt freely to demand. The main problem is to ensure equal access to markets and to prevent governments reserving their home markets for domestic producers by import restrictions of all types. The 1972–73 world boom and the impact of the 1973 Middle East war on oil supplies combined to create a new problem—a problem with which international institutions were not equipped readily to cope. In a world in which basic material shortages may inhibit economic growth the basic problem is likely to be not import, but export controls. The main industrial countries will be anxious to reserve sufficient raw materials and finished products to ensure full employment and relative price stability. A revaluation of their currency would ensure this by making their exports more expensive, but might be totally inappropriate on other grounds. In 1973 the US temporarily imposed an export ban on soya beans, and this could well presage a general tendency.

This is one aspect of the problems associated with the Arab oil embargo following the 1973 war. Oil lies at the centre of international economic developments in other ways. During the 1960s the USA switched from being in energy surplus to being in energy deficit, and the oil market changed from a buyer's market to a strong seller's market. The geographical concentration of available reserves in the Middle East gave a small number of producers monopoly powers which they seized after the 1973 Arab–Israeli war. Not only could they raise prices sharply, but the general currency unrest meant that oil in the ground became more valuable to them than monetary reserves. Many leading producers, such as Kuwait and Saudi Arabia, have minute populations and limited absorptive capacity for industrial development funds. Yet the sums involved are immense; by 1980 the annual revenues of the Middle Eastern oil producers will easily exceed $100 billions. In the past, Arab oil money has normally been invested on a short-term basis in the eurocurrency markets and has moved in response to interest rate differentials.

One consequence of the steep oil price increases from October 1973 was a dramatic switch in the distribution of balance-of-payments surpluses and deficits between countries, with energy rich countries gaining at the expense of the rest. When combined with weak commodity prices and slack world trade the problems have been particularly onerous for those developing countries without oil. The continued current account surpluses of the Organisation of Petroleum Exporting Countries (OPEC) dropped from $65 billion in 1974 to $37 billion in 1976, but this compares with a deficit in 1972. Other developing countries ran a deficit of $22 billion in 1976, and the industrial countries other than Japan and Germany, which each had a $4 billion surplus, a $31 billion overall deficit. The oil producers' surpluses have been flowed through financial intermediaries, to those in need, and especially through the major US banks. Some countries, though, have not benefited and face chronic endemic deficits. Partly to bridge this gap the IMF has established a large supplementary facility for those with severe balance-of-payments problems accentuated by their oil imbalances. This facility is separate from normal quota borrowings, though subject to usual IMF safeguards. It is designed to bypass the commercial markets in recycling balance-of-payments surpluses and to aid the poorer countries.

Monetary union and the EEC

As already mentioned the EEC has grandiose plans for achieving full monetary and economic union by 1980. This involves the full co-ordination of economic policies, the gradual pooling of national gold and foreign exchange reserves, the creation of a form of European central bank, and the development of a common currency. In short, it requires a considerable abdication of national sovereignty on the part of member

States and the subordination of national economic aims to the wider aims of the Community as a whole.

A series of detailed timetables to meet the objective were drawn up by the EEC Commission in 1969, and a more detailed proposal (the Werner Plan) in 1971. The enlargement negotiations and the accession of the UK, Denmark, and Ireland in January 1973 delayed any action on these proposals. Also the currency chaos evolving from the 1971 dollar devaluation caused further delays. National interests and preoccupations have in the last resort nearly always overridden Community objectives. Whilst countries have gained from tariff elimination and to a greater or lesser extent from the Common Agricultural Policy there is no clearcut beneficiary of full monetary and economic union. Also the proponents of the Plan seem to have fastened on a common currency as the lynchpin of union without fully exploring the consequences.

It was envisaged that permissible variations in the relative exchange rates of the member currencies would be gradually reduced until they became freely convertible amongst themselves and their parities between each other irrevocably fixed. The logic of this was that the EEC would be one economic unit with no frontiers, with no capital controls, no internal balance-of-payments statistics, no variations in fiscal structure or tax rates, and completely harmonised economic systems. Parallels are drawn with the USA, but the significant differences between the various states of the Union are ignored. To stress a common currency is to put the cart before the horse; this has in the past always evolved from economic union rather than vice versa. If all the preconditions of free movement of goods, labour and capital, and fully harmonised economic policies were met a common currency would tend to evolve naturally, as it did in Germany in the nineteenth century or in the UK or the USA. To press for a common currency before meeting these preconditions in the hope its very creation will by itself bring forth these preconditions will solve little, and is foredoomed to failure. Yet this appeared to be the EEC approach. For example, a common currency without structural harmonisation would lead to a massive regional problem. Labour and capital would migrate to the most economically attractive areas and large areas would be relatively starved of resources. Those countries with relatively high inflation rates and low productivity growth would become progressively less competitive, with no power to change their exchange rates to offset differential inflation. A vast regional development fund would be needed to offset this natural trend, but governments appear unwilling to finance this.

Proposals for monetary union were swamped in the mid 1970s by more urgent questions caused by the repercussions of the recession and the oil crisis. Nonetheless they remain on the agenda for the later 1970s as an aspiration of the European Commission.

The New International Economic Order and commodities

Resurgent economic rationalism in the resource rich countries in the early 1970s, the example of OPEC in oil, fears over the possible early exhaustion of non-renewable resources engendered by the Club of Rome's gloomy prognostications, dissatisfaction with traditional aid mechanisms, the intractable balance-of-payments problem of many developing countries especially since oil prices rose, and the collapse of the 1972–73 commodity price boom in the subsequent recession, combined in demands by third world countries for the establishment of a New International Economic Order. Initially couched in Marxist rhetoric, their demands were formulated by the Group of 77 (which now comprises 114 developing countries) and expanded at a United Nations Special Session in December 1974. The demands were subsequently elaborated in the United Nations Conference on Trade and Development (UNCTAD) and formed the main subject of UNCTAD 4 at Nairobi in May 1976, and with energy were the subjects of the CEIC meetings in Paris in 1976–77.

The claims re-echo the debate that has persisted since the 1930s on the most appropriate means of organising international trade in primary commodities. Prices are liable to fluctuate widely as supply and demand often move out of balance. The weather, strikes, transport disruptions, wars, national disasters, and the lumpy nature of additions to capacity affect supply, which cannot quickly be altered in the short run. Demand though, moves independently in line with world economic activity, with fluctuations accommodated by varying stockpiling needs. The developing countries seek greater stability in the market, and would also like a higher level of prices moving in line with world inflation. The Group of 77 has expounded an Integrated Programme for Commodities, which includes a Common Fund to finance buffer stock or similar price stabilisation arrangements for eighteen commodities, arrangements for greater technical and other assistance for local downstream processing of the developing countries' raw materials, easier and more assured access to the markets of the industrial countries, and curbs on the activities of the multinational companies. The aim of buffer stocks is literally to act as a buffer between supply and demand, buying in times of surplus and selling in times of shortage to even out the price. Most commodity markets, however, are far more complex than this simple idea suggests, and considerable skill would be needed to set the intervention prices to ensure a long term equilibrium between supply and demand. The UNCTAD proposals insist on a Common Fund and an attack on all commodities at once because, it is argued, the past piecemeal approach to agreements has been unproductive. Only tin has had a moderately effective agreement, helped by large United States market intervention, and has not in any case adequately restricted prices. A Common Fund would require less finance, because not all commodities fluctuate in concert; some are depressed whilst others are booming.

The industrial countries have recognised the need for more equitable arrangements in commodity markets, and the urgent requirement to support those developing countries most seriously affected by oil price rises and weak commodity prices. They have too, grudgingly accepted the case for some form of common fund, but a narrower and less interventionist one than that conceived by UNCTAD. They prefer a case by case approach to commodities, arguing strongly that each has specific problems which are not amenable to standard prescriptions. They fear bureaucratic encroachment on world commodity markets, and believe that intervention would tend to create persistent over capacity. Direct methods of stabilising producing countries' export incomes are preferred, rather than indirect support through commodity prices, which will greatly benefit industrial country producers rather than those most in need.

The debate on commodities is still actively continuing. From being neglected during most of the post war period, commodity problems have again emerged into the prominent position they occupied during the 1930s and 1940s. They will now remain an important topic in international economic discussions and negotiations, as the problems raised are at the heart of the relations between the industrial and the less developed countries. They are the kernel of the North–South dialogue, full discussion of which lies outside the scope of our book.

IX

INDUSTRY AND TRADE

Introduction

Chapters II to V have set out the economic theories of how companies operate, and Chapters VI to VIII have described their broad economic environment. This chapter, and the next, discuss some of the practical problems of economic policy which impinge on a company's operations. In particular, this chapter describes some of the main areas where governments regulate industrial activity in order to meet their policy objectives. Often these objectives may be based on some ill-digested theory totally unrelated to existing circumstances, but that does not in any way moderate the resultant impact on the organisation.

Before turning to these policy questions, the preliminary section of this chapter describes some of the key attributes of modern industry, with especial reference to the United Kingdom.

Concentration in British industry

Reliable and up-to-date information about concentration in British industry is extremely difficult to obtain, as the main sources of information, the detailed *Censuses of Production*, are only fully processed after a lengthy delay. In consequence any debate on the size and concentration of firms in British industry tends to generate more heat than light. Quite apart from the sparseness of the statistical sources, there is also disagreement over what the statistics that are available actually mean. One important point is that trends, apparent in the past, will not necessarily continue unchanged into the future. It is always highly dangerous to formulate policy prescriptions on the basis of a continuation of past trends. A major disturbance, such as an energy crisis, nearly always intervenes.

There are two broad measures of industrial concentration in general use. The first involves examining 'individual industries and calculating concentration ratios'. These show the proportion of an industry's total output, or employment, accounted for by the largest firms (usually the largest five or seven) in the industry. Such ratios, calculated across the broad spectrum of industry, reveal a wide diversity of experience, with the degree of concentration rising markedly in some industry groups, but falling in others, as Table 9.1 demonstrates.

Table 9.1   Changes in UK industrial concentration 1958–68

Industry group	Number of industries in which concentration* increased by 3% points or more		decreased by 3% points or more	
	1958–63	1963–68	1958–63	1963–68
Food and drink	15	11	1	10
Chemicals and allied industries	6	13	4	11
Metal manufacturing	7	13	3	3
Engineering and electrical	17	40	17	12
Vehicles	5	4	—	—
Metals not elsewhere specified	8	10	1	2
Textiles	17	24	3	2
Leather, clothing, footwear	11	13	1	1
Bricks, pottery, glass, cement	6	12	2	—
Timber, furniture	1	2	—	2
Paper, printing, publishing	5	4	1	3
Other manufacturing	3	8	3	1
Total	101	154	36	47

* As measured by concentration ratios for five leading firms.

sources: K. D. George. 'The changing structure of competitive industry', *The Economic Journal*, March 1972 (Supplement) and Report on the Census of Production for 1968, Part 158, HMSO, 1974.

The 1958–63 figures were based on 208 individual industries, and the 1963–68 results on 340. There has been a general tendency for the direction and size of the change in concentration to be inversely related to the level of concentration existing at the start, the higher the initial concentration, the greater the tendency for it to decline. Examination of US statistics discloses a similar diversity. Over 400 industry groups, the shares of the four leading firms rose in 204, fell in 153, and remained constant in 43.

Concentration ratios are a useful indication of the degree of competition existing in industry, but no more. They do not, for example, indicate the degree of product differentiation between firms within the industries as defined; yet each of the five leading firms within an industry may be a monopolist for its own products. The level of tariffs protecting the industry and the degree of penetration by imports may be important checks on highly concentrated industries. The UK or USA car industries are examples, where importers tend to set the pace for highly concentrated markets, as measured by concentration ratios. The growth of the market and the difficulties facing new entrants are also crucial. More important, it is impossible to compress all the facts about an industry into a single figure; the five firms may have equal shares, or one may have 90%, whilst a few relatively large firms may control the remainder of the industry, or there may be a very large number of small firms. Also no account is taken of the possible diversification of a small number of multiproduct firms into a wide range of industries. They might not have a significant share of any single industry, even though they could exert considerable market power.

The second general measure of concentration deals with this problem. It shows the share of output, assets or employment, throughout industry, in the hands of a specified number of larger firms. As far as this aggregate concentration is concerned there has undoubtedly been a large increase in this century. The hundred largest manufacturing firms in the UK increased their share of manufacturing net output from 16% in 1909 to roughly 20% in 1948. By 1963 their share was 38%, and by 1970 it had risen to 45–50%. Thus most of the increase in concentration has occurred since the Second World War, with an actual decline between 1935 and 1949. Similar trends have been apparent in the US, although they have not proceeded as rapidly, or as far. The 100 largest manufacturing firms increased their share of manufacturing industry value added from 23% in 1947 to 30% in 1954, and 1958, and 33% in 1963 and 1967. The much greater scale of the US economy allows the peaceful coexistence of a greater number of economic sized firms, than in the UK. The far more rigorous US anti-trust laws have also had an important effect in preventing concentration.

The impressions conveyed by the *Census of Production* data are supported by details of company balance sheets:

Table 9.2   Shares of specified groups in total net assets of all UK quoted companies

In percentages	1948	1957	1968
10 largest	16.5	18.7	23.7
50 largest	35.0	39.9	50.8
100 largest	46.5	50.7	63.7

SOURCE: K. D. George, Changing structure of British industry' in *A New Era in Competition* (ed. T. M. Rybczynski), Blackwell: 1973.

The 100 largest quoted companies have greatly increased their share of the net assets of all UK quoted companies, particularly since 1957. There has been considerable fluidity within this overall trend; only 52 of the 100 largest companies in 1948 remained in this category in 1968. Of the remaining 48, 12 had been relegated to a lower ranking, 9 had been taken into public ownership, and the other 27 had been taken over or merged into other companies. Mergers and takeovers came into prominence in the second half of the period; all the 24 disappearances from 1948's top 100 which occurred in the 1957–68 period resulted from takeover, merger, or nationalisation. Directly comparable figures for subsequent periods are not available. By 1970 though the largest 50 quoted companies had increased their share of total net assets to 53.8%, and the largest 84 had 64.3%. In 1974 the top 68 firms, which accounted for a similar percentage of the total as the 84 of 1970, controlled 63.2% of total net assets. The number of companies dropped 17% between 1970 and 1974, for similar reasons to the 1957–68 decline.

Temporarily leaving the question of mergers to one side, it is often argued that increasing industrial concentration is inevitable in the present industrial environment. The relevant theory starts off with a given number of firms of equal size. Every year, half the firms remain unchanged in size, a quarter increase in size by a fixed amount, and a quarter decrease in size. The degree of concentration measured by the proportion of employment or output taken by, say, the largest five firms will rise annually. These assumptions are, however, totally artificial. They ignore the general growth of industry, the changing nature of an industry's products, the possibility of new entrants, whether as new small firms or as larger firms widening their product range, and assume a fairly static industrial structure, without major new industries growing in response to new technologies or changed market needs. The statistics show lengthy periods when industrial concentration has remained constant, or has declined.

The exploitation of economies of scale might require greater concentration in some sectors of British industry, if it is to remain internationally competitive. The relatively small size of the domestic market, for example, will not support as many producers of basic organic chemicals as the US. It is questionable, however, whether many of the mergers and takeovers of the past twenty years have greatly raised efficiency. Often they merely transfer ownership and increase the economic power of the acquiring firm, without any noticeable improvement in productivity. The competitive process should, itself, force the closure of sub-standard plants and reward the most efficient and profitable producers. Takeovers frequently concentrate scarce managerial resources on relatively easy growth and financial manipulation, and do not necessarily improve the economy's overall efficiency. Investment in new productive assets or internal growth are more likely to raise national productivity, but are often much harder work. Quite apart from efficiency, mergers have in recent years raised serious social problems, with the sudden closure of apparently efficient plants, and mass redundancies.

Control of monopolies, restrictive practices and mergers

Post-war British governments have been concerned to prevent firms in highly concentrated industries from acting against the public interest, whether through an undue abuse of monopoly powers, or through collusive behaviour. More recently, they have also vetted mergers between larger companies to ensure that these do not work against the public interest. The milestones in the development of official controls are the Monopolies and Restrictive Practices Act of 1948, the Restrictive Trade Practices Act of 1956, the Resale Prices Act of 1964, the Monopolies and Mergers Act of 1965, the Restrictive Practices Act of 1968, and the Fair Trading Act of 1973. This last measure replaced the 1948 and 1965 Monopolies Acts and substantially affected the remaining statutes. British membership of the EEC has also subjected British industry to the Rules of Competition of the Rome Treaty as interpreted by a growing body of case law.

Prior to 1973, and after 1956, the regulation of restrictive practices resulting from agreements between firms was through a Registrar of Restrictive Trade Practices, working through a Restrictive Practices Court, whilst control of monopolies and mergers was through a completely separate Monopolies Commission. The 1973 Fair Trading Act created a Director General of Fair Trading, with his own department, to undertake a central role in applying all competition policies. He took over the responsibilities of the Registrar, and can also make references to the Monopolies and Mergers Commission.

Restrictive Practices were defined under the 1956 Act as agreements between two or more persons restricting prices of goods, quantities, descriptions, processes, conditions of supply, or areas or persons supplied. All such agreements had to be registered, were presumed to work against the public interest and were declared illegal unless judged otherwise by the Restrictive Practices Court. Agreements relating to wages and employment, nationalised industries and other public bodies, and the supply of services were outside the scope of the Act. To gain exemption from the outright prohibition, parties to an agreement had to satisfy the Court that the agreement passed through one or more of seven gateways or escape clauses, and, furthermore, that the benefits to the public from its continued operation offset any detriments. The gateways were that a restriction protected the public from injury, gave benefits to consumers, was necessary to counteract measures taken by others to restrict competition, or to offset a monopolist seller or monopsonist buyer, avoided local unemployment, promoted exports, or was necessary to maintain an agreement that the Court had already passed. In practice, the Court adapted a rigorous attitude, and passage through these gateways was difficult. The 1968 Act added a further escape clause—that ăn agreement did not directly or indirectly restrict or discourage competition to any material degree. Reflecting the preoccupations of the time when it was passed, it exempted agreements intended to hold down prices, or deemed by the Government to be in the national interest. All information agreements, and agreements relating to standards of dimension, quality, or design were made registrable. The 1973 Fair Trading Act further extended the legislation to cover restrictive agreements and information agreements affecting the supply of commercial services, removed the immunity previously enjoyed by patent- or design-pooling agreements, and empowered the Court to make interim orders prohibiting an agreement pending a final decision on it. The Restrictive Practices legislation only applies to agreements affecting goods supplied within the UK. Export agreements are exempt from registration, although particulars of such agreements must be lodged with the Director General.

Whilst the 1956 Act prohibited the collective enforcement of resale prices, *resale price maintenance* (RPM) was still allowed by individual suppliers. This is a practice whereby the manufacturer sets the prices which must be charged by retailers for final sale, and enforces these prices by withholding supplies or even recourse to legal action. It is argued that RPM inhibits consumer choice, between service and price for example, and discourages innovation and competition in retailing. The 1964 Act made all resale price maintenance illegal, with specific exceptions possible through a small number of gateways. There was a general exception to the outright prohibition, where suppliers acted to prevent 'loss leader' selling. The specific gateways were where it could be proved in the Restrictive Practices Court that abandonment of RPM would result in a loss of quality, substantially reduce the number of shops, cause price increases in the long run, present a danger to health, or result in the withdrawal of necessary services. In addition, any benefits accruing had to outweigh the general disadvantage. As a result of the Act, RPM has been voluntarily abandoned in many fields, and has been prohibited in most others. Its general abandonment appears to have been associated with a once-for-all improvement in productivity in retailing, and has, in many areas, encouraged greater competition. The consumer has often benefited from the spread of discount selling, as in electrical appliances. In many industries, manufacturers ditched strict RPM and substituted widely advertised recommended prices, ostensibly unbacked by any legal sanctions.

Britain has adopted a much more pragmatic approach to the control of monopolies than the USA. The basic tenet of UK legislation has been that monopoly by itself is not necessarily harmful, but only the abuse of monopoly power. Apart from the progressive outlawing of specific practices as already mentioned, there has been no general attack on monopoly, but a case-by-case study of individual monopolies on their merits. The 1948 Act established an independent tribunal, the Monopolies Commission, reporting to the Government to enquire into particular cases referred to it and to make recommendations. It was unable to initiate enquiries and its recommendations were not enforceable at law. The Commission had to decide whether the monopolies referred to it were against the public interest. This was widely defined in the enabling act as 'the production, treatment and distribution, by the most efficient and economic means of goods of such types and qualities, in such volume and at such prices as will best suit the requirements of home and overseas markets'. More detailed specific guidelines were also set out. Monopolies were defined for the purpose of the Act as firms controlling one-third or more of the market for a particular product class. The hearings of the Commission were private and confidential. Its members, who were part time, could only sit as a body, and their investigations usually covered several years. Minor changes were made in 1953 and 1956, but the first major revision was in 1965 when the legislation was extended to cover the supply of services as well as goods. The government was also given power to dissolve monopolies, to regulate prices, and to require the publication of price lists.

The *1973 Fair Trading Act* repealed the 1948 and 1965 Acts. It altered the definition of a monopoly by reducing the qualifying market share from $33\frac{1}{3}$% to 25%. Whilst monopoly references were previously framed either in relation to the UK as a whole, or a substantial part, the market can now be defined in terms of a purely local monopoly. Under the earlier legislation nationalised industries and other statutory trading bodies were exempted from scrutiny by the Monopolies Commission, but this exemption no longer applies. The 1973 Act redefined the guidelines that the Commission should follow in considering the public interest. Competition is now explicitly defined as the best means of achieving various desirable economic ends. The Act requires the Commission to report within a specified period. It gives Ministers power to prohibit the recommending of prices or changes, and also to invite enquiries into restrictive labour practices—but merely to stimulate informed discussion.

Under the 1973 Act, the Director General of Fair Trading was given the task of collecting information about market structure and firms' behaviour. Not only was he empowered to initiate investigations by the Monopolies Commission, but also to call for factual information to assist him to decide whether to make a reference. He is required, once a reference is made, to assist the Commission in any way possible. Once the Commission has reported, the Director General has the task of negotiating undertakings with firms, advising Ministers on the use of restrictive orders, and supervising the observance of any undertakings or orders. He thus has considerable independence, although the final word rests with Ministers, who can continue to initiate monopoly references. They alone can refer public-sector industries, and make statutory orders, and have a reserve veto over the Director General's references. To a considerable extent, the 1973 Act took control of monopolies out of the political arena, although it is inevitably an area in which Parliament remains deeply interested.

Mergers were uncontrolled before 1965, even if they would have resulted in a one-third market share. The 1965 Act enabled the government to refer actual or intended mergers creating, or intensifying, a technical monopoly and involving assets worth more than £5 million to the Monopolies Commission, and to make orders either directly prohibiting or imposing conditions on future company takeovers. Ministers retained the sole power to refer mergers under the 1973 Act, although the Director General of Fair Trading was given important advisory powers. Both the 1965 and 1973 Acts instituted a special procedure for newspaper mergers. The Ministers' consent, after a reference to the Monopolies and Mergers Commission, strengthened by outside members, is an essential prerequisite of any merger affecting newspapers. There is no compulsion on firms to seek permission for a merger, or even inform the government, but they may subsequently find their merger disallowed. The government does not refer all normal mergers to the Commission, but aims 'to single out the small minority of cases of real economic importance which raise significant public interest questions'.

In the case of 'horizontal' mergers between suppliers of similar goods and services, the government closely examines those which might significantly reduce competition. Where firms seek to take over their customers or suppliers—vertical mergers—the government considers whether serious doubts are raised about the effects of the ensuing increase in market power on competitors or final consumers. Mergers prompted by diversification are examined more closely than others, with particular attention to mergers motivated mainly by a desire to minimise tax liabilities or to make large capital gains by selling off under-utilised assets of the company taken over (asset stripping). Whereas this last practice was regarded with some favour in the late 1960s, it was increasingly condemned in the early 1970s because of its potentially adverse social implications. The general attitude to mergers also changed. In the mid-1960s there was a general presumption in favour of mergers to create bigger units better able to finance modern large-scale industry and counter foreign competition. The social costs of mergers were often ignored, but they have since assumed increased prominence.

Not only is UK industry covered by British legislation but it must also have regard to the *EEC's rules*. In regulating competition, the EEC appears to have adopted a more rigid and doctrinal attitude towards the presumed virtues of competition than have successive UK governments. Articles 85 and 86 of the Rome Treaty prohibit all restrictive practices and abuses of dominant positions which affect trade between EEC member states, unless they can satisfy fairly rigorous criteria. To obtain exemption, agreements must contribute to technical or economic progress, or improve productive efficiency, and must allow consumers a reasonable share of the benefits. Prohibition of agreements is enforced through Commission decisions, backed by the sanction of substantial fines. A notification procedure allows parties to an agreement to seek exemption through the escape clauses, or to obtain 'negative clearance', meaning that the Commission can find no grounds to intervene. Failure to notify agreements, or provision of false information can result in fines. There is, nonetheless, substantial indirect evidence that a considerable number of agreements have not been notified.

The Commission acts on agreements either as a result of notification, at the request of member states, or aggrieved parties, or if prima facie evidence of restraints exists. To simplify its work it has issued guidelines on the agreements for which it will issue negative clearance. Most of the cases have been on exclusive dealer arrangements which prevent third parties from selling the goods under contract in the distributor's territory or make it more difficult for the distributor to sell the goods under contract outside his agreed territory. There have also been several price-fixing cases in which substantial fines imposed by the Commission have been upheld by the European Court.

Although the Commission is actively interested in extending its powers, it has not yet formulated an effective merger policy. It holds that Article 86 of the Rome Treaty, which prevents abuse of dominant positions, gives the necessary authority to prevent mergers that result in control of a large part of the market becoming vested in one firm. This view is, however, controversial to say the least, and is widely challenged. The Commission is studying this area as part of a wider study on possible controls over the activities of multinational companies.

Control of restrictive practices, monopolies, and mergers in the United Kingdom is part of a wider attempt to improve the lot of the consumer. The 1973 Fair Trading Act concentrated consumer-protection policies in the hands of the Director General of Fair Trading. He was given a watching brief over commercial activities, so as to identify practices which might adversely affect the economic interests of consumers. The Act provided for statutory orders banning or regulating particular consumer trade practices, which might adversely affect consumer interests 'whether they are economic interests, or interests with respect to health, safety, or other matters'. The Director General was also empowered to take remedial action against any individual who persists in a course of business action which is detrimental and unfair to consumers. The Act also outlawed pyramid selling and similar trading schemes unless they met very tight criteria. Pyramid selling is the practice whereby a complex selling organisation is built up with each salesman buying his goods from someone at a higher level; the main way for investors to recover their outlay is by obtaining commission directly or indirectly from recruiting others rather than by selling to the public.

The size of firms

Despite the growing concentration of British industry, the average size of plant, and of firm, is not particularly large when measured in terms of numbers employed. In 1973, for example, the average UK manufacturing unit employed only 123 workers. Table 9.3 sets out some of the main relevant statistics from the 1968 Census of Production, the latest for which details are available for firms as opposed to establishments.

There is an overwhelming preponderance of small firms in terms of numbers, but the largest firms (employing more than 5000 workers) accounted for nearly 47% of total employment, and 51% of net output. The size of firm and the degree of concentration varies considerably according to the relevant industry; small firms are the general rule in some sectors, whereas large enterprises dominate in others. In many industries, both large and small firms coexist, with the smaller companies

Table 9.3   UK manufacturing firms classified by size of employment in 1968

Size of firm (No. employed)	Number of firms	%	Employ-ment '000	%	Net output £m	%	Number of establish-ments	%
1– 99	55 234	89.5	981	13.5	1 632	11.5	58 092	70.5
100– 199	2 964	4.8	409	5.6	669	4.7	4 429	5.4
200– 999	2 714	4.4	1 114	15.4	1 979	13.9	6 753	8.2
1000– 4999	638	1.0	1 352	18.7	2 721	19.2	5 563	6.8
5000– 9999	103	0.2	714	9.8	1 515	10.7	2 331	2.8
10000–49 999	79	0.1	1 534	21.2	3 209	22.6	3 552	4.3
50 000 and over	13	—	1 145	15.8	2 466	17.4	1 623	2.0
Total	61 745	100.0	7 249	100.0	14 190	100.0	82 343	100.0

SOURCE: *Report on the Census of Production for 1968*, Part 158, HMSO, 1974.

performing specialist services or producing specialist products between the interstices of the larger firms.

Averages can, of course, be misleading, but Table 9.4, based on the above table, shows average employment and net output per firm in each size range. The overall totals are very heavily influenced by the very large number of small firms.

Table 9.4   Average employment and output per firm

Size of firm (No. employed)	Average employment per firm	Net output per firm £'000	Number of establish-ments per firm	Average employment per establishment
1– 99	17.8	29.5	1.1	16.9
100– 199	138.0	225.7	1.5	92.3
200– 999	410.5	729.2	2.5	165.0
1000– 4999	2 119.1	4 264.9	8.7	243.0
5000– 9999	6 932.0	14 708.7	22.6	306.3
10000–49 999	19 417.7	40 620.3	45.0	431.9
50 000 and over	88 076.9	189 692.3	124.8	705.5

SOURCE: Table 9.3.

What the table does clearly show is that the larger firms are usually an agglomeration of smaller establishments, or workplaces. The 13 firms employing more than 50 000 workers each had an average 125 establishments per firm. The average employment per establishment, which can obviously be deceptive, was well under 1000 workers. Even many of the smallest firms had more than one establishment.

In general, the industrial, regional and fiscal policies of successive UK governments have been directed towards the needs and likely responses of medium-sized and large firms. The crucial importance of the small-firm sector was all too often ignored. The *Report of the Committee of Enquiry on Small Firms*—the Bolton Committee—issued in November 1971 (Cmnd 4811) helped redress the emphasis. It was set up by the then Labour Government in July 1969, 'to consider the role of small firms in the national economy, the facilities available to them, and the problems confronting them; and to make recommendations'.

One of the most useful functions of the Bolton Committee's report was to concentrate attention on the importance of small firms to the national economy, particularly outside manufacturing industry.

Table 9.5 The importance of the small-firm sector

	Statistical definition of small firms	Small firms as % of all firms		
		No. employed	Net output	No. of firms
Manufacturing 1968	200 employees or less	19	16	94
Retailing 1971	Turnover £50000 p.a. or less	40	29	92
Wholesale trades	Turnover £200000 p.a. or less	25	11	77
Construction 1968	25 employees or less	23	19	90
Mining/quarrying 1968	25 employees or less	18	20	76
Motor trades	Turnover £100000 p.a. or less	32	29	87
Miscellaneous services	Turnover £50000 p.a. or less	82	68	99
Road transport	5 vehicles or less	36	26	85
Catering	All except multiples and brewery-managed public houses	75	73	96
Total all groups		31	21	93

1963 unless stated
SOURCES: *Bolton Report*, Tables 1.I and 3.I; *1958 Census of Production*, Part 158, HMSO, 1974; *Business Monitor*, SD 22, Part 1, HMSO.

Small firms are relatively less important in Britain than in most other industrial countries. Furthermore, their relative importance has declined more rapidly, as Table 9.6 brings out. The figures refer to the size of establishments, rather than firms, and are not always strictly comparable, but they clearly illustrate trends.

The Committee concluded that the small-firm sector is vital to the country's economic health. Small firms are, in many ways, highly efficient, being 'better adapted to the exploitation of certain kinds of economic opportunity than larger firms, and having some special advantages which derive from the intense commitment of the owner manager'. They are a productive outlet for the energies of people who value independence highly; they are often the most efficient form of organisation in industries where the optimum size of sales outlet or production unit is small; they can flourish in limited or specialised markets uneconomic for the large firm and thereby improve consumer

Table 9.6 The shares of manufacturing employment in small establishments (percentages)

	Years	Beginning	End
UK	1954–63	33	31
Germany	1953–63	40	34
USA	1954–63	37	39
Canada	1955–64	46	47
Belgium	1962	—	51
France	1954–63	58	51
Sweden	1950–65	56	53
Japan	1956–66	59	54
Netherlands	1962	—	58
Australia	1953–63	62	60
Switzerland	1955–65	66	61
Norway	1953–67	70	64
Italy	1961	—	66

SOURCE: *Bolton Report*, Tables 6.I and 6.III.

choice; they act as specialist suppliers to larger companies, often producing at lower costs than their customers could achieve; they provide competition to ever larger multiproduct firms and act as some check on monopoly profits and inefficiencies, thus lubricating the economic system; they are an important source of innovation and the traditional breeding ground for new industries; they are the seedbed for new entrepreneurial talent and new large companies to challenge established giants.

The Committee did not find that the small-firm sector was in need of special support despite its post-war decline, provided it is given a fair crack of the whip. This presupposes at least equal treatment for the sector with the elimination of the disincentive effects of the fiscal system. A good general economic climate with an improved growth rate, and an encouragement of more effective competition, are the best guarantors of the sector's health. Whilst governments have not actively discriminated against small firms, the Committee found that their interests have been neglected because no one was charged with looking after them. It proposed action to remedy this neglect through the setting up of a small firms' division within government. Many of the Bolton Committee's organisational proposals have since been acted upon. There is now a much greater awareness of the importance of small firms to the national economy, but finance remains a problem.

The public sector

Britain, in common with most industrial nations, has a large and growing public sector responsible for a significant proportion of national economic activity. In 1976 public corporations, which are broadly the nationalised industries, accounted for some $11\frac{1}{4}\%$ of Britain's Gross Domestic Product. The public sector as a whole, including the activities of central and local government, produced about 31%. The public sector, including the armed forces, provided 30% of all the jobs available in the economy, with the generally capital intensive public corporations providing rather less than 8%. The sector is of greater importance when it comes to capital spending on plant and equipment. The public corporations accounted for 20% of all investment in fixed assets, and the public sector as a whole for 43%. Within this overall picture, the latter financed 52% of capital spending in all new buildings and works other than private dwellings.

Quite apart from those industries such as steel, coal, gas, electricity, and transport in public ownership, the government can exert significant control over other sectors through its purchasing activity and its research and development contracts. Recently shipbuilding, aerospace and much oil production has been taken directly into public ownership. Also the State, through the National Enterprise Board, has built up majority stakes in many companies as a condition of financial assistance. The NEB hold 95% of British Leyland for example. Such holdings are not included in the statistics cited above. Some industries, such as computer production, or construction of nuclear power plant may not be publicly owned but are totally dependent on public sector patronage. Most industries can feel the effects of government actions at various times, even if no direct impact is intended. For example, car safety regulations such as tyre thickness requirements or compulsory seat belts profoundly affected the industries supplying tyres and seat belts and dictated their production and investment strategy, at least for a limited period.

In most industrial countries the State has increasingly intervened in strategic industries in which there are considerable economies of scale, and very heavy capital requirements. There are strong barriers to the entry of new competitors in such industries and a general tendency towards monopoly. Moreover, the technical characteristics of the industry concerned often require a monopoly or something approaching it, at least in part of its operations. The duplication of investment in gas or water pipelines or electricity cables needed to provide competition between suppliers would involve a colossal waste of resources. The history of Britain's railways shows that there is still a tendency to monopoly even with such duplication. Also in the UK there has been strong competition between substitutes which has alleviated the monopoly power of some industries, as between gas and electricity in supplying domestic consumers. The general message is that governments can ill afford the unregulated pursuit of private economic advantage in key industries vital to their countries' economic wellbeing. Inevitably they will intervene to guide investment and regulate prices, so that the actual ownership of the equity becomes almost irrelevant.

Not all public sector industry need necessarily be of this monopolistic infrastructure type. Even in Western Europe there are many examples of highly profitable publicly controlled firms competing effectively with private industry. British Petroleum, in which the UK government is the predominant shareholder, is one example, and the French car producer, Renault, is another. Where there is no outside profitability yardstick against which to judge an industry's progress, however, there are considerable difficulties in controlling and regulating nationalised industries.

Under the various nationalisation statutes, most British nationalised industries are indirectly responsible through a minister to Parliament. They are required to meet demand for their products or services in the most efficient way and to conduct their finances so that over time they at least break even, after making a contribution to reserves. No efficiency or profitability criteria were set out in these vague statutes, and successive governments have attempted to provide more clearcut financial objectives for the nationalised industries. The most recent detailed restatement was in the November 1967 White Paper (Cmnd 3437) *Nationalised Industries: A Review of Economic and Financial Objectives*.

A basic trouble has been that the nationalised industries have been periodically saddled with 'national interest' commitments, often at the expense of their commercial viability. Thus, British Rail has had to keep open commercially unremunerative branch lines in rural areas for social reasons, and the National Coal Board has been obliged to delay the closure of uneconomic and worked out pits because of consequent unemployment problems. The 1972–73 requirement that nationalised industries should observe the appropriate price-control legislation and hold prices down, often below allowable cost increases, was an example of an overriding national economic, as opposed to social, objective. The 1967 White Paper explicitly stated that the Government would henceforth accept responsibility if the industry concerned had to act against its own commercial interests in order to take account of significant social or wider economic costs or benefits.

Apart from this very important proviso, each industry was set an overall financial target for a period of years (usually five) at a time. In most instances targets were set as percentage returns on the whole industry's net assets, although the Coal Board, British Rail, and London Transport Board were set specific monetary objectives. The LTB's objective, for example, was to earn £4 million a year after interest and historic cost depreciation. Beyond their overall targets all the industries were required to use discounted cash flow methods of investment appraisal, and to set an 8% pass mark for new projects. This was later raised to 10%. It was argued that the figure was 'broadly consistent, having regard to differing circumstances in relation to tax, investment grants, etc., with the average rate of return in real terms looked for on low-risk projects in the private sector in recent years'. The pass mark represents the 'minimum rate of return to be expected on a marginal low-risk project undertaken for commercial reasons'. The industries were required to carry out sensitivity analyses and to use a more stringent criterion for exceptionally risky projects. Social cost–benefit analysis was to be used where financial criteria alone would be insufficient.

The White Paper also set out appropriate pricing policies for the nationalised industries. Although prices had to cover overall accounting costs wherever possible, pricing policies had to be devised with reference to the costs of the particular goods provided. The aim was to ensure that consumers paid the true costs of providing goods for their consumption and that cross subsidisation was avoided. In particular prices had to be related to long-run marginal costs wherever possible. These costs were to include a satisfactory return on capital employed and provide for the replacement of fixed assets. Where there was ample spare capacity, prices might be based on short-run marginal costs, and there is always the need to recover accounting costs. As far as possible, the pricing system had to provide adequate incentive to encourage users to spread demand and even out peaks and troughs. Two-part tariffs and differential pricing systems were encouraged for industries such as electricity with a peak-load problem. In addition to requiring more rational pricing policies, the White Paper encouraged the nationalised industries to reduce their costs through productivity schemes and manpower planning. If changes in output per man are any guide to efficiency the nationalised industries as a whole have performed consistently better than the private sector, although this partly reflects their greater capital intensity.

With British membership of the EEC from 1 January 1973, the coal and steel industries have come under the pricing and investment regulations of the European Coal and Steel Community (ECSC). To a considerable extent, these have overridden the established UK position, and have greatly modified the powers exerted over these industries by the responsible Minister. For example, both industries were required to adopt the European basing-point pricing system, and were exempted from the various price controls of the 1973 Counter Inflation Act, even though the government continued to exert indirect pressure on their prices.

Industrial location

According to the classical profit-maximising theory of the firm, industry will tend to locate at the place where its costs are minimised. Leaving aside any artificial inducements such as favourable planning decisions or government grants, the initial siting of a factory will be based solely on economic cost considerations. Firms will balance the availability of sufficient factors of production of suitable quality against the costs of transporting their products to markets, and site accordingly. In general, transport is the most important cost factor. Thus the development of pipelines and very large crude carriers in the past decade greatly reduced the transport costs of crude oil, so that it made economic sense to site oil refineries near the main industrial centres, rather than in the oil-producing countries. The costs of transporting products were infinitely greater than the cost of moving crude oil. In the aluminium industry the main cost element is the electricity needed for refining, rather than the raw material bauxite, or the intermediate alumina. Hence aluminium smelters tend to be located in areas with cheap electricity, preferably near the markets rather than near the bauxite mines. In the case of steel, proximity to consumers and the transport costs of finished pro-ducts are key considerations, and steel mills are usually located near the main markets. In contrast, much copper ore, which is not so energy inten-sive, is smelted near the mine and transported in a semi-finished state.

Often industries require special resources which determine their initial location. For example, the cotton industry was originally developed in

Lancashire because of the suitability of the climate for cotton processing. Shipbuilding, naturally, developed on estuarial sites. Cost considerations dictated the historical location of much British industry. Iron and steel are good examples. When iron was smelted with charcoal, the industry was located in the Weald close to the necessary raw materials, but the exhaustion of these resources and the switch to coal in the eighteenth century prompted a move to the industrial regions of the North, close to coal and iron-ore deposits. More recently, the switch to foreign ore sources has prompted the location of steel mills near deep water, and the development of electric arc furnaces has eliminated the strong pressure to locate on the coal fields. Returning to the cotton industry, another requirement, at least at the cheaper end of the market, is an abundant supply of low-cost labour. In post-war decades Far Eastern countries such as Japan initially, and then India and Taiwan, have made huge inroads into Western cotton industries because they possess cheap labour in abundance. On a world scale the cotton textile industry has moved in accordance with classical cost considerations.

These examples at an industry level support the classical location theory. Nonetheless, there are considerable impediments to the free movement of industry in response to relative costs. Once a firm has set up a factory in a certain area, it is subject to what might be called 'locational inertia'. Unless there are compelling reasons, such as expiry of a lease, or a refusal of planning permission for an extension, firms will greatly prefer to expand on existing sites, even if their costs might be theoretically lowered by moving. Whilst heavy industry is generally responsive to relative cost considerations, firms supplying consumer goods are often less influenced by cost factors. They will tend to plump for a location which is congenial to employees, and especially to senior management, provided there are no serious cost disadvantages. This applies particularly in a relatively small geographical area such as most West European economies. In France, for example, the congenial area tends to be the Paris basin, in the United Kingdom it is somewhere along the Manchester–Birmingham–London axis, in Italy it is the Milan area, and in Germany and the Low Countries the Rhine basin.

The strength of social and prestige factors as opposed to strictly economic considerations is shown by the experiences of the Location of Offices Bureau. This agency had only limited success in persuading firms to relocate their offices outside Central London. The LOB had all the cost arguments well and truly on its side, but was often unable to overcome an irrational reluctance to move. This implies that the traditional profit-maximising theory is an insufficient explanation of location for new investments made by established firms. These are located in accordance with past relative costs which may be irrelevant to modern conditions.

Since the 1939–45 war, governments of most Western economies have intervened to steer firms to given locations through a mixture of stick and carrot. Their regional policies, discussed in more detail below, have aimed to even out regional discrepancies by overcoming firms' reluctance to move. Such official intervention presupposes that governments can guide industry more efficiently than market mechanisms. The supposition is that the social benefits of encouraging firms to locate in a particular area exceed the private costs to the firms of moving to that location.

Certainly, the costs and benefits of a particular location to an individual firm need not necessarily coincide with the costs and benefits to a society as a whole. The existence of external economies and diseconomies has already been mentioned in the discussion of pollution in Chapter VI, but they are particularly important in any study of location. Furthermore, Chapter III has described the impact of economies of scale on firms' cost structures, whilst ignoring any external effects. Yet these external effects of scale are often decisive factors behind a firm's location decision. It is simplest to take a concrete example such as an oil refinery which might initially be sited on a deep-water estuary near a large population centre. As the refinery grows in size its output of non-fuel and by-products will increase to the scale where it will be economic for chemical producers to set up alongside the refinery fence. In time the growing oil–chemical complex will be large enough to warrant the setting up of specialist contractors, offering particular skills more economically than each chemical factory can supply by itself. For example, one firm might specialise in installing pipework, or in inspecting pressure vessels. As the output of the complex grows, producers of specialist rather than commodity chemicals might be attracted by the availability of specialist materials which were previously uneconomic to process.

This theory of industrial agglomeration around an original nucleus underlies many official regional development policies. The theory is that the establishment of a few viable large-scale industries in a few key growth points or regions well supplied with good communications, a well educated and abundant labour force, and adequate land and water, will start off a self-sustaining growth process, and enable the regions to become economically viable. The theory is that external economies of scale, as the original nuclei grow, will attract other, perhaps more labour-intensive, firms.

Not only may there be external economies of location but there may easily be major diseconomies. The most obvious is congestion, raising transport costs and accentuating pollution and environmental degradation. Firms may individually argue that their offices should be located in a major commercial centre such as London, because of the need, for example, to be in close contact with other firms in the same industry. The net result may, however, be severe traffic congestion with greatly overloaded public-transport facilities, coupled with a scarcity of office accommodation with rents to match. These diseconomies may outweigh the initial advantages to each firm of locating in the city centre. An individual firm might be unable to lower these costs by moving. Sometimes the external diseconomies of a particular firm's location are more tangible. Thus the opening of a limestone quarry in a country area of outstanding natural beauty might adversely affect the environment at no cost to the quarrying firm.

In discussing industrial location, it is useful to make a distinction between firms that are theoretically able to move their factories in accordance with relative costs and those which are not. This is particularly relevant in any discussion of multinational companies. Too often all companies operating outside their home country are grouped together, yet a very real distinction can be made between those companies that are multinational by choice and those that are multinational by necessity. The latter are predominantly natural-resource companies who can only operate where the appropriate raw materials exist or geographical conditions permit. Their options are much narrower than those of the former group.

Regional policies

Regional policies are here used to mean conscious attempts to steer industry to particular locations. In the UK a predominant motive, since the 1930s, has been to reduce the great disparity between levels of unemployment between particular localities, by lowering unemployment rates in the peripheral regions. This objective was the main guideline probably until the early 1960s. Scotland, Wales, and the North were the main centres of Britain's traditional industries, such as coal mining, shipbuilding, and textiles which had been in persistent decline since the early 1920s. The newer industries had been repelled by the dereliction and physical unattractiveness of these older industrial areas. Their labour requirements differed and they tended to set up in more congenial physical surroundings nearer the main population centres of the South East. This added to the prosperity of the latter areas, and hastened the run-down of the older regions.

Since the early 1960s the emphasis of government policy has broadened to cover the rehabilitation of areas of industrial dereliction, and the elimination of congestion from the prosperous areas. The British concern with faster economic growth has drawn attention to the potential resources being under-utilised in the less developed regions. Not only has their unemployment been higher, but a smaller percentage of the population, particularly women, has been at work. Migration from these areas has meant that their social and physical capital, such as schools and hospitals, has been relatively under-utilised, whilst greater strain has been placed on the facilities of the more prosperous regions. A self-perpetuating cycle of decline has often been created, with migration causing under-utilisation leading to a lack of improvement, leading to further migration, and so on. A more even spread of employment opportunities throughout the country, it was believed, might allow the economy to be run at a higher pressure of demand without setting up inflationary tendencies. The theoretical justification for government intervention by all governments, regardless of party, has been the divergence between private and social costs of location already mentioned.

Laudatory though these aims might have been, the execution of policy has been less so. A major defect of the British governmental system is the persistent tendency to pull up a plant and examine its roots before it has become established. Industrial companies assume that they have an unlimited life and tend to plan accordingly. A decision to locate a factory in a particular area is usually based on a long-term assessment of costs. Firms want certainty about the legal and fiscal environment they will face over the life of their investment and possible extensions. Yet UK government policy on regional incentives has tended to change frequently. Certainty and continuity have been notable by their absence. This has undoubtedly greatly reduced the effectiveness of any regional incentives; none has been given sufficient time to prove itself. After all, it takes a considerable time for the vast mass of industry even to become fully acquainted with the incentives that are available, let alone to take advantage of them. Moreover, the restrictions that have been imposed on development in congested areas have often been unduly rigid, and may have hampered the growth of small firms.

The main restrictions, which are still in force, are the need to obtain Industrial Development Certificates for all new factories or extensions to existing premises above a certain floor area. The exemption limit below which an IDC is not required has been 15 000 square feet since 1972, with 10 000 square feet in the South East. Previously it was 3000 feet in the Midlands, East Anglia and South East, and 10 000 feet elsewhere. Certificates are now not needed in development and special development areas. They are now more readily granted for modernisation schemes involving staff increases than was previously the case. Office building in the South East is controlled through Office Development Permits, and all commercial and industrial building is subject to normal planning constraints.

A catalogue of the frequent changes in regional incentives would be both lengthy and tedious. A general feature has been the stress on attracting work to the workers, rather than persuading workers to move to jobs. This is because the latter, except within limited areas, would heighten rather than reduce regional disparities, and because the locational inertia of the vast mass of workers is probably greater than that of industry, at least at the margin. This is despite the considerable degree of labour mobility apparent between population censuses in the UK. Incentives have fluctuated between outright grants to firms locating in development areas and tax incentives, through attractive depreciation provisions. Most incentives, except the regional employment premium, have favoured capital-intensive industry, rather than labour-intensive firms with large labour requirements. Whereas French incentives have always linked the size of grants to the number of new jobs created by the investment, there has been no such link in the UK. A result has been the attraction of highly capital-intensive projects to certain regions, without any great impact on their unemployment levels. Such incentives may also have encouraged firms to install an inappropriate capital–labour mix. Since British industry tends to be less capital-intensive than its American or European counterparts, any such trend might not have been harmful. Most of the general regional incentives introduced since 1963 have favoured all firms in a particular region, whether they were already established there or not. This has involved subsidising firms who would have expanded in the assisted areas irrespective of the incentives, as well as those attracted by the incentives. It could be argued strongly that this has misused national resources.

The present UK regional incentives introduced in 1972 were to remain in force at least until 1978. The exception is the regional employment premium, which is a subsidy to the labour costs of all manufacturing firms in the assisted areas. This was introduced in 1967 for a guaranteed period of seven years, and was due to be phased out from 1974. It was given a reprieve by the March 1974 change in government, and was doubled in the July 1974 mini-budget to £3 per head per week for adult male employees in manufacturing and certain other industries. The basic regional incentives in force since the 1972 budget apply to Wales, Scotland, the South West, and most of England north of a line from the Wash to the Dee. Chart 9.1 shows the assisted areas, which were last changed in April 1977.

Free depreciation is allowed on all investment in plant and machinery throughout the country. This means that firms may write off such investments for tax purposes at whatever rate best suits them. In addition, there is a 40% initial allowance for all spending on new industrial buildings. To preserve a favourable differential for the assisted areas, cash grants are available in the latter both to firms already

Chart 9.1   The assisted areas in Great Britain

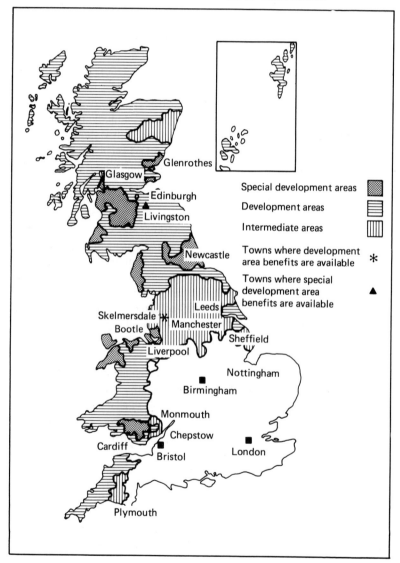

established and to those setting up in these areas. The rates of grant are 22% for buildings, plant and machinery, and mining works in special development areas, and 20% in development areas, with 20% for buildings alone in intermediate areas, and 20% for buildings in derelict land-clearance areas for two years only (i.e. to 1974). The Special Development Areas were primarily old coal-mining districts particularly affected by colliery closures and lacking abundant alternative employment opportunities although Merseyside was added in April 1977. The Intermediate Areas are areas without the deep-seated social and economic problems of the development areas, but which suffer similar problems if not on the same scale. Essentially there was a problem, when development area grants were greatly increased in the mid-1960s, of shading off from full regional incentives to none. The Hunt Committee which reported in 1969 recognised that these grey areas might become worse off than the assisted areas without some limited assistance. Derelict land-clearance areas are places with good natural advantages but which are so affected by the ravages of past industrialisation that their attractiveness to new firms is greatly impaired. In April 1977 Aberdeen was demoted from a development area to an intermediate area in recognition of the effects of the North Sea boom, but the Hull–Grimsby area was promoted.

The regional grants are, broadly speaking, available to all manufacturing and mining and quarrying activities, and to the construction industry. Under the various local-employment Acts, additional selective assistance has been available since early post-war years to firms wishing to locate in development areas. This assistance has included the provision of advance factories, cash grants, and loans on favourable terms. An important qualification has been the creation of additional employment. From 1972, however, this selective assistance has also been available for the modernisation of industry. It has also been extended to firms in intermediate areas as well as to those in the Development and Special Development Areas. The administration of this aid is concentrated in the regions through Regional Industrial Development Boards. An Industrial Development Executive was also set up in 1972 responsible for private-sector industry generally and industrial development in assisted areas.

One of the main drawbacks to the relocation of industry has been the lack of sufficient skilled and semi-skilled labour in the development areas. Workers made redundant in traditional industries have to re-learn new skills. The 1972 revamping of regional assistance measures improved the grants available to firms for retraining workers. Additionally, removal and rehousing grants were greatly increased to encourage retrained workers to move to jobs where they can use their newly acquired skills.

Rehousing grants were also introduced to encourage any workers in the assisted areas to move in search of work.

The recasting of regional incentives in 1972 was an integral part of the government's strategy for raising Britain's rate of economic growth and preparing for entry into the EEC. The United Kingdom has always hoped that it will gain from a common EEC approach to regional policy as a counterweight to the considerable costs to Britain of the Common Agricultural Policy. Community progress has been slow and halting, with countries such as Germany, who have no serious regional problems, unwilling to supply unlimited funds to countries such as Italy, Ireland and the UK, who have. Some assistance has been available since the 1950s through the European Coal and Steel Community for areas adversely affected by changes in the coal and steel industries. The European Social Fund and the Investment Bank have also provided finance for the underdeveloped Southern Italy whose regional problem is of a totally different nature and scale to that of Britain. Under the Common Agricultural Policy, grants have been awarded on a very small scale to diversify backward rural areas and to rationalise uneconomic small holdings.

The main EEC instrument to date is a provision that all EEC regional assistance should be 'transparent' and should be readily calculable. There should be no hidden subsidies or under-the-counter payments. In the central areas of the EEC, which in the UK means all non-assisted areas, any regional aids above those available in the country as a whole are limited to 20% of the after-tax cost of the investment. The UK government argues that all its regional aids, except perhaps the regional employment premium, meet these criteria. An effective EEC regional policy is an essential accompaniment of any quick movement to monetary and economic union. The problems involved have already been discussed in the final section of Chapter VIII; like many problems regional development policies were overtaken as priority items in 1973–74 by the aftermath of the energy crisis and the existing recession.

Emphasis on regional policy gave way in the mid 1970s to attempts to sustain Britain's manufacturing base and its employment through a deep and prolonged recession. Various temporary employment subsidies were introduced, initially in areas enjoying regional assistance, but later throughout the country. The first temporary subsidy, in August 1975, was £10/week for each worker retained on the company payroll rather than made redundant, and was for three months with a further three months, extension. The scheme was extended periodically as unemployment increased, both geographically, temporally and financially. Job creation schemes were introduced simultaneously, mainly to reduce heavy unemployment amongst teenagers. The April 1977 budget introduced a £20/week subsidy for six months to small firms employing less than 50 workers. The main purpose of these and similar schemes was to act directly on the level of unemployment without causing general reflation that would have conflicted with other objectives.

X

LABOUR AND THE UNIONS

Introduction

Various aspects of wage determination and employment patterns have already been discussed in previous chapters. In particular, Chapter VI has commented on prices and incomes policy and on some of the pressures underlying wage demands in an inflationary climate. The previous chapter briefly discussed not only the regional policy aspects of employment but also gave some details of employment by size of firm. The present chapter falls into two main parts; first a general discussion of employment patterns in the United Kingdom, followed by sections on trade unions and collective bargaining, wage determination, and the relative importance of capital and labour.

Patterns of employment

There are many ways of analysing employment—for example, by industry, by region, and by social class. The total working population of the UK in March 1977 was very close to 26 million. This covers all those gainfully employed, or registered as unemployed, but excludes retired persons and students. The working population is subdivided as shown in Table 10.1.

There are approximately $1\frac{3}{4}$ million people who are described as employers and self-employed, and roughly $22\frac{1}{2}$ million employees in civil employment, of whom three-fifths are male. The total working population has risen fairly steadily in line with the UK's total population, although annual trends are affected by the general level of economic activity, and by specific legislative changes. For example, the 1973 raising of the school-leaving age held a year's school leavers off the labour market and kept back the growth of the labour force. When the pressure of demand is weak and registered unemployment increases, a large number of marginal workers leave the labour force. People over sixty-five, for example, who have continued to work may give up, those near retiring age may retire early, and married women may stop a part-time job.

These and other similar factors, partly of a statistical nature, depressed the apparent growth of the working population between 1966 and 1972 when demand conditions were weak.

Over the longer term there have been somewhat divergent trends in the factors affecting the percentage of the population economically active. Obviously, changes in the age structure of the population have an important effect, particularly if the proportion of older people increases. Extensions of full-time higher education also work to lower activity

Table 10.1   Working population of UK March 1977

	'000
Working population	26 014
Unemployed excluding adult students	1 383
Employed labour force	24 631
HM Forces	330
Self-employed (with or without employees)	1 886
Employees in employment	22 415
of which male	13 269
female	9 146

SOURCE: *DE Gazette*, August 1977, HMSO.

rates—the proportion of the total population gainfully employed. Against this, there has been a lowering of social pressures preventing married women from going out to work. Domestic appliances, convenience foods, and modern materials have greatly lessened the burden of housework. Educated to a much higher standard, women have often been unwilling merely to sit at home. Table 10.2 shows how activity rates have moved since 1951.

As the previous chapter has indicated, activity rates, particularly for women, vary markedly between regions. In part this is a function of the economic structure of the regions; for example, there are few female steel workers or coal miners, but many female secretaries. It also reflects social attitudes, however, with some regions less willing than others to countenance working wives. The Lancashire cotton industry has a long tradition of female operatives, whereas there is no such tradition in the Welsh mining valleys or on Tyneside. Table 10.3, which shows the relative size of each region in terms of employment, also shows the marked variations in female activity rates. These, for males, mainly reflect the proportion of retired people in the population at large—the reason for the relatively low male activity rate in the South West for example.

Table 10.2   Activity rates. Economically active population (HM forces and civilian labour force as percentage of total population) in each group aged 15 and over[a]

	1951	1961	1971 Census	1971 GHS	1974 GHS
Males	87.6	86.0	81.4	82.3	80.8
Females married	21.7	29.7	42.2	44.0	49.0
Females other	55.0	50.6	43.7	45.3	42.4

(a) 16 for 1974 because of 1972 rise in school-leaving age.
The GHS figures are samples from the General Household Survey.
SOURCE: *Social Trends* 1973 and 1976, HMSO

The table clearly brings out the differences in unemployment levels between the regions. The UK economy was depressed in 1977, which accounts for the high national figure. The South and Midlands had unemployment levels well below the national average, with the South East around three quarters. By contrast, the rate was near double the national average in Northern Ireland, and substantially higher in the North and

Table 10.3   Regional employment, unemployment and activity rates

	Employees in employment '000 '77 March	Average % Unemployment '77 July (b)	Activity rates 1971 (a) Males over 15	Females over 15
South East ⎱	7 885	4.5	81.9	44.8
East Anglia ⎰		5.3	80.0	38.7
South West	1 504	6.6	78.1	37.6
West Midlands	2 181	5.6	84.1	45.4
East Midlands	1 477	5.0	82.3	43.3
Yorkshire and				
Humberside	1 975	5.5	81.2	41.7
North West	2 631	7.0	81.6	44.4
North	1 246	7.8	80.2	40.0
Wales	980	7.6	78.5	35.7
Scotland	2 043	7.8	81.2	42.4
N. Ireland	494	10.7	79.9	36.0
United Kingdom	22 415	5.9	81.3	42.6

(a) Civilian labour force and armed forces.
(b) Seasonally adjusted.
SOURCES: *DE Gazette*, August 1977; *Regional Statistics*, 1975, HMSO.

Scotland. These comparisons highlight the justification for government assistance to the regions.

The occupational breakdown of the labour force is only available in detail from the Censuses of Population, and then after a considerable delay. Table 10.4 gives the broad analysis from the 1971 census for heads of households.

Skilled manual workers form the largest single category, followed by the semi-skilled, and junior white-collar workers such as clerical workers, and shop assistants. The table brings out the fairly small size of the professional and managerial classes. The pattern for female workers not shown here differs considerably from that for males. Here junior non-manual workers make up some three-eighths of the total, and personal service workers are of much greater relative importance.

The industrial pattern is shown in Table 10.5, which covers employees in employment in the UK. Regular annual information is unavailable about the industrial spread of self-employment and a somewhat notional

Table 10.4   Economic activity of chief economic supporters of households analysed by socio-economic groups 1971, Great Britain

	'000	%
Employers and managers in large establishments	681	3.7
Employers and managers in small establishments	1 366	7.5
Professional workers—self-employed	137	0.8
Professional workers—employees	625	3.4
Ancillary workers and artists	936	5.1
Foremen and supervisors—non-manual	133	0.7
Junior non-manual workers	2 306	12.7
Personal Service workers	363	2.0
Foremen and supervisors—manual	613	3.4
Skilled manual workers	4 247	23.4
Semi-skilled manual workers	2 077	11.4
Unskilled manual workers	1 167	6.4
Own account workers (non professional)	686	3.8
Farmers—employers and managers	146	0.8
Farmers—own account	131	0.7
Agricultural workers	209	1.1
Not elsewhere described	1 338	7.4
Students	55	0.3
Other economically active	971	5.3
Total	18 187	100.0

SOURCE: *Social Trends*, 1974, HMSO.

figure is used for the estimates of working population. In periods where the number of self-employed rises rapidly at the expense of paid employment, estimates of the working population will be distorted. This happened particularly in the construction industry in the late 1960s with the spread of labour-only sub-contracting (the lump). The exclusion of the self-employed from the table means that the numbers working in industries such as construction, distribution, agriculture, and some service trades are under-estimates of the total number of workers in those industries. Against this, the figures include an element of double counting of those who hold two jobs. 'Moonlighting', as it is called, is especially

Table 10.5   Employees in employment in Great Britain March 1977

	Total '000	% females working full time	part time
Agriculture, forestry, fishing	358.9	13.0	9.3
Mining and quarrying	341.3	3.2	0.9
Food, drinks and tobacco	695.6	26.3	14.0
Coal and petroleum products	38.1	9.4	1.6
Chemicals and allied industries	429.6	22.7	5.5
Metal manufacture	479.8	9.1	2.1
Mechanical engineering	920.8	12.7	2.9
Instrument engineering	147.4	29.1	7.0
Electrical engineering	741.3	30.0	6.8
Shipbuilding and marine engineering	171.0	5.6	1.5
Vehicles	751.6	10.6	1.5
Metal goods not elsewhere specified	539.6	22.0	6.4
Textiles	490.8	36.5	9.0
Leather, leather goods and fur	41.9	34.1	10.3
Clothing and footwear	380.9	63.2	13.1
Bricks, pottery, glass, cement, etc.	262.5	19.3	3.9
Timber, furniture, etc.	260.1	14.8	4.6
Paper, printing and publishing	533.9	25.5	6.7
Other manufacturing industries	334.7	26.8	9.5
Construction	1 190.2	5.3	2.8
Gas, electricity and water	330.7	15.5	4.5
Transport and communication	1 435.6	13.7	3.3
Distributive trades	2 635.3	29.0	26.5
Insurance, banking, finance and business services	1 096.1	37.8	13.6
Professional and scientific services	3 549.4	35.8	32.5
Miscellaneous services	2 118.2	26.1	31.1
Public administration and defence	1 645.9	28.7	11.4
Total	21 921.0	25.1	15.7

SOURCE: *DE Gazette*, July 1977, HMSO.

common in the distributive trades, and other service industries. Because of an unwillingness to disclose part-time earnings to the tax authorities much moonlighting remains unreported.

Another factor distorting the figures shown in Table 10.5 is that part-time workers are shown as whole units irrespective of the hours they work. Some countries, such as Australia, adjust their statistics for this and also treat female workers as less 'valuable' than men. Australian statistics are sometimes expressed in terms of 'equivalent male units' with each female employee the equivalent of 0.55 males. The apparent justification is that women are paid less, although their relative wages are not necessarily a reflection of their relative productivity—a conclusion no doubt hotly disputed. In the UK part-time employment is especially prevalent amongst married women, and is again most common in the service industries. The final column of Table 10.5 shows what percentage of the employees in each industry is women working part time. One in eight of all workers in the food industry and one in ten of those in clothing and footwear are female part-time workers. The share of women working full time in each industry is also shown in the table. Even with the Equal Pay Act in full effect from the end of 1975, women workers tend to earn less than men for equivalent work. Those industries with a proportion of female workers well above the overall average tend to pay lower average wages. This is discussed more fully in a later section of this chapter.

In the table the industries identified are the main Orders of the Standard Industrial Classification, the classification system for all industrial statistics. A much wider range of industries is distinguished for which full employment statistics are available. Employment in manufacturing industry totalled just over 7.2 million, or one third of all UK employees. Agriculture, forestry and fishing accounted for under 2% of employees. There have been marked changes in the industrial composition of employment over the years, with a noticeable trend towards greater employment in service trades, and in white-collar occupations within manufacturing industry. In October 1976 administrative, technical, and clerical staff made up 26.5% of all male employees in manufacturing industry compared with 15.2% in December 1948, and 22.1% in April 1963. The growth rate has levelled off though; the percentage was 26.5% in April 1973. In 1948 manufacturing industry, defined on a slightly different basis to the present definition, provided work for nearly 40% of all employees, and in 1963 for 38%. In contrast the service industries, defined for this purpose as the last four rows in Table 10.5, accounted for 24.4% of 1948 employment, 27.6% of employment in 1963, and 38.4% of workers in 1977. Looking at it another way, the total number of employees rose by roughly 1.5 million between 1948 and 1977, but the number in these service industries increased by 3.4 million. Against this, agricultural employment halved over this period. The decline in the coal industry is reflected in the drop in mining and quarrying manpower from 879 000 in 1948 to 1977's 341 000. There were some equally dramatic changes within manufacturing industry which has in total provided declining employment opportunities in recent years. Shipbuilding and marine engineering employment fell from 330 000 in 1948 to 171 000 in 1977, and the number of workers in textiles from just under 1 million to under $\frac{1}{2}$ million. These structural declines in Britain's traditional industries are a major explanation of the continuing regional problem. The magnitude of the changes that have occurred in industrial patterns of employment is rarely mentioned, yet their accomplishment with such relatively little upheaval is a major achievement.

Unemployment

The level and percentage of unemployed are some of the most used and abused of all economic statistics. A sharp rise is castigated as a failure of official economic policy, and a decline is heralded as a major political victory. Indeed to the extent that full employment remains one of the country's basic economic objectives, the maintenance of relatively low and stable unemployment is important. Chapter VI has already shown how economic objectives can conflict and how governments must juggle between these objectives. A basic complication is that unemployment does not instantaneously reflect changed economic conditions, but only does so after a lengthy time lag, estimated at nine months or more. Firms are loath to lay-off workers immediately when there is a business downturn, but will first reduce overtime, and often introduce short time before reducing the labour force. The reverse process applies in an economic upturn. Such lags are usually totally ignored in press comment, and governments are often urged to take actions to correct a situation which has already been reversed.

The unemployment figures are also poor indicators for various statistical reasons. What they show are the number of workers who register for unemployment benefit, not the number who would be willing to work if work were available. This cuts both ways. At the beginning of the chapter we mentioned how many workers might retire early rather than register as unemployed, or, if married women, may temporarily live off their husband's salary. Also there may be concealed unemployment as a result of firms hoarding workers who are not fully employed. One result of the mid-1960's introduction of the Selective Employment Tax, which was a poll tax on numbers employed in distribution and services, was a once-for-all shake out in employment as firms released hoarded labour. Against these factors making the registered unemployment figures look too low, is the fact that the register may include adult students who are only available for temporary work in holidays. Also there is a hard core of 'unemployables' who will never be suitable for employment, mainly for health reasons.

In discussing unemployment it is useful to distinguish between several different types. First there is *frictional* unemployment of people who register as unemployed whilst changing jobs. The raising of social-security benefits and the introduction of compulsory redundancy pay have allowed workers to take more time and care in choosing new jobs. The amount of frictional unemployment has thus tended to rise. Even in periods when the total amount of unemployment has remained roughly constant there have been substantial changes in its composition. Every month some 0.3 to 0.4 million adults join the unemployment register and a similar number leave. Even during periods when unemployment has risen sharply, as in 1976–77, there has been a large monthly outflow of some 0.3 million from the register. This emphasises that unemployment is a problem of marginal workers. The same point is made by an analysis of unemployment by duration. In July 1977 there was a total of over $1\frac{1}{2}$ million unemployed in Great Britain. Of these, nearly one-fifth had been out of work less than three weeks and one-eighth a fortnight or less.

At the other extreme, roughly three-fifths or some 0.9 million had been out of work for eight weeks or more and just over 0.3 million had not been working for over a year. This covers the hard core of unemployables, but also includes those unemployed for structural reasons. *Structural* unemployment is the most intractable, and lies at the heart of the regional problem. Workers declared redundant in industries such as coal mining or shipbuilding may not have alternative employment opportunities in their immediate locality. Also their skills, acquired after many years of practice, may be ill-adapted to any alternative employment. This latter problem can, to a limited extent, be overcome by the provision of appropriate training facilities. Often, however, workers declared redundant in such declining industries are too old to adapt to new situations yet too young to retire permanently. The degree of structural unemployment is difficult to judge, but it obviously varies between the regions.

To a degree the amount of frictional or structural unemployment depends on the pressure of demand and on the overall state of the labour market, and the distinctions are artificial. Nonetheless, the third type of unemployment distinguished is *cyclical* unemployment. Workers are thrown out of work or taken on according to whether the economy is in boom or slump. This cyclical trend is used as one of the main indicators of demand pressures despite all the warnings listed at the beginning of this section. Thus the percentage of adult employees out of work, adjusted for seasonal variations, rose from 2.3% in September 1969 to 3.8% in the winter of 1971–72 and had fallen back to 2.2% by November 1973. It then began rising again to 2.8% in November 1974, 4.8% in November 1975, and 5.6% in December 1976. By July 1977 it had reached 5.9%; unimaginable figures even three years earlier. The amount of cyclical unemployment can be altered by changes in the government's economic policy.

In the post-war decades the proportion of males out of work has been greater than the number of females, this despite the very rapid rise in the number of women who have entered the labour force, compared with the relatively stable number of men. Movements in unemployment have been broadly spread across all occupational groups. For example, the proportion of labourers or managerial classes out of work has been the same as for all groups of workers. Within the age ranges, unemployment is most prevalent in the under-20s and in the over-60s. In general, however, increased prospects for early retirement have given the over-60s an alternative option and the greatest rise in unemployment has occurred in the youngest age group.

Working hours

Too great a concentration on numbers employed diverts attention from the important economic variable, which is the number of hours actually worked. These are influenced not only by numbers employed but also by the length of holidays, statutory or otherwise, and by the length of the working week. The UK has far fewer statutory holidays than most other advanced industrial nations and paid holidays also tend to be lower. As for weekly hours of work, British employees also tend to work longer than their counter-parts, as Table 10.6 shows:

Table 10.6 Average weekly hours of work in manufacturing

	1970	1972	1974	1976
UK	44.9	44.1	44.0	43.5
Germany	43.8	42.7	41.9	41.4
France	44.8	44.0	42.9	41.6
USA	39.8	40.6	40.0	40.1
Canada	39.7	40.0	38.9	38.7
Japan	43.3	42.3	40.0	40.2
Australia	39.5	38.7	38.8	37.7

SOURCE: *UN Monthly Bulletin of Statistics*, July 1977

It is necessary to make a distinction between average hours actually worked and normal hours of work. The latter is merely the number of hours for which workers are paid at normal rates before overtime payments are made. It is normal hours which union negotiators aim to reduce even if the average hours actually worked do not fall. In a sense this gives a partly concealed wage increase. Since the 1939–45 war the UK has seen two general cuts in normal hours of work, which have been mirrored by cuts in actual hours. There was a marked drop in the early 1960s and again in the late 1960s when the 40-hour week became prevalent throughout industry. Normal hours of work in the metals group of industries remained roughly stable at around 45 from 1947 to mid-1960, and then again until they dropped to the present 40.

Average hours actually worked depend not only on the number of hours negotiated in wage contracts but also on the pressure of demand. Nonetheless, the average hours of operatives in manufacturing fell by about 10% between 1956 and 1976. At any one time there tend to be a large number of people working overtime, which fluctuates around one-third of all manufacturing industry operatives. The average overtime per operative has remained fairly stable at some eight hours, although the number working overtime fluctuates cyclically. The amount of short-time working is much more variable.

There appears to be a trade-off between wages and leisure. Whereas there has been a long-term trend towards a shorter working week, technical changes and widened spending opportunities have meant that workers continue to hanker after higher real incomes. Despite widespread prophecies in the early 1960s increased mechanisation and the spread of computers have not greatly reduced the length of the working week.

Collective bargaining

Whereas the earnings and conditions of work of many salaried employees are set by individual negotiation with their employers, those of wage earners are typically fixed by collective bargaining. In the heyday of capitalism in the nineteenth century when they lacked the political and economic power they have acquired today, most individual workers were in a very weak position *vis-à-vis* their employers. Governments were not committed to the maintenance of full employment and labour was much like any other commodity in being responsive to supply and demand conditions. Employees had no capital on which to fall back if they were unwilling to accept the going rate of wages. Also they could not, unaided, resist employers playing off one worker against another. There was no vast system of social-security benefits on which workers could rely. In these conditions it made economic sense for workers to band together in trade unions to present a united front to much more powerful employers.

This is still the basic justification for trade unions today. In combination, workers can extract more favourable terms and conditions from employers than they can individually. Trade unionism developed most rapidly in the nineteenth century in the skilled trades. The large general industrial unions such as the Transport and General Workers Union, which cover a wide range of industries, only became fully effective in this century. Since the second world war there has been a spread of trade unionism into white-collar occupations and into the salaried professions. The doctors and air-line pilots are two examples of professional groups with very successful unions. In all cases the motive is the same—to obtain a better deal for the workers acting in concert.

Collective bargaining was originally restricted to wages and hours of work and terms of employment considered narrowly. Its scope has steadily widened, however, with accelerating speed in recent years, to cover nearly all aspects of the working situation. This feature, as has already been noted in Chapter I, distinguishes Britain and North America from the European mainland. Industrial relations are strongly regulated by statute in Europe, and working conditions are legally defined. Britain by contrast has a strong voluntary tradition with a minimum of legal interference. Working conditions are fixed by a wide range of collective agreements, which are not strictly enforceable at law, but are accepted by custom and practice. Such agreements may be concluded at a national, regional, local or plant level by unions and management. In practice British unions have probably achieved almost as much by collective bargaining, at least in substance, as their European contemporaries have gained through statute. Unions have often been weak or divided in Europe and the law has had to intervene on their behalf.

This difference between Britain and Continental Europe will inevitably cause problems in the Common Market context. One example is in attitudes to workers' participation in management. As Chapter I has already indicated, German unions lay great stress on workers' involvement in management through membership of supervisory boards. Many British unions have tended to distrust this involvement, arguing that their members' interests are best served through an extension of collective bargaining. The fashion for productivity bargaining in the late 1960s shows just what unions can achieve. In the most spectacular cases workers were able to give up traditional and out-of-date working arrangements in exchange for substantial wage increases. It was, of course, debatable how often this significantly raised productivity.

The original role of trade unions was as friendly societies aiding sick and injured workers, and giving death benefits and pensions. As the welfare state grew this role dwindled in importance, although it is a strong feature of some unions such as some of the craft printing unions or the miners. The number of workers covered by trade unions has grown steadily and is now nearly 12 million. The unions have increasingly recruited white-collar workers so that over half of all employees are unionised. This is a much higher proportion than in other industrial countries, and the number of unionists in the United Kingdom in fact exceeds those of all other EEC members put together. The trade unions have not escaped the trend towards increased concentration apparent in industry as a whole. Table 10.7 shows trends during the past decade and Table 10.8 the size distribution of unions in 1975.

Between 1965 and 1975 the number of unions shrank from 630 to 488 whilst membership grew by 1.6 million. This drop resulted mainly from amalgamations rather than from unions going out of existence. Most trade unions are affiliated to the Trade Union Congress, which represents labour in dealings with government. Although influential, it has no powers to control its members except through persuasion or through its members' consent. Table 10.8 shows that a handful of large unions contain most unionists—25 unions have nearly four-fifths of all members.

Although Britain has retained a primarily voluntary system of industrial relations, the law has intervened at times to hold the ring. It has particularly regulated the right to strike and the right to picket, and has also governed wages in poorly organised industries through Wages Councils, and the payment of Redundancy Payments. More recently, the 1971 Industrial Relations Act marked a fundamental change in the law governing collective bargaining and trade unions. This Act developed out of concern over the mounting power of the unions and their apparent ability to exert overwhelming pressure at key points in the economy. It was felt that the growth of a small number of highly influential unions had tipped the balance too far away from employers towards organised labour. The Industrial Relations Act followed, after a lengthy delay, the report of a Royal Commission appointed in the mid-1960s to examine trade unions and employers' associations.

The Commission reported in favour of strengthening the existing voluntary system of collective bargaining. It felt that the problem of unofficial strikes at plant level might be resolved by integrating shop stewards' organisations more fully into the union apparatus. The recognition and development of plant bargaining on a more formalised basis might, it argued, also contribute to a reduction of wage drift. The

Table 10.7   Trade union membership (end of year)

	1965	1970	1975
No. of Unions	630	540	488
Membership '000s			
males	8 084	8 440	8 508
females	2 241	2 740	3 442
Total	10 325	11 179	11 950

SOURCE: *DE Gazette*, November 1976, HMSO.

Commission did not press for any changes in the law, except for the establishment of a Commission on Industrial Relations to assist voluntary change. Although the then Labour Government introduced legislation incorporating most of the Royal Commision's proposals, this was overtaken by the 1970 General Election. The new Conservative Government favoured a much closer legislative control of union activities. The Industrial Relations Act required unions to register if they were to continue enjoying immunity from prosecution, although most unions refused to register. Registered unions might be granted an agency-shop basis in particular plants. This requires workers once recruited to join a union, although, unlike the closed shop, it does not make union membership a pre-condition of recruitment. Unless either party said otherwise, collective agreements were assumed to be legally binding. Strikes or similar actions introduced without sufficient agreed notice during the course of such an agreement were unfair industrial practices which might be declared illegal by the National Industrial Relations Court. Unions could be fined because of illegal acts by their officers, and unions not directly in dispute with a firm were forbidden to boycott that firm. The Court could require unions to hold a secret ballot on, for

Table 10.8   Distribution of trade unions 1976

No. of members	Number	Total Membership ('000)	% of all union members
250 000 or more	11	7 264	60.8
100 000 to 250 000	14	1 995	16.7
50 000 to 100 000	15	1 045	8.7
1 000 to 50 000	190	1 572	13.2
Under 1 000	258	74	0.6

SOURCE: *DE Gazette*, November 1976, HMSO.

example, an employer's wage offer or a strike decision, and could impose a cooling-off period.

In essence the aim of the Industrial Relations Act was to circumscribe the power of the unions. In practice the unions ignored many of its provisions, and its clauses on compulsory ballots and cooling-off periods fell into disuse. The government's use of these powers during a rail strike in 1972 boomeranged against it. Experience with the Act, and especially its boycott by the unions, showed that the law cannot provide a substitute for voluntary agreement. No law will work effectively if it is disregarded by a large section of the population. That being said, many of the Act's provisions, particularly on union recognition, and on the encouragement of plant-level bargaining, were welcome additions to the law governing collective bargaining. The 1971 Act was substantially repealed in July 1974 by the Labour Government, and replaced by an Employment Protection Act that gave substantial benefits to organised labour.

Strikes

Most discussions of trade union activity inevitably focus on the incidence of strikes. Despite popular opinion, Britain's long-term strike record is better than that of many industrial countries. The year 1972, which saw widespread strikes in the UK, was something of an exception. Table 10.9 shows comparative estimates of days lost through strikes per 1000 persons employed for several countries.

Table 10.9 Days lost through strikes: selected international comparisons (days lost per 1000 persons employed)

	1966–70 Average	1971–75 Average	1975	
United Kingdom	404	1 146	540	
United States	1 500	1 173	1 480	(1974)
Japan	166	328	400	
Germany	12	92	10	
France	263*	342	390	
Italy	1 822	1 730	1 640	
Australia	608	1 464	1 390	
Canada	1 836	1 862	2 840	

* excluding 1968.

SOURCE: *DE Gazette*, December 1976, HMSO.

Table 10.10   Length of strikes in the UK in 1976

	% of total stoppages	% of workers involved	% of days lost
Under 1 day	19.7	16.9	2.8
1 to 6 days	48.6	50.2	27.2
6 to 12 days	16.7	16.0	20.0
12 to 18 days	6.0	6.9	8.7
18 to 24 days	3.1	4.8	10.6
24 to 36 days	2.7	2.4	6.5
36 to 60 days	1.9	2.0	13.1
Over 60 days	1.3	0.8	11.1
Totals	2 016	669 800	3.509 m

SOURCE: *DE Gazette*, June 1977, HMSO.

Because 1968 is ignored for France the table greatly understates the days lost by strikes in France. The table clearly shows that Britain's long-term strike record has been considerably better than that of North America, even if worse than that of many European economies.

During this century the incidence of strikes has tended to move in waves, with the average number of days lost being particularly high in the early 1920s, and also in the years immediately prior to the first world

Table 10.11   Analysis of UK stoppages of work by cause (percentage of strikes by number)

	1945	1953	1960	1972	1976
Wage disputes	43.2	45.3	48.9	59.2	43.2
Hours of work	3.9	2.6	2.5	1.7	3.3
Demarcation disputes			2.3	2.2	
Disputes concerning employment or discharge (inc. redundancy)	12.7	13.0	8.1	14.1	47.2(a)
Other personnel disputes			2.5	2.2	
Other working arrangements, rules and discipline	35.9	36.7	32.0	15.9	
Trade union status	3.3	1.7	2.2	3.3	
Sympathetic action	1.0	0.7	1.6	1.4	0.7
	100.0	100.0	100.0	100.0	100.0

SOURCE: *DE Gazette*, February and June 1973, June 1977, HMSO.

(a) Definitions have changed. In 1976 this was divided as follows: Redundancy questions 4.3; Trade union matters 8.0; working conditions and supervision 10.6; manning and work allocation 19.6; dismissal and other disciplinary measures 10.3.

war. The incidence has been comparatively low since the second world war, at least until the early 1970s. Many UK strikes are of comparatively short duration, and are unofficial in the sense that they do not have official trade union support. Table 10.10 analyses strikes by duration in 1976; well over half the strikes lasted under a week.

A study of post-war strikes by cause shows considerable changes over time. Some figures for selected years are shown in Table 10.11.

Over the period the proportion of straightforward wage disputes has tended to increase, whilst there has been a decline in disputes over working arrangements and discipline. Sympathy strikes and disagreements over trade union status have always been of minor importance.

The importance of labour

References have been made in previous chapters to the degree of capital or labour intensity of a particular investment or industry. This is a very difficult concept to measure, although the general principle is simple. Some industries rely very heavily on capital equipment, and labour is a relatively unimportant proportion of the total cost structure. Others in contrast need a great deal of labour and the share of labour is well above average. Table 10.12 shows some statistics for UK manufacturing industries in 1975–76 based on census of production information.

As a general guide, industries in which wages and salaries make up a higher percentage than the average of manufacturing industry as a whole are relatively labour intensive, and those in which it is lower are capital intensive. This is shown in the second column of the table. Thus chemicals and allied industries are on average capital intensive whilst instrument engineering or clothing or footwear are labour intensive. Obviously the degree of capital and labour intensity can vary markedly within these broad industrial headings. Candle manufacture is more labour intensive, for example, than petrochemicals production.

Workers in capital-intensive industries have a much greater amount of capital at their disposal. As a general rule they will each tend to produce more in terms of net output than workers with lower amounts of capital. The first column of the table shows average productivity by industry in terms of net output per head. There is indeed a rough correspondence between this and the share of net output going in wages and salaries.

There is much less correspondence between net output per head and average weekly earnings which are shown in the final column. Certainly the lowest productivity industries do tend to pay the lowest average wages but there are important exceptions such as, for example, shipbuilding. As one might expect, other factors considered in the next

Table 10.12 Some UK employment statistics

	Net output per employee 1975	Wages and salaries as % net output 1975	Average gross weekly earnings full-time manual men Oct. 1976
	£	%	£
All manufacturing industry	4 928	52.1	67.8
Food, drink and tobacco	6 210	37.6	66.8
Coal and petroleum products	22 698	15.5	76.8
Chemicals and allied industries	8 549	36.5	71.7
Metal manufacture	5 034	59.6	73.7
Mechanical engineering	5 065	53.6	63.1
Instrument engineering	4 000	59.8	61.6
Electrical engineering	4 613	54.8	63.5
Shipbuilding and marine engineering	3 698	78.8	72.1
Vehicles	4 080	74.8	72.5
Metal goods not elsewhere specified	4 305	55.1	64.9
Textiles	3 430	61.4	61.2
Leather, leather goods and fur	3 495	54.7	55.9
Clothing and footwear	2 701	56.8	53.3
Bricks, pottery, glass, cement, etc.	5 891	45.9	68.8
Timber, furniture, etc.	4 513	53.4	61.5
Paper, printing and publishing	5 048	54.2	73.9
Other manufacturing industries	4 601	51.7	66.3

SOURCES: *Business Monitor*, PA. 1000, 1975, HMSO; *DE Gazette*, March 1977, HMSO.

section often outweigh the productivity element. In one sense, however, workers in capital-intensive industries do have some advantage. In general they not only have more capital equipment at their disposal at any given point in time, but new investment in their industries tends to be higher than elsewhere. Investment in new and more efficient capital equipment is one of the primary sources of rising productivity. Employers in high-productivity industries are able to raise their wage levels more easily than other firms without eating into profits. In the absence of strong market pressures or official controls, firms in high-productivity industries will be able to determine wage levels. In theory, national price stability requires workers in high-productivity industries to hold back to the advantage of the lower-productivity workers. If they do not, the overall result will be a degree of inflation; market forces will raise earnings in the low-productivity industries faster than their productivity growth warrants, causing an increase in the general price level. Looking at it from the workers' point of view in a high-productivity industry, however, their restraint would mean a rise in the share of profits in total value added in their industry, which might be totally unacceptable. The economic system has not yet found a satisfactory method of coping with these equity problems. They are some of the major difficulties underlying the design of a completely effective prices and incomes policy.

Some issues in wage determination

Detailed analysis of all the basic issues of wage determination is beyond the scope of this book. Some have already been mentioned in preceding sections. Despite the strong pressures of trade unions, the share of wages and salaries in total gross domestic product has been relatively stable at some two-thirds, not only over time but also between different economies. Obviously there have been fluctuations over the course of the business cycle. In 1976, for example, total incomes from employment amounted to 72.1% of GDP compared with 67% in 1956 and 69% in 1966. In normal times firms have been able to pass on wage increases in higher prices and thereby preserve their profit margins. Where trade-union activity has been effective is in raising the wages of organised labour at the expense of the unorganised. Statistics here are difficult to obtain, but it is clear that skilful use of the closed shop and other restrictive practices has raised the wages of many craftsmen above that of other less organised workers with broadly similar skills. The printing unions are a good case in point.

Economic theory suggests that labour is like any other good, or factor of production, in that its price in alternative uses will tend to equality at the margin. This implies that under perfectly competitive conditions income, suitably discounted, will tend to equality for similar occupations. In practice there are numerous imperfections in the labour market, not least of which are trade unions, which distort its free workings. Quite apart from their attempts to control all prices and wages to reduce inflation or regulate the pressure of demand, governments may intervene to regulate wages. For social reasons they may fix minimum wage levels in industries which are poorly unionised. The lack of organisation usually results from the fragmented nature of the job, the lack of large bargaining units, and the willingness of potential labour market entrants to work for low wages. Catering is an industry in which minimum-wage legislation has proved essential.

Not only may unions regulate a closed shop, but the government may require entry examinations and evidence of professional standards which have the same effect. The medical professions are a classic case. Also governments may intervene in labour markets to further some popular policy. A typical example is equal pay for women. Under the Equal Pay Act, employers are required to pay identical wages for equivalent work. Traditionally women's wages have tended to be well below those of men, quite frequently for identical work. To a limited extent there are sound economic reasons. Because female workers often have family responsibilities, their rate of absence tends to be higher, and their sickness rates are often greater than those of men. Also the welfare facilities required for them tend to be more expensive. Women tend to change jobs more frequently, at least before their children have grown up, and this imposes costs on employers. Women, once married, tend to be less mobile than men, and their educational qualifications tend to be lower. It is further argued that their productivity is lower, but there is little justification for this argument. Certainly they have been less willing than men to join trade unions and press for higher wages, probably because men have traditionally been the breadwinners and the wives' earnings have been supplementary. Many of these arguments fall down when subject to close scrutiny, but they do not alter the fact that women's average wages have been lower than those of men, even in similar occupations. The introduction of equal pay has been spread over several years, but even then causes hardships for many employers.

Wages are particularly influenced by competitive supply and demand pressures at a local level. Union activity has placed a floor on wages and prevented large pools of unemployed from bidding down wage levels. On the other hand, firms at local level often have to pay higher wages than their local competitors, even in different industries, to attract sufficient workers, particularly those possessing scarce skills at least in the short run. Over the longer term, wages must tend to equality at the margin. Whilst wage agreements are often negotiated centrally these usually only refer to basic wage rates. Regional, local, and plant agreements add various supplements and bonuses to these basic rates. Up to a point these result from long-forgotten reasons but they are also designed to reflect local supply and demand factors. These plus payments help explain the difference between basic wage rates and average earnings, although the existence of overtime payments helps raise the latter even more. Normally average earnings tend to rise faster than wage rates, a phenomenon known as *wage drift*.

The different wages paid to workers in different occupations or industries, or *wage differentials*, in theory reflect different economic conditions. Certainly over the long term wage differentials have remained remarkably stable, even though at any point in time particular groups of workers may gain temporary advantage. Quite apart from supply and demand, these differentials reflect a whole host of factors, including established custom and practice. Relative wages reflect the amount of training or education required for a particular occupation, with premium paid to these with long training periods. Those with higher skills tend to be paid more than the unskilled.

Often there is no apparent relationship between a worker's skill or the effort and risk involved in his job and his wage. Professional footballers and pop stars are paid what might be considered as exorbitant rewards for very little work. This reflects their relative scarcity, and their rewards include a large element of economic rent. In many cases relative incomes incorporate intangible factors such as congenial working conditions or innate satisfaction which offset comparatively low wages. Often, however, as with nurses and teachers, society has tended to place too great an emphasis on these psychic rewards and insufficient on pecuniary satisfaction. Other factors reflected in wage differentials include the risk, danger or inconvenience attached to a job. Also there may be compensation for dirty and unattractive working conditions as it might be necessary to pay premium rates to attract sufficient labour.

The preservation of adequate wage differentials, and more important the alteration of existing differentials, is the rock on which all attempts to secure a long-term prices and incomes policy have foundered. In the last resort no adequate substitute has yet been found for the market. Whilst wages can be restrained for short periods, rigidities and inconsistencies inevitably creep in which become more glaring with the passage of time. It then becomes necessary either to relax restrictions on wages or else re-invent something approaching market mechanisms. This certainly became apparent in the 1972–74 experiments in incomes policy, as in all previous attempts both in the UK and elsewhere. The 1975–77 Social Contract also foundered in mid 1977 for the same reasons.

MAIN SOURCES OF STATISTICS
AND INFORMATION

1. United Kingdom: Government Sources

A GUIDE

The Central Statistical Office, in 1976 published a comprehensive *Guide to Official Statistics*, a well laid out and cross-referenced report that greatly simplifies the location of official statistics, broadly defined. The first guide includes developments up to June 1976, and will be kept up to date at regular intervals. It includes a full list of government statistical sources, and details of appropriate contact points within Government departments.

GENERAL PUBLICATIONS

Monthly Digest of Statistics and *Annual Abstract of Statistics*. These two publications bring together most of the main economic and social statistics for the United Kingdom, with the *Annual Abstract* containing more series and providing a longer run of years. Statistics on a regional basis are contained in the *Scottish Abstract of Statistics* (annual), the *Digest of Welsh Statistics* (annual), the *Northern Ireland Digest of Statistics* (biannual) and the *Abstract of Regional Statistics* (annual).

Trade and Industry, weekly from the DTI, contains regular statistics on a wide range of industries, and also general economic and trade information.

Economic Trends each month provides a broad background to UK economic trends in the form of charts and tables. It includes quarterly articles and tables on the national income and balance of payments, which are annually detailed in *National Income and Expenditure* (the Blue Book) and the *UK Balance of Payments* (the Pink Book). Details of incomes, wealth, and taxation are contained in the annual *Inland Revenue Statistics,* and *Report of the Commissioners of HM Customs and Excise.*

INDUSTRIAL PRODUCTION AND SALES

Business Monitors, obtainable from HMSO, are the primary source for the latest monthly or quarterly figures, usually in greater detail than is published elsewhere. Separate Monitors cover individual industries, giving latest figures of sales, exports, stocks and prices, etc. The annual censuses of production are also published in the Business Monitor series in the form of separate industry reports providing information on the structure of industry. There are also Monitors dealing with service and distributive trades and a number of miscellaneous series.

Census of Production. The last of the quinquennial surveys, now superseded by a system of quarterly and annual figures, was for 1968. Results are published in over 170 industry volumes including a 13-volume directory of businesses classified by broad industry groups.

The results of the annual census are now published in the *Business Monitor* series.

Digest of UK Energy Statistics. Annual publication containing tables and charts of energy demand in the United Kingdom and production and consumption of individual fuels. Further statistical information on energy can be obtained from the annual report and accounts of each of the nationalised industries.

EMPLOYMENT, EARNINGS, ETC.

Department of Employment Gazette (monthly) including tables and charts on employment, unemployment, hours worked, manpower, earnings, wage rates, stoppages, retail prices, together with special articles on related subjects.

British Labour Statistics: Historical Abstract (1886–1968); *Yearbooks* (from 1969). These volumes contain, for easy reference, both a description and a run of figures relating to each of the main official series of labour statistics, together with notes on new developments year by year.

New Earnings Survey. These booklets describe and give comprehensive results of the survey now held annually. Main results are first published in the *Department of Employment Gazette.*

Time Rates of Wages and Hours of Work (annual).

EXTERNAL TRADE

Overseas Trade Statistics of the United Kingdom. Monthly publication giving detailed overseas trade statistics, the December issue of which carries cumulative totals for the whole calendar year. Annual volumes are also produced. Special analyses of imports and exports in greater country and commodity detail can be obtained direct from HM Customs and Excise.

HOUSING AND CONSTRUCTION

Housing and Construction Statistics and *Local Housing Statistics*—two quarterly publications from the Department of the Environment.

FINANCIAL AND COMPANIES

Financial Statistics. A monthly publication bringing together all the key financial and monetary statistics of the United Kingdom.

Business Monitors. (M3) Company Finance. An annual analysis of the accounts of quoted companies. (M5) Insurance companies' and private pension funds' investment. (M7) Acquisitions and mergers of companies.

Local Government Financial Statistics (annual).

INLAND TRANSPORT

Passenger Transport in Great Britain and *Highway Statistics*—two annual publications from the Department of the Environment.

DISTRIBUTION

Census of Retail Distribution and Other Services 1971 provides data on the numbers, sizes, type, turnover, etc., of shops. Monthly indices of retail sales are included in *Trade and Industry.*

AGRICULTURE AND FOOD

A comprehensive guide to sources of agriculture, food and fisheries statistics is published by HMSO as No. 14 in the series *Studies in Official Statistics.* The Ministry publishes much of its information through Statistical Information Notices and in a more permanent form in two annuals: *Agricultural Statistics: England and Wales,* and *Agricultural Statistics: United Kingdom.*

Household Food Consumption and Expenditure. Annual report on food consumption, expenditure and nutrition by type of household. (Quarterly reports appear in MAFF's *Food Facts* and elsewhere.)

POPULATION AND HOUSEHOLD

Census of Population 1971. Reports giving national and local analyses of information on population and households, including separate volumes on a variety of subjects including immigration, economic activity, workplace and transport to work, qualified manpower, household composition, fertility, etc.

Population Projections—national figures. United Kingdom and constituent parts. Prepared by the Government Actuary annually.

General Household Survey. A continuous sample survey of households relating to a wide range of social and socio-economic policy areas. First results were for 1971.

Family Expenditure Survey. Annual report of income and expenditure of type of household.

SOCIAL STATISTICS

Social Trends (annual). Selection of key statistics relating to all aspects of social policy.

Health and Personal Social Service Statistics (annual).

Annual Report of the Department of Health and Social Security.

Statistics of Education (six volumes a year).

Scottish Educational Statistics (annual).

Education Statistics for the United Kingdom (annual).

Criminal Statistics (annual).

NOTE: All the above (unless otherwise indicated) are published by Her Majesty's Stationery Office and are available at Government bookshops. Mail orders to Her Majesty's Stationery Office, PO Box 569, London SE1 9NH.

2. United Kingdom: Non-Government Sources

ASLIB

3 Belgrave Square, London, SW1X 8PL. Tel: 01–235–5050.

Aslib is the principal British source of authoritative information and advice on the systematic acquisition and use of specialised information. Its name is derived from the initial letters of its original title, Association of Special Libraries and Information Bureaux.

THE BRITISH INSTITUTE OF MANAGEMENT

Management House, Parker Street, London W.C.2. Tel: 01–404–3456.

BIM is an independent, self-governing, non-political, non-profit-making body. Founded in 1947 its object is to promote the highest standards of management in every sector of the economy, both private and public. The Institute is supported by more than 13 500 organisations and over 32 000 Individual Members. The services available include a large and well equipped library; an experienced team of information officers; wide range of publications and advisory services on salaries and consultants.

THE ECONOMIST INTELLIGENCE UNIT

Spencer House, 27 St. James's Palace, London SW1A 1NT. Tel: 01–493–6711.

The primary object of EIU publications is to be relevant to the information requirements of commerce and industry. Independent analysis, interpretation and comment, based on the latest available economic indicators, are published by the EIU in a range of regular reviews and bulletins covering most of the business spectrum.

IMRA

28 Bore Street, Lichfield WS13 6LL. Tel: Lichfield 3448.

The Industrial Marketing Research Association consists of 1100 individual members who conduct research into the marketing of goods and services to industrial and institutional consumers. The Association is the representative body of the profession in the UK. Its aims include improving technical standards and quality in industrial marketing research, creating a greater awareness of the value of IMR and liaison with Government organisations and other bodies to promote the flow of information.

THE INSTITUTE OF MARKETING

Moor Hall, Cookham, Berks. Tel: 062–85–24922.

The Institute of Marketing is a professional body for senior executives engaged in marketing management. Its main objects are to develop the body of knowledge about marketing, to provide services for members and to make the principles and practices of marketing more widely known and effectively used throughout industry. The Institute's Information Department provides a wide range of information on every aspect of marketing.

NATIONAL INSTITUTE OF ECONOMIC AND SOCIAL RESEARCH

2 Dean Trench Street, London SW1P 3HE.

The reviews of, and predictions for, the UK economy published by the NIESR in the *National Institute Economic Review* are, together with those published in the *Bank of England Quarterly Review,* the most important independent assessments available.

THE MARKET RESEARCH SOCIETY

51 Charles Street, London, W.1. Tel: 01–499–1913.

The Market Research Society is the incorporated professional body for those using survey techniques for market, social and economic research. Founded 25 years ago, it is the largest body of its kind in the world. The

Society maintains a permanent secretariat and an information service for members and non-members on matters concerned with the profession.

NATIONAL ECONOMIC DEVELOPMENT OFFICE (NEDO)

Millbank Tower, Millbank, London S.W.1. Tel: 01–834–3811.

The popular name for the National Economic Development Council is Neddy; it is the national forum for economic consultation between government, management (CBI) and trade unions (TUC). Little Neddies, formally referred to as Economic Development Committees, are the industry offshoots of Neddy. They are made up of leading representatives of management and unions, together with government officials and independent members. The National Economic Development Office (NEDO) is the secretariat to Neddy and the Little Neddies. NEDO is not a government department or agency and is not involved in implementing government decisions.

3. Other Information Sources

EUROPEAN COMMUNITY INFORMATION OFFICE

20 Kensington Palace Gardens, London W8 4QQ (Tel: 01–727–8090).

Issues a number of publications free of charge and provides other information. Maintains a catalogue of all published works and documents on the European Communities.

DEPARTMENT OF TRADE AND INDUSTRY LIBRARY

European Communities Secondary Legislation Documentation Centre, Room LG27, 1 Victoria Street, London SW1H 0ET (Tel: 01–222–7877, ext. 3693).

Available to all enquirers. Supplies detailed information on secondary legislation enacted by the Communities. Photocopies of documents may be obtained.

DEPARTMENT OF TRADE AND INDUSTRY

Statistics and Market Intelligence Library, Export House, 50 Ludgate Hill, London, E.C.4 (Tel: 01–248–5757, ext. 368).

The largest source of statistical information on overseas countries with comprehensive trade statistics and general statistical publications.

OECD

Information Service, 2 Rue André-Pascal, Paris XVIe (Tel: 524 82–00).

INDEX